WONDERFUL WORDS OF LIFE

The Calvin Institute of Christian Worship Liturgical Studies Series, edited by John D. Witvliet, is designed to promote reflection on the history, theology, and practice of Christian worship and to stimulate worship renewal in Christian congregations. Contributions include writings by pastoral worship leaders from a wide range of communities and scholars from a wide range of disciplines. The ultimate goal of these contributions is to nurture worship practices that are spiritually vital and theologically rooted.

Available

Gather into One: Praying and Singing Globally
C. Michael Hawn

Discerning the Spirits
A Guide to Thinking about Christian Worship Today
Cornelius Plantinga Jr. and Sue A. Rozeboom

My Only Comfort: Death, Deliverance, and Discipleship in the Music of Bach
Calvin R. Stapert

Christian Worship in Reformed Churches Past and Present
Lukas Vischer, Editor

WONDERFUL WORDS OF LIFE

Hymns in American Protestant History and Theology

Edited by

Richard J. Mouw & Mark A. Noll

WILLIAM B. EERDMANS PUBLISHING COMPANY
GRAND RAPIDS, MICHIGAN / CAMBRIDGE, U.K.

Wm. B. Eerdmans Publishing Co.
255 Jefferson Ave. S.E., Grand Rapids, Michigan 49503 /
P.O. Box 163, Cambridge CB3 9PU U.K.

Printed in the United States of America

09 08 07 06 05 04 7 6 5 4 3 2 1

Library of Congress Cataloging-in-Publication Data

Wonderful words of life: hymns in American Protestant history and theology /
edited by Richard J. Mouw & Mark A. Noll.
p. cm.
Includes bibliographical references and index.
ISBN 0-8028-2160-X (pbk.: alk. paper)
1. Evangelicalism — United States — History.
2. Hymns, English — United States — History and criticism.
3. United States — Church history.
I. Mouw, Richard J. II. Noll, Mark A., 1946-

BR1642.U5W65 2004
264'.23'0882804 — dc22

2003068571

www.eerdmans.com

Contents

Series Preface

Taken together, the eleven essays in this volume, many of which were first presented at a conference sponsored by the Institute for the Study of American Evangelicals (ISAE), make a strong case that hymns are both a fascinating and an irreplaceable type of primary source document for both intellectual and social religious history. If Richard Mouw can't give a speech without quoting hymns, I can hardly imagine teaching a course in Christian theology or the history of Christianity without studying them.

But the study of hymns belongs in one other type of academic class, too: any class on the history, theology, and practice of Christian worship. While hymns are forged in private moments of poetic and musical inspiration by their writers and composers, and while they may be whistled and sung privately in prisons and hospitals, at home and at work, they gain their force and staying power through corporate singing, most often in worship.

Thus, while the reputation of the editors and authors of this collection will, no doubt, put this volume on the radar screen of American religious historians, we hope that its place in a series of books on liturgical studies will help the growing group of interdisciplinary worship scholars take notice.

Liturgical history has most often been developed as the history of official liturgical texts, such as the *Book of Common Prayer,* the Catholic Mass, or Methodist or Reformed service books — which are subject to painstaking source and redaction criticism or phenomenological analysis. Recent interest in ritual theory has helped scholars think beyond official texts to incorporate a sense of space, time, gesture, and posture into our understanding of worship. But we also need a wider view of the texts and sounds that shape our worship, including attention to sermons, extemporaneous prayers, and congregational songs of all types. It may be that congregational song gives us one of the best points of access to understanding worship from the point of view of worshipers rather than clergy.

Thinking of hymns at least partly as liturgical documents also helps us consider the link between liturgical and devotional prayer. The hymns studied in this volume may be among the most successful efforts in the history of Christianity to develop a truly "liturgical spirituality" — in which common worship leaves an unmistakable imprint on the piety of individual believers and serves as a kind of "source and summit" of Christian spirituality (to borrow language from the Second Vatican Council).

Many Christians are formed to think of their own private prayer life as primary and to consider Sunday worship as effective to the extent that it ignites or deepens their personal piety. In this way of thinking, the question "what did worship do for me?" is completely natural, even if it is a bit self-centered and individualistic.

Yet it may be more profound and more spiritually healthy to think in precisely the opposite way: that corporate worship — in which the whole is greater than the sum of the parts — is our primary and most essential form of prayer, one that gathers up and completes necessary forms of personal piety. This is especially true in times when our individual mental or emotional reserves are depleted. At minimum, this more corporate vision of piety provides a new way to think about and experience the unmistakably corporate language that the Bible gives us for the church as the people of God, the body of Christ, and the temple of the Spirit.

For three thousand years or more congregational song has been one tool for nurturing a genuinely corporate and liturgical spirituality. It is a tool that is responsive to local needs and yet one that transcends local experience. Our singing even gives us a way to pray alongside of Christians from centuries ago or half-a-globe away. Anyone who seeks the long-term health of Christian congregations is wise to attend to what songs are sung in common. And one of the best ways to gain perspective on that task of musical stewardship is to learn from the many fascinating chapters in the history of congregational song. May this volume be not only a means for better understanding the history of Christian practice but also a catalyst for more pastoral and profound stewardship of congregational song today.

John D. Witvliet
Calvin Institute of Christian Worship
Calvin College and Calvin Theological Seminary
Grand Rapids, Michigan

Contributors

Susan Wise Bauer teaches writing and American literature at the College of William & Mary in Virginia. She is the author of *The Well-Educated Mind: A Guide to the Classical Education You Never Had* (W. W. Norton) and is at work on a four-volume world history, also for Norton.

Thomas Bergler is Assistant Professor of Educational Ministries and Associate Director of the Link Institute for Faithful and Effective Youth Ministry at Huntington College in Huntington, Indiana. He is currently writing a book on the history of Christian youth ministry in America during the 1950s.

Virginia Lieson Brereton, a lecturer in English at Tufts University, is currently at work on a history of religion in Chicago and on a study of mountain spirituality. Her most recent book was *Women and Twentieth-Century Protestantism* (University of Illinois), co-edited with Margaret Lamberts Bendroth.

Esther Rothenbusch Crookshank has served on the faculty of The Southern Baptist Theological Seminary since 1994, where she is Associate Professor of Church Music (Hymnology and Musicology) in the School of Church Music and Worship. Her areas of research include nineteenth-century gospel hymnody in the U.S. and in Germany, Baptist hymnody, the hymns of Watts, and the music of the praise and worship movement.

Kevin Kee is Assistant Professor of Canadian History and Social Studies at McGill University, Montreal, Canada. He is preparing for publication a manuscript focused on revivalism in Canada from the late nineteenth century to the 1950s.

Richard J. Mouw is President and Professor of Christian Philosophy at Fuller Theological Seminary. His most recent book is *He Shines in All That's Fair: Culture and Common Grace* (Eerdmans).

Mark A. Noll is McManis Professor of Christian Thought at Wheaton College. He has recently published *America's God, from Jonathan Edwards to Abraham Lincoln* (Oxford).

Felicia Piscitelli is an original cataloger at the Sterling C. Evans Library at Texas A&M University, College Station, Texas, with the faculty rank of Associate Professor and specialties in Romance languages and in music. She is an organist at St. Thomas Aquinas Catholic Church in College Station, and at present is helping a faculty member at the university to develop a course on hymnody to be offered in Spring 2004.

Robert A. Schneider is Assistant Vice Provost for Core and Transfer at Temple University in Philadelphia, Pennsylvania, and has taught American religious history there and elsewhere. He is writing an article detailing the emergence of American Protestant missionary hymnody in the 1820s.

Rochelle A. Stackhouse serves as an Interim Pastor in the UCC in northeastern Pennsylvania as well as Adjunct Professor at Moravian Theological Seminary. She recently published an article entitled "Spirituality and Extroverts" and is working on a book on the same subject.

Jeffrey VanderWilt is an assistant professor of theological studies at Loyola Marymount University, Los Angeles, California. He specializes in the theology of Christian worship and is the author of *Communion with Non-Catholic Christians: Risks, Challenges, and Opportunities* (Liturgical Press).

Introduction

Richard J. Mouw

These days, when appearing at events where I am scheduled to speak, I am often asked whether any hymns will be quoted. I think it is fair to say that I have gotten a reputation of sorts for doing that kind of thing, but it is a reputation that comes naturally. My preacher-father, who regularly quoted some lines from a hymn to nail down a point he was trying to make in a sermon, schooled me in the practice.

Sometimes I wonder, though, whether I was born a little too late to be doing this sort of thing. My father's congregations were well educated in the contents of their hymnbooks. It was a regular practice at our Sunday evening services to have "request time," and there was never a lull during that part of the service. Typically several favorites would be called out at once, and we usually did not have enough time to sing all of the hymns that were requested. When my father quoted a hymn, he was drawing on material that was familiar to his hearers.

But when you quote a hymn to a contemporary congregation, you now risk getting a wall of blank stares in response. These days many evangelical congregations do not even possess hymnbooks. Or the books may be there in the pew racks, but the words of hymns to be sung are either projected onto a large screen or printed in the bulletin. None of this is conducive to the spontaneous quoting of favorite hymns. Indeed, in many congregations, gathered worshipers sing more praise songs than hymns, if they sing any hymns at all.

Not that I want to be counted among the cultured despisers of praise songs. Many of the criticisms of this form of music strike me as misguided. Yes, they are repetitious. But evangelicals have always been fond of repetition — as those of us from the generation raised on "Do, Lord" and "I have the joy, joy, joy, joy" know only too well. Besides, Gregorian chant is also nothing if not repetitious.

Indeed, one of the merits of praise music, which is too-seldom acknowledged, is that it represents a partial revival of psalmody. To be sure, the use of the biblical psalms in praise music is not nearly as comprehensive as what we find in the Genevan Psalter. There is almost no lament, for example, in contemporary Christian music. But for all of that, much praise music is simply phrases from the Psalms and other biblical texts put to music. This is a good thing, although it is regrettable when such music simply replaces the contents of the hymnbooks.

I do think the trend away from more traditional music will be reversed sooner rather than later. The older hymns, I predict, will make a comeback. Maybe we will sing them to a different beat, accompanied by different instruments than in the past. Chances are we will not hold hymnbooks in our hands as often as we once did. But I am convinced that hymn singing will eventually loom large again in evangelical worship. I hope I am right in my optimism, because if we do abandon the older hymns we will have lost a precious treasure in the life of the believing community.

There are some Christian leaders, of course, who are convinced that the hymns of the past are actually an obstacle to our spiritual well-being. In the summer of 2001 *The Los Angeles Times* ran a piece about a pastor who organizes his services around show tunes, accompanied by dialogue with the gathered worshipers about various lines in the songs. The pastor admitted that some members of his congregation were uneasy with this style of worship. "How's this got anything to do with religion?" they ask him. His response: "If you are sitting in church for an hour, reciting words and singing hymns you hardly know, what's that got to do with religion?"

An Evangelical Testimony about the Importance of Hymns

The pastor apparently meant his question as a rhetorical one, but I can think of several good answers. For one thing, hymns are an important means of theological pedagogy. My mentor David Hubbard was fond of saying that hymns contain "compacted theology." His favorite example was the line from Edward Mote's hymn, "My hope is built on nothing less" (ca. 1834), which reads: "His oath, His covenant, His blood, / Support me in the whelming flood." "There are several centuries of theology packed into those lines," Hubbard would say.

My own theological reflection is greatly enriched by thinking about the contents of hymnody. An illustration is this verse from Matthew Bridges' "Crown Him with many crowns" (1851):

Crown Him the Lord of love;
Behold His hands and side,
Rich wounds, yet visible above,
In beauty glorified:
No angel in the sky
Can fully bear that sight,
But downward bends His wond'ring eye
At mysteries so bright.

The imagery here not only captures important theology, but it does so in a way that impresses the theological point on your consciousness as no scholarly treatise can do. I may know theologically that Christ ascended into the heavens as the victorious Crucified One, the Lamb who was slain. But the theological point is underscored — it becomes graphic — through the marvelous words about his "Rich wounds, yet visible above, in beauty glorified" — wounds that create a sight so full of mysteries that the celestial hosts cannot bear simply to fix their gaze on them.

In some worship settings that I have suffered through, the hymns have been the only available expression of theological orthodoxy. Once I participated in an ecumenical service where the preacher of the day made it clear that he had no use for the idea of a substitutionary atonement. I was sitting in the front row next to the worship leader, a Roman Catholic friend. Halfway through the homily I whispered to her, "This is awful!" She whispered back: "Be patient. I'm the one who chose the hymns!" At the end of the service she invited us to sing all of the verses of Carl Boberg's "How great thou art" (translated 1949). Her enthusiastic singing was a striking contrast to the preacher's obvious discomfort when we got to the third verse:

And when I think, that God, His Son not sparing;
Sent Him to die, I scarce can take it in;
That on the Cross, my burden gladly bearing,
He bled and died to take away my sin.

Hymns are also an important record of the past spiritual experiences of the believing community. It is not uncommon to hear critics complaining about the extensive use of the first person in evangelical hymnody — although these same people seldom extend that critique to the same pattern as it appears in the biblical psalms! To be sure, evangelical religion has often operated with a much too individualistic understanding of the Christian faith, and evangelical hymns can certainly be a force for encouraging a one-dimensional egotism. But there are also strengths in the first-person character of many evangelical hymns. For evangelicals who take seriously the need for a *personal* relationship to Jesus Christ, the fact that many hymns speak of person-specific experiences is not necessarily a defect. Indeed, we should expect that people who have important things to say about their specific faith journeys would want to put their testimonies to music. Properly understood, the resultant records of individual spiritual experiences can actually promote a sense of community. By attending to ways in which the hymnal serves as an archive for the rich diversity of Christian narratives, we gain the kind of empathy that is crucial for the formation of what the philosopher Hannah Arendt liked to refer to as "the expanded consciousness." In this sense, singing "I"-centered hymns can be an important means for experiencing the communion of the saints.

For example, I am a Fanny Crosby enthusiast, and her employment of the first person often inspires me precisely because of the uniqueness of the "I" that is the subject of her hymnic testimonies. Her frequent use, as a blind person, of visual imagery expands my own understanding of the character of spiritual sight. When she expresses the conviction, for example, that "I shall see in His beauty the King in whose Law I delight" — the One who presently gives her "songs in the night" — I am drawn into an experience of spiritual empathy that enhances my sense of the communion of the saints.

While participating not long ago in a service in Beijing, China, with a large congregation of about five thousand people, hymn singing resulted in a memorable experience of spiritual empathy. We had met the evening before with someone who described — reluctantly at first, but eventually in some detail — what it had been like for believers during the enforced suppression of Christian worship during the Cultural Revolution. These matters were still on my mind the next morning as I sat in the worship service. The first hymn announced was the old gospel song, "There is sunshine in my soul today" by Eliza E. Hewitt. As we sang, I watched a row of elderly women who, of course, were singing in Chinese. But since I knew the words I sang along in English. Like me, the women obviously knew the words by heart, and I choked up when I thought about their experiences in the Cultural Revolution and the message of these words in the hymn: "There is music in my soul today, a carol for my King / And Jesus, listening, can hear, the songs I cannot sing."

In my own experience, hymns have also served as a powerful resource for thinking about issues in social ethics. When some of us began, in the 1960s and 70s, to insist that evangelicals should be actively committed to such things as racial justice and the task of peacemaking, we were often met with hostility from other evangelicals. The resistance to such concerns was so strong that it was easy to start wondering whether one had missed a warning from the Lord against Christians getting caught up in such matters. In times of discouragement, though, it was the hymnbook that provided much encouragement.

As I compared the dominant evangelical social attitudes of the time with the message of many evangelical hymns, I was struck by the gap between what we talked about and what we sang. One preacher, for example, having issued a bold call for Christians to support military crusades as the only way to defeat the godless forces in the world, then called on the congregation to sing Ernest W. Shurtleff's "Lead on, O King eternal" (1888), which contains this most interesting proclamation:

For not with swords loud clashing,
Nor roll of stirring drums,
With deeds of love and mercy,
The heavenly kingdom comes.

The hymn proved to be a perfect antidote for the sermon!

Many of the best lessons in evangelical hymnody concerning the scope of Christian discipleship came from the "altar call" hymns of evangelistic crusades and revival meetings. These are the hymns featured in chapters that follow by Kevin Kee and Thomas Bergler. They call for a radical kind of self-examination before the face of God. Typically the preacher would ask that every head be bowed and every eye closed. Then we would sing Judson W. Van DeVenter's "I surrender all" (1896). Such moments made up some of the most sacred experiences of my life. It was precisely the "all-ness" of those times of self-examination that exerted a profound influence in the deep places of my soul — so much so that I have never been tempted to doubt the power of those moments, but rather to expand the scope of self-examination that hymns encouraged in those sacred moments of my youth.

There is much about that older evangelical ethos to which many of us would never want to return. But the songs that we learned to sing will reside forever in a very deep place. Perhaps new generations will find equally — or even more — effective ways to sing about the basic issues of life. But those generations would do well to pay at least some attention to testimonies from the past. The essays in this book are a contribution to that spiritual exercise.

The Shape of This Book

Historians have only just begun to describe the profound connections that hymnody sustains to other spheres of existence. As my own experience suggests, and as is documented at great length through the chapters that follow, hymns and gospel songs have enjoyed the deepest possible connections with personal experience — domestic, intergenerational, and social, as well as religious. They are also a full expression of theology — especially as popularized for mass consumption. They comment at unexpected length on relations between churches and society — particularly as a barometer of shifting cultural standards. And they act powerfully to form identities — for individuals and groups and as markers of inclusion and exclusion.

Yet hymns and hymn singing are difficult to write about because the very act of singing is so important for the affective weight borne by the hymns. The chapters that follow, which deal only incidentally with music and singing, nonetheless contribute substantially to understanding the centrality of hymn singing in many dimensions of American Protestant and evangelical life. As such, they join a small but growing body of literature that attempts to explain the wider dimensions of hymn experiences that reflect basic personal-social-religious realities of Western Christian history.[1]

This book focuses on hymns that have meant the most for Protestants, especially in Caucasian and evangelical traditions in the United States. Yet because the effects of hymn singing are so protean, it is entirely appropriate that the book also includes chapters on Isaac Watts and other British hymn writers who provided the first great impetus to the hymn traditions of the United States; on the use of gospel songs in English Canada, where traditions overlap significantly with the United States; and on the powerful attraction of African-American gospel music for whites of several religious persuasions (and none). The center of attention, however, is the large body of American Protestants, especially in evangelical traditions, for whom hymn writing, hymn editing, hymn adapting, hymn abridging, and above all hymn singing have constituted something very like the heart of their Christian experience.

The first section of the book uses only mild hyperbole by describing Isaac Watts as the *fons et origino* of Anglo-American Protestant hymnody as a whole. Mark Noll explains in brief why a "new hymnody" was so important in the great religious changes of the eighteenth century and also how that hymnody was able to provide a platform of common theological affirmation for the otherwise fractious evangelical movement. Then come

1. For this effort, an older and flourishing genre of books about hymn writers and hymn texts, viewed more narrowly, offers welcome support for broader historical efforts. The first among those works remains John Julian, *A Dictionary of Hymnology* (New York: Charles Scribner's Sons, 1892), but among many other helpful examples, see also Theron Brown and Hezekiah Butterworth, *The Story of the Hymns and Tunes* (New York: American Tract Society, 1906); Louis F. Benson, *Studies of Familiar Hymns*, 2 vols. (Philadelphia: Westminster, 1923, 1926); Henry Wilder Foote, *Three Centuries of American Hymnody* (Cambridge, MA: Harvard University Press, 1940); Erik Routley, *I'll Praise My Maker* (London: Independent Press, 1951); William James Reynolds, *Hymns of Our Faith* (Nashville: Broadman, 1964); Albert Christ-Janer and Charles Williams Hughes, *American Hymns Old and New*, 2 vols. (New York: Columbia University Press, 1980); and Ian Bradley, ed., *The Penguin Book of Hymns* (London: Penguin, 1989). Many of the notable examples of broader historical analysis are cited in the notes to the chapters that follow, including Susan S. Tamke, *Make a Joyful Noise Unto the Lord: Hymns as a Reflection of Victorian Social Attitudes* (Athens: Ohio University Press, 1978); Sandra S. Sizer, *Gospel Hymns and Social Religion: The Rhetoric of 19th Century Revivalism* (Philadelphia: Temple University Press, 1978); Lionel Adey, *Class and Idol in the English Hymn* (Vancouver: University of British Columbia Press, 1988); and Donald Davie, *The Eighteenth-Century Hymn in England* (New York: Cambridge University Press, 1993).

two chapters on the incredibly influential work of Watts. Esther Rothenbusch draws on the best literature concerning the use of Watts in America, as well as her own research, to detail the extraordinarily deep, long enduring, but occasionally ironic impression of Watts on American Protestant religious thought and experience. Rochelle Stackhouse, using in part her own pioneering dissertation, explains how the passage of time muffled, and even reversed, the stern political message found in one of Watts's most memorable hymns, "Our God, our help in ages past." Stackhouse underscores the importance of that transition by showing also that the same experience took place with the best-known hymn of Timothy Dwight, who also happened to be one of the most important early publishers of Watts in America.

The book's next section presents five carefully researched papers that, as full as they are, can still only hint at the many dimensions of American religious life that are opened up by a serious attention to hymns. Robert Schneider shows how absolutely crucial hymns — written, sung, exemplified — were in the opening two generations of the American missionary movement. Kevin Kee explains the centrality of gospel songs in a long tradition of leading Canadian evangelists, especially how song became an index to the commodification of revival in urban Canada. Thomas Bergler's study of the post–World War II development of Youth for Christ (YFC) picks up where Kee's last evangelist, Charles Templeton, left off. Bergler extends his argument, however, to suggest that the contemporary debate over music in church, often styled "worship wars," actually began with the musical innovations pioneered by YFC in the 1940s and 1950s. Felicia Piscitelli uses the hymnbook to frame a path-breaking account of Protestant-Catholic ecumenical relations over the last several decades; her research shows how much and yet how selective Catholic borrowing of Protestant hymns and gospel songs has been. This section closes with Virginia Brereton's sensitive essay on the reasons for white enthusiasm for black gospel music that began with the emergence of Mahalia Jackson and other African-American headliners. Her chapter also points to the fact that, if this book could have come closer to a comprehensive account, it would have included several more papers on the critically important development of hymnody, including those of Isaac Watts, in African-American traditions.

The last section of the book is more directly theological. It begins with Jeffrey VanderWilt's explanation of how hymns reveal important changes in Protestant attitudes toward death from the early nineteenth to the late twentieth century. Susan Wise Bauer performs a similar task in exploring the debates, largely within conservative Protestant circles, over the merits of narrative versus systematic hymns. VanderWilt and Bauer both do significant digging into what has been sung by American Protestants, but also theologize themselves with considerable cogency about what they have found through a study of the hymns. My own chapter on the themes of rescue in the nautical images that were once so popular in evangelical hymns allows me to engage with some of the most important academic writing on American hymnody and also to make a theological statement of my own.

Most of the chapters in this book were first prepared for a conference, "Hymnody in American Protestantism," sponsored by the Institute for the Study of American Evangelicals (ISAE) at Wheaton College with generous funding from the Lilly Endowment. It is a commentary on the riches to be found in serious study of hymnody that many of the chapters have had to be abridged considerably from the papers first prepared for this conference.

For the ISAE's American Protestant Hymns Project, Professor Stephen Marini of Wellesley College prepared an extensive database of the most often reprinted hymns in 175 popular Protestant hymnals that were published from 1737 to 1960. Marini's database is put to use by several of the contributors to this volume (especially Schneider, Piscitelli, VanderWilt, and Bauer). Abbreviated results from the Marini survey, along with considerable tabular information from the authors who employed the database for their own purposes, are found in the appendices that bring the book to a close.

IN THE BEGINNING WAS WATTS

CHAPTER ONE

The Defining Role of Hymns in Early Evangelicalism

Mark A. Noll

In May 1731, the English Congregationalist Philip Doddridge wrote to his older colleague in the Nonconformist ministry, Isaac Watts, about a midweek worship service he had recently conducted in a barn for "a pretty large assembly of plain country people." Doddridge's text was from Hebrews 6:12 — "That ye be not slothful, but followers of them who through faith and patience inherit the promises." After the sermon Doddridge sang with his humble congregation a hymn by Watts that began,

> Give me the wings of faith to rise
>   Within the veil, and see
> The saints above, how great their joys,
>   How bright their glories be.

The effect of the singing was the occasion for Doddridge's letter: "I had the satisfaction to observe tears in the eyes of several of the auditory, and after the service was over, some of them told me that they were not able to sing, so deeply were their minds affected with it."[1]

Although this incident took place in an out-of-the-way venue with a congregation of no special account, Doddridge was nonetheless regis-

1. Doddridge to Watts, in Geoffrey F. Nuttall, *Calendar of the Corespondence of Philip Doddridge DD (1702-1751)* (London: His Majesty's Stationery Office, 1979), 61-62. For the text of the hymn, see E. Paxton Hood, *Isaac Watts: His Life and Writing* (London: Religious Tract Society, 1875), 165.

tering a sea change in Western Christianity. Ordinary believers had begun to find their voice, and that voice was expressed in song. Watts was the founder of the new hymnody that the people were beginning to sing, but Doddridge, with hymns like "Awake, my soul; stretch every nerve" and "O happy day, that fixed my choice," was an important contributor too. Soon both Watts and Doddridge helped open the way for leading evangelicals like John and Charles Wesley, George Whitefield, and Jonathan Edwards, who proclaimed that true Christianity meant not just intellectual recognition of Christian dogma or formal acknowledgment of the church, but the experience of repentance and faith in Jesus Christ. Oceans of ink have been spilled in analyzing virtually all aspects of the evangelical movements that arose from that insistence. Only rarely, however, has the significance of song been given its full place in this story. Yet nothing was more central to the evangelical revival than the singing of new hymns written in praise of the goodness, mercy, and grace of God.

Hymns in the Early Evangelical Movement

For the early generations of evangelicals, hymn singing became almost sacramental. It was the one physical activity that all evangelicals shared, and it was the one experience that bound them most closely together with each other. In fact, it is difficult to discover any significant event, person, or structure of early evangelicalism that did not involve the singing of hymns. It is likewise difficult to discover any significant experience of singing where the hymns had not been freshly written by the evangelicals themselves (or by Isaac Watts who befriended them and whose hymns they embraced enthusiastically from the start).

Venue, time, social locale, and place hardly made a difference. Hymn-singing played a critical role during the Moravian revivals in the late 1720s, far in the eastern German lands, that eventually exerted a great impact in Britain and North America.[2] Jonathan Edwards was one of New England's earliest promoters of Isaac Watts's hymns, and his paradigm-making account of the 1734-1735 revival in Northampton, Massachusetts,

2. W. R. Ward, *The Protestant Evangelical Awakening* (New York: Cambridge University Press, 1992), 127.

specified hymn-singing as a key element of this awakening.[3] The critical role in early Methodism that was played by Charles Wesley as hymn writer and John Wesley as hymn publisher is very well known. Yet observers at the time made more of Methodism singing than do historians — in the words of one American Congregationalist who wanted his colleagues to move more quickly in imitating the Methodists: "We sacrifice too much to taste. The secret of the Methodists lies in the admirable adaptation of their music and hymns to produce effect; they strike at once at the heart, and the moment we hear their animated, thrilling choruses, we are electrified."[4] After George Whitefield had preached to huge crowds in Philadelphia in 1739, Benjamin Franklin noted how "one could not walk through Philadelphia in the evening without hearing psalms sung in different families of every street."[5] Hymns composed in Welsh and Gaelic fueled the evangelical revivals in Wales and Scotland.[6] And hymnody provided a lifeline during the forced migrations of African-American evangelicals.[7] The hymns that were sung, moreover, constituted for almost all evangelical subgroupings what John Wesley wrote in 1780 about his landmark *Collection of Hymns for the Use of the People Called Methodists* — these hymns were "in effect a little book of experimental and practical divinity . . . [a] distinct and full . . . account of scriptural Christianity."[8]

An indication of how important hymn singing became as a result of promotion by evangelicals like Wesley can be found in modern bibliogra-

3. On Watts, see Edwards to Benjamin Colman, 22 May 1744, in *The Works of Jonathan Edwards, Vol. 16: Letters and Personal Writings,* ed. George S. Claghorn (New Haven: Yale University Press, 1998), 144-45; on singing in 1734-35, see Edwards, *A Faithful Narrative of the Surprising Work of God* (1737), in *The Works of Jonathan Edwards, Vol. 4: The Great Awakening,* ed. C. C. Goen (New Haven: Yale University Press, 1972), 151.

4. Quoted in Leland Howard Scott, "Methodist Theology in America in the Nineteenth Century" (Ph.D. diss., Yale University, 1954), 132n81.

5. Luke Tyerman, *The Life of the Rev. George Whitefield,* 2 vols. (London: Hodder & Stoughton, 1876), 1:338.

6. See Glyn Tegai Hughes, *Williams Pantycelyn* (n.p.: University of Wales Press, 1983), and R. Parry, ed., *Hymns of the Welsh Revival* (Wrexham: Hughes & Son, n.d.); along with Donald Maclean, *The Spiritual Songs of Dugald Buchanan* (Edinburgh: John Grant, 1913).

7. John Saillant, "Hymnody and the Persistence of an African-American Faith in Sierra Leone," *The Hymn* 48 (January 1997): 8-17.

8. John Wesley, *A Collection of Hymns for the Use of the People Called Methodists* (1780), in *The Works of John Wesley, Vol. 7,* ed. Franz Hildebrandt and Oliver A. Beckerlegge (Nashville: Abingdon, 1983), 74.

phies. One of the most extensive and helpful of such guides is *The Hymn Tune Index,* which catalogues the tunes in published works from the mid-sixteenth century to the early nineteenth. Although other factors were involved in accelerating the rate of hymnbook publication — like a general upsurge in publishing, the growth of population, and the energetic contributions of American printers — the gross figures are still impressive. From 1701 to 1740, English-language publishers brought out an average of approximately sixty hymn tune books per decade. From 1741 to 1780, the years when evangelical movements began to emerge, the number per decade doubled to about 120. From 1781 to 1820, when evangelicalism began to exert a pervasive effect on the religious life of England, Wales, Scotland, Ireland, and the new United States, the number of hymn tune books brought out each decade skyrocketed to about 310. Such enumerations indicate the shape of a cultural, as well as a religious, revolution.[9]

The Religion of the Evangelical Hymns

The hymns of the early evangelical movement proclaimed a rich understanding of Christian faith, but also a somewhat restricted one.[10] Although most of the major hymn-writers of the eighteenth century composed verses on the nature of the church, the sacraments of baptism and communion, the configuration of events at the end of time, as well as the particular convictions of their own subgroups, the hymns that were sung widely, that were reprinted time after time, and that won their way deep into the heart of popular evangelicalism did not concern these potentially divisive subjects. Rather, the enduring hymns featured the need of sinners

9. Nicholas Temperley, *The Hymn Tune Index: A Census of English-Language Hymn Tunes in Printed Sources from 1535 to 1820,* 4 vols. (Oxford: Clarendon, 1998), 1:409-57 ("Chronological List of Sources").

10. The following paragraphs present an edited version of work being prepared for a book on eighteenth-century evangelical history (forthcoming InterVarsity Press, 2004). They follow in paths pioneered by Stephen A. Marini in, for example, "Rehearsal for Revival: Sacred Singing and the Great Awakening in America," *Journal of the American Academy of Religion: Thematic Studies* 50 (1983): 71-91; "Evangelical Hymns and Popular Beliefs," *Dublin Seminar for New England Folklife: Annual Proceedings* 21 (1996): 117-26; and especially "Hymnody as History: Early Evangelical Hymns and the Recovery of American Popular Religion," *Church History* 71 (2002): 273-306.

for Christ the savior, the love of God in Christ, the saving power of Christ, the refuge and healing found in Christ, the joy of redemption in Christ, and the hope of eternal life in Christ. All efforts to illustrate the themes of the most popular evangelical hymns must be arbitrary, but Stephen Marini's catalogues of the hymns that were most often reprinted across the evangelical spectrum has made possible a greater degree of specificity. His database for hymnals published from 1737 to 1960 is used by other contributors to this book and is presented in Appendix I. For this chapter, a different Marini compilation is used that was drawn from eighty-six Protestant hymnals published in North America from 1737 to 1860. In the first instance, these hymns illustrate the strong bonds that religious song constructed across the Atlantic, since the vast majority were composed by English authors of the eighteenth century. Even more importantly, the texts of the most often reprinted hymns in this list illustrate forcefully the character of evangelical faith, or at least the depiction of this faith that ordinary evangelicals chose to sing about in many different places and through many decades.

The eleven hymns reprinted most often in the books canvassed by Professor Marini (there was a tie for tenth place) included four by Isaac Watts ("Come we that love the Lord" [Come we], "Am I a soldier of the cross" [Am I], "When I can read my title clear" [When title], and "He dies the friend of sinners" [He dies]); two by the Methodist-turned-Moravian John Cennick ("Jesus my all to heaven is gone" [Jesus] and "Children of the heavenly king" [Children]); one each by the Cambridge Baptist Robert Robinson ("Come thou fount of every blessing" [Come thou fount]), Charles Wesley ("Blow ye the trumpet blow" [Blow]), the London Baptist Samuel Stennett ("On Jordan's stormy banks I stand" [Jordan]), and the maverick Methodist Edward Peronnet ("All hail the power of Jesus' name" [All hail]); and one anonymous hymn from the influential *Collection* by the London Baptist John Rippon from 1787 ("How firm a foundation" [How firm]).[11]

If the popular hymns shied away from some controversial subjects,

11. For the list, see Marini, "Hymnody as History," 280. Short titles are for references in the text. Hymns are quoted below from *The Baptist Hymnal for Use in the Church and Home*, ed. W. Howard Doane (Philadelphia: American Baptist Publication Society, 1883); *The Methodist Hymnal* (Baltimore et al.: Methodist Publishing House, 1939); and *Trinity Hymnal* (Philadelphia: Orthodox Presbyterian Church, 1961).

they were not in the least timorous about affirming the full sinfulness of humanity and the desperate need for a Redeemer.

> My grief a burden long has been,
> Because I was not saved from sin.
> The more I strove against its power,
> I felt its weight and guilt the more;
> Till late I heard my Saviour say,
> "Come hither soul, I am the way." (Cennick, Jesus)

Realism about the sinful state continued after conversion, for even those who favored perfection did not deny the powers of human corruption:

> Nothing but sin have I to give:
> Nothing but love shall I receive. (Cennick, Jesus)

More generally, the life of faith was regarded as a battle requiring constant divine support:

> Prone to wander, Lord, I feel it,
> Prone to leave the God I love;
> Here's my heart, O take and seal it,
> Seal it for thy courts above. (Robinson, Come thou fount)

In almost all evangelical hymns the love of God in Christ for ordinary women and men was central, which is why so many of the hymns of Isaac Watts were so popular for so long.

> He dies! — the Friend of sinners dies;
> Lo! Salem's daughters weep around:
> A solemn darkness veils the skies;
> A sudden trembling shakes the ground.
>
> Here's love and grief beyond degree:
> The Lord of glory dies for men!
> But lo! what sudden joys we see, —
> Jesus, the dead, revives again! . . .
>
> Break off your tears, ye saints, and tell
> How high our great Deliverer reigns;

Sing how he spoiled the hosts of hell;
And led the tyrant Death in chains. (Watts, He dies)

For the work of God on behalf of sinners, the merits of Christ's death were central, whether for the Baptist Robert Robinson:

Jesus sought me when a stranger,
Wand'ring from the fold of God:
He, to rescue me from danger,
Interposed his precious blood. (Robinson, Come thou fount)

Or the Methodist Charles Wesley:

Jesus, our great High Priest,
Hath full atonement made. (Wesley, Blow)

Many of the hymns depicted joyful responses to the work of God more than detailed description of it:

Sinners! whose love can ne'er forget
The wormwood and the gall,
Go — spread your trophies at His feet,
And crown Him Lord of all. (Perronet, All hail)

Blow ye the trumpet blow!
The gladly solemn sound
Let all the nations know,
To earth's remotest bound:
The year of jubilee is come;
Return, ye ransomed sinners home. (Wesley, Blow)

The men of grace have found
Glory begun below;
Celestial fruits on earthly ground
From faith and hope may grow. (Watts, Come we)

Come, thou Fount of every blessing,
Tune my heart to sing thy grace;
Streams of mercy, never ceasing,
Call for songs of loudest praise. (Robinson, Come thou fount)

The hymns also say much about the life of faith, and in realistic terms. In response to the question whether "I" should "be carried to the skies / On flowery beds of ease?" the answer was unequivocal:

Sure I must fight if I would reign:
Increase my courage, Lord;
I'll bear the toil, endure the pain,
Supported by thy Word. (Watts, Am I)

The standard expectation was that life would be difficult, but also that God-in-Christ would make it possible to go on with hope.

Fear not, brethren; joyful stand
On the borders of your land;
Jesus Christ, your Father's Son,
Bids you undismayed go on. (Cennick, Children)

When through fiery trials thy pathway shall lie,
My grace, all sufficient, shall be thy supply;
The flame shall not hurt thee; I only design
Thy dross to consume and thy gold to refine. (Rippon, How firm)

The end in view, repeated in many hymns, was an eternal life of joy and peace gained through final identification with Jesus Christ:

Jesus, my all, to heaven is gone,
he whom I fix my hopes upon;
His track I see, and I'll pursue
The narrow way, till Him I view.
The way the holy prophets went,
The road that leads from banishment,
The King's highway of holiness,
I'll go, for all His paths are peace. (Cennick, Jesus)

Fixation on heaven was strong in the most popular evangelical hymns, but that fixation was grounded in broader doctrines of the Christian life.

The soul that on Jesus hath leaned for repose,
I will not, I will not desert to his foes;

That soul, though all hell should endeavor to shake,
I'll never, no, never, no, never, forsake. (Rippon, How firm)

On Jordan's stormy banks I stand,
And cast a wistful eye
To Canaan's fair and happy land
Where my possessions lie.
O the transporting, rapturous scene
That rises to my sight!
Sweet fields arrayed in living green,
And rivers of delight. (Stennett, Jordan)

When I can read my title clear
To mansions in the skies,
I bid farewell to every fear,
And wipe my weeping eyes. (Watts, When title)

A few other themes were adumbrated in these hymns, for example, the reliability of Scripture: "How firm a foundation . . . Is laid for your faith in his excellent Word!" (Rippon, How firm) But for the most part, the hymns that were most often reprinted held to their narrow focus on the great acts of redemption that disturbed complacent sinners, turned them with longing to Christ, encouraged them in the life of faith, and joined them to Christ eternally.

The Broader Connections of Hymnody

The eighteenth-century upsurge in hymnody constituted an index for many aspects of the new evangelical era. As only three of many possible indications of what hymn singing revealed, we will examine how hymns mediated between differences of class and race, how hymns offered a public voice to women, and how they functioned to pacify intra-evangelical disputes.

If hymn singing was one of the strongest trans-Atlantic evangelical activities, it also provided one of the few bridges between the classes and the races. Samuel Davies in America, for example, took a particular pleasure from the fact that converted African Americans and American Indians became adept at singing his and other hymns of the evangelical revival. In 1756, he informed a British correspondent that, after the welcome reception of some hymnals sent by the Wesleys from England, "Sundry of them ["the *poor Slaves*"] have lodged all night in my kitchen; and, sometimes, when I have awaked about two or three o-clock in the morning, a torrent of sacred harmony poured into my chamber, and carried my mind away to Heaven. In this seraphic exercise, some of them spend almost the whole night."[12]

Hymns were also one of the few means open to women for the public expression of their faith. Although there were not too many women hymn writers in early evangelicalism, the English Baptist Ann Steele (1716-1779) and the Welsh Calvinist Methodist, Ann Griffiths (1776-1805), were forerunners of what later became a long line of productive author-composers.

Ann Steele was permanently injured by a fall from a horse when she was just a teenager, and thereafter enjoyed anything but an easy life.[13] Yet she wrote steadily about Christian confidence in God and eventually published three volumes of sacred poetry. Her most poignant verses were occasioned by the tragic drowning of her fiancée only hours before their wedding:

Father, whate'er of earthly bliss
Thy sovereign will denies,
Accepted at thy throne of grace,
Let this petition rise: —

Give me a calm, a thankful heart,
From every murmur free;
The blessings of thy grace impart,
And make me live to thee.[14]

Ann Griffiths, whose memory for Scripture and sermons was phenomenal, composed hymns that she recited to her household. After she

12. From *Letters from the Rev. Samuel Davies, etc. Shewing the State of Religion in Virginia, Particularly among the Negroes* (London, 1757), 16, as quoted by George William Pilcher, "Samuel Davies and the Instruction of Negroes in Virginia," *Virginia Magazine of Biography and History* 74 (1966): 298.

13. See Virginia Hampton Wright, "Anne Steele," *Christian History* 31 ("The Golden Age of Hymns") (1991): 22.

14. *Baptist Hymnal* (1883), no. 374.

died giving birth to her first child, one of her servants repeated those hymns to her husband, who wrote them down and saw them published. They made unusually full use of biblical imagery, as in these verses describing Jesus and his work in terms of the "tent of meeting" and the "Presence" of God taken from the history of ancient Israel:

Sinner is my name and nature,
Fouler none on earth can be;
In the Presence here — O wonder! —
God receive me tranquilly;
See him there, his law fulfilling,
For his foes a banquet laid,
God and man "Enough!" proclaiming
Through the offering he has made.

Boldly I will venture forward;
See the golden sceptre shine;
Pointing straight towards the sinner;
All may enter by that sign.
On I'll press, beseeching pardon,
On, till at his feet I fall,
Cry for pardon, cry for washing
In the blood which cleanses all.[15]

The early evangelical hymns also possessed an almost magical power to smooth over the often sharp theological differences that emerged within the movement. No example of this power serves better than the very strained relationship between the Arminians, John and Charles Wesley, and the Anglican Calvinist, Augustus M. Toplady (1740-1778). Toplady and the Wesleys were prime antagonists in a fresh bout of Arminian-Calvinist disputes beginning in the late 1760s. During this struggle, Toplady roundly denounced John Wesley and one of his colleagues, Walter Sellon, as perpetrators of the very same heresies that others had earlier proclaimed in the history of the church. According to Toplady, Wesley was "the John Godwin of the present age," and Sellon "stands in the same relation to Mr. John Wesley, that Caelestius did to

15. A. M. Allchin, *Songs to Her God: Spirituality of Ann Griffiths* (Cambridge, MA: Cowley, 1987), 100-101.

Pelagius, and Bertius to Arminius; viz. of retainer-general and whitewasher in ordinary."[16] For his part, Wesley blasted right back. In a pamphlet pretending to give Toplady's view of the contested issues, Wesley summarized his opponent's views like this: "One in twenty (suppose) of mankind are elected; nineteen in twenty are reprobated. The elect shall be saved, do what they will: The reprobate shall be damned, do what they can. Reader, believe this, or be damned. Witness my hand, A— T— ."[17]

Toplady and Charles Wesley were fully up to the challenge of putting this kind of acerbic theological exchange into verse. One of the hymns Toplady published during this time of theological strife was entitled "Arminianism Renounced"; it began with what Toplady took to be the typical Arminian stance:

How have I proudly scorn'd to stoop,
And cried the Pow'rs of Nature up,
And trusted to my legal Deeds![18]

Earlier Charles Wesley had written a hymn about the Calvinist doctrine of the decrees of God, which John Wesley had reprinted in the *Arminian Magazine* not long after his own fierce polemic against Toplady. It included many stanzas that left no doubt about the Wesleys' opinions, including this one:

Still shall the *Hellish Doctrine* stand?
And Thee for its dire Author claim?
No — let it sink at thy Command
Down to the Pit from whence it came.[19]

In a word, the antagonism between the Wesleys and Toplady was almost as sharp, and as fundamentally theological, as one could imagine.

16. Toplady, *Works* (1794 ed.), 280, 47, as quoted in Alan P. F. Sell, *The Great Debate: Calvinism, Arminianism, and Salvation* (Grand Rapids: Baker, 1983), 123n.36.

17. John Wesley, *The Doctrine of Absolute Predestination Stated and Asserted. By the Reverend Mr. A— T—* (1770), in *The Works of John Wesley*, ed. Thomas Jackson, 14 vols. (London: Wesleyan Conference Office, 1872), 14:198.

18. Augustus M. Toplady, *Hymns and Sacred Poems, on a Variety of Subjects* (London: Daniel Segwick, 1860), 149.

19. Frank Baker, ed., *Representative Verse of Charles Wesley* (New York: Abingdon, 1962), 31.

And yet not too many years after Toplady first published his hymn, "A Living and Dying Prayer for the Holiest Believer in the World," which he intended as a frontal attack on the Wesleyan doctrine of Christian perfection, Methodist hymnals had joined the hymnals of almost all other evangelicals in reprinting it:

> Rock of Ages, cleft for me,
> Let me hide myself in Thee!
> Let the Water and the Blood,
> From thy riven Side which flow'd,
> Be of Sin the double Cure,
> Cleanse me from its Guilt and Pow'r.[20]

Similarly, hymnals of all evangelical varieties, militantly Calvinist, militantly Arminian, and at all points in between just as eagerly reprinted the Marseille Hymn of Methodism that was printed as the first entry in all of the Wesleys' later hymnbooks:

> O for a thousand tongues to sing
> My dear Redeemer's praise!
> The glories of my God and King,
> The triumphs of his grace! . . .
> He breaks the power of cancelled sin,
> He sets the prisoner free;
> His blood can make the foulest clean —
> His blood availed for me.[21]

Although much did divide evangelicals from each other, hymnody served as a powerful ecumenical counterforce. It was precisely those themes in the hymns that spoke most directly of the sinner's experience of divine grace ("Let the water and the blood cleanse me from [sin's] guilt and power"; "His blood can make the foulest clean — His blood availed for me") that exerted the strongest unifying power.

* * *

20. Toplady, *Hymns and Sacred Poems,* 163.
21. Wesley, *Collection of Hymns,* in *Works,* 7:74.

Much else remains to be said about how the new hymnody of the eighteenth century created a dynamic engine of great emotional and cognitive power for virtually all later Protestant groups in the English-speaking world, and through indirect ways for many Roman Catholics as well. The next two chapters return, as is only proper, for concentrated attention to Isaac Watts, with whom it all began. By the end of the book, it will be obvious that Philip Doddridge's humble rural folk who in 1731 were so affected by singing one of Watts's hymns were but the vanguard of an army whose numbers cannot be counted.

CHAPTER TWO

"We're Marching to Zion": Isaac Watts in Early America

Esther Rothenbusch Crookshank

Hymns even apart from music — read aloud, memorized, and contemplated — found a place in the inner lives of nineteenth-century Americans that seems to have been closer to Scripture than to anything else. In 1872 Henry Ward Beecher, America's most loved preacher at that time, claimed that hymns, particularly those of Isaac Watts, shaped Americans' theology in his day more powerfully than even the Bible did.

> When believers analyze their religious emotions, it is as common to trace them back to the early hymns of childhood as to the Bible itself. At least until very recently, most English-speaking Protestants who thought about heaven did so more in the terms of Dr. Watts than of the *Revelation* of St. John.

Beecher's assertion contains a strong thesis about the roots of "religious emotions," particularly of those Americans who had learned hymns from childhood. He also addressed concepts of heaven, naming as the genesis of those images — for the average churchgoing American — the hymnody of Isaac Watts even before biblical revelation. Supporting this opinion is a passage from the greatest American fiction work of the era, *Uncle Tom's Cabin,* by the clergyman's famous sister, Harriet Beecher Stowe: "Something in the voice penetrated to the ear of the dying. He moved his head gently, smiled, and said, 'Jesus can make a dying-bed Feel soft as downy pillows are'."[1]

Watts's Theology and Language of Worship

Exactly how American Protestants of the mid-nineteenth century did "land in Dr. Watts," to quote Beecher once more, is the subject of this chapter. This study will trace the path of four of Watts's texts in Protestantism from the colonial period through ca. 1900: "Alas and did my Saviour bleed," "Am I a soldier of the cross," "Come, we that love the Lord," and "When I survey the wondrous cross." I will address the questions of (1) the nature of Watts's system of public worship; (2) how and why his psalms and hymns took root on American soil; (3) how Watts's theology and language affected American worship and was altered by it; (4) the role of Watts's texts in the two Awakenings and in related musical styles and practices; (5) the place of Watts in school education through the nineteenth century; and (6) the centrality of Watts in African-American worship and the shape-note singing tradition. My conclusions will address the cultural work that Watts's writings accomplished in American life and worship through these contexts.

Between 1707 and 1739 in Southampton the young British clergyman and scholar of logic and philology, Isaac Watts, produced four publications by which he hoped to achieve a systematic reform of congregational song in England's dissenting churches of his day. The four books were: *Hymns and Spiritual Songs, in Three Books* (London, 1707), *Psalms of David Imitated* (1719), *Horae Lyricae,* and *Divine and Moral Songs for Children.* Accomplishing far more and reaching beyond what he could have anticipated, his achievement indelibly stamped Protestant worship on both sides of the Atlantic for more than the next two centuries.

In his famous Preface to *The Psalms of David Imitated,* Watts disclosed the essence of his "Grand Design": "to teach my Author to speak like a Christian."[2] His case was powerfully reasoned and irrefutably scriptural:

1. Isaac Watts, *Hymns and Spiritual Songs, Book II,* "Christ's Presence makes Death easy." Cited in Selma L. Bishop, *Isaac Watts: Hymns and Spiritual Songs, 1707-1748* (London: Faith Press, 1962), 190.

2. Isaac Watts, Preface to *The Psalms of David Imitated in the Language of the New Testament* (London: Printed for J. Clark, R. Ford, and R. Cruttenden, 1719), [iii]-xxxii. Cited in David W. Music, *Hymnology: A Collection of Source Readings* (Lanham, MD: Scarecrow, 1996), 130.

Watts the logician argued that Old Testament Scripture viewed in New Testament light both allowed and obligated him to Christianize the psalms. After systematically "ransacking" existing metrical psalters, church histories, and psalm commentaries, Watts developed a new approach, what he called the psalm imitation, by which to shape the Psalms into christological declarations and prayers. Watts's preface demonstrates a clear awareness of how radical his plan was and also why it had such enormous influence. It also expressed his unshakable confidence in the soundness of his underlying "great Principle": "But still I am bold to maintain the great Principle on which my present work is founded; and that is, That if the brightest Genius on Earth or an Angel from Heaven should translate *David,* and keep close to the Sense and Style of the inspired Author, we should only obtain thereby a bright or heavenly Copy of the *Devotions of the Jewish King;* but it could never make the fittest *Psalm-Book for a Christian People.*"[3] At the end of the same volume he included the groundbreaking article entitled "A Short Essay Toward the Improvement of Psalmody." Although Watts had intended to revise and republish it later, this is the only volume in which it appears. Biographer Harry Escott views it as the manifesto of Watts's work. In it Watts argued that while the integrity of scriptural text be preserved in public reading, it was just as important that worship song must be non-literal, i.e., the congregation's own response: "By Reading we are instructed what have been the Dealings of God with Men in all Ages, . . . but Songs are generally Expressions of our own Experiences, or of his Glories. . . . We breath *[sic]* out our souls towards him."[4]

Armed with the Pauline mandate to sing with understanding, Watts approved only singing "with due knowledge and Conviction";[5] reason itself, he claimed, demanded that the psalter and all congregational song must be true for the congregation singing it. He saw the need in public worship of his day for what Escott calls "something approaching uniformity of interpretation." For Watts, the beauty of scriptural songs was that they met the needs or expressed the feelings of people in individual situations — they had concreteness, particularity, and specificity.[6] On that ba-

3. Cited in Music, *Hymnology,* 135.

4. Watts, *Psalms of David,* 243. Cited in Harry Escott, *Isaac Watts: Hymnographer: A Study of the Beginnings, Development, and Philosophy of the English Hymn* (London: Independent, 1962), 122.

5. Watts, *Psalms of David,* 266. Cited in Escott, *Isaac Watts,* 127.

6. Escott, *Isaac Watts,* 124.

sis, Watts took it upon himself not only to gospel-ize but to modernize, nationalize, and concretize the psalter for his world of Great Britain and his target audience, the Dissenting churches. Watts's *Psalms* provided his generation with an equivalent of Kenneth Taylor's *Living Bible* set to music — neither a literal translation nor a metrical versification (and he made no apologies on either count) but a new model, for which he adopted the literary word "imitation." As Escott points out, Watts was writing in England's Augustan Age, "when the Imitation was a literary genre popular in intellectual circles. Watts did for the Hebrew Psalmists what Pope had done for Horace, and what Johnson was shortly to do for Juvenal." As Pope applied to the personalities and events of the Georgian era Horace's descriptions, "so Watts set forth the Christian worship and life of his own age in terms descriptive of Hebrew life and . . . worship in the days of David and Hezekiah."[7] Thus in Watts, Psalm 100 became: "Sing to the Lord with joyful voice, / Let ev'ry land his name adore; / The British isles shall send the noise / Across the ocean to the shore."

Finally, insisting that even the Christianized Psalter could not meet every need of New Testament worship, particularly for Communion, Watts argued that the gospel by its nature called for "hymns of human composure." Did not the epistles proclaim that the church had a higher revelation of God than David or the prophets? He clinched his argument for hymns with the line: "Where can you find a Psalm that speaks the Miracles of Wisdom and Power as they are discover'd in a crucify'd Christ?"[8]

The second underlying premise of Watts's "Essay," after affirming comprehensibility and realism in song, was the principle of liberty in Christ as developed in Paul's Epistle to the Galatians. Watts read this epistle as freeing Christians from a bondage to singing only New Testament texts just as surely as it broke the Calvinist shackles of metrical psalmody. Liberty in the Spirit rejected neither psalms nor hymns, but proclaimed an open season for singing either scriptural or non-scriptural texts, in sum, freedom from all "fixed forms of praise."[9] For Watts, as Escott explains, "it is the breath of reality in our praises that matters most of all to God . . . before using [the Psalms] we must make them our own." Nothing less could be true new covenant worship.

7. Ibid., 121-131.

8. Watts, *Psalms of David,* 258; cited in Escott, *Isaac Watts,* 125.

9. Escott, *Isaac Watts,* 126-127.

Watts's system of congregational song, while influenced by his study of earlier metrical and even medieval models, was most shaped by his exhaustive command of Scripture in the original languages. His principles for worship were also shaped by his passionate mastery of both logic and philology; as the author of a logic textbook that would be used at Oxford for over a century, he exercised great care in his use of language.

Equally important, however, was his deep distress over the confusion about singing that he observed among lay working-class worshipers in England's Nonconformist congregations. As a result, he resolved to adapt his language, when writing poems for congregational use, to the understanding of the common Christian, resulting in what he called "sunk expression." Harry Escott has described Watts's stylistic development as a process of "artistic *kenosis.* Watts had to lay his poetic glories aside and dress the profound message of the gospel in the homespun verse and language of the people."[10] Ronald Tajchman, by analyzing Watts's use of Aristotelian rhetorical schemes and devices, explains the tension in the poet's hymns: "On the one hand, [Watts] sought to elevate his fellow believers by means of language. On the other hand, he wanted to reach the lowest level of understanding." By yoking his theological and scriptural prowess to his rhetoric skills, Watts could navigate a middle path.[11]

Like earlier psalm versifiers, Watts divided longer psalms into parts, to facilitate congregational use. He divided some psalms still further by inserting the rubric "Pause." Escott notes the astounding metric variety and options in Watts's psalter. While adhering, as he promised, to the best-known meters, Watts provided multiple versions in different meters for many psalms for a total of 338 psalm versions, of which 164 are in common meter, 121 in long meter, 34 in short meter, and several each in assorted others.[12] Nearly 50 psalms, or one third of the Psalter, are provided with two versions; 13 psalms are cast in all three favorite meters; many other psalms or sections of psalms appear in four, five, and even six different meters. Although prevented by his theology from using twelve entire psalms and 285 verses of other psalms, which he declared unfit for the New Testament church, Watts was nonetheless remarkably inclusive for

10. Ibid., 26.

11. Ronald Tajchman, "Isaac Watts's Communion Hymns: An Application of Classical Rhetoric," *The Hymn* 46, no. 1 (January 1995): 22.

12. For example, 6 8's, 6 10's, 6.6.8.6.6.8. and 6.6.6.6.4.4.4.4.

the rest of the Psalter. According to Escott's tabulations, of the 2,461 total verses in the book of Psalms, Watts treats fully 2,050.[13]

While poets since the Middle Ages had written devotional and communion hymns and had also made limited efforts to bring Christ into the Psalms, Watts's brilliant system was a quantum leap forward. He was not surprised when some denounced this revolutionary step. Appearing early on among pamphlets from his opponents were *A Vindication of David's Psalms from Mr. I. Watts's Erroneous Notions* and *Reasons wherefore Christians ought to worship God, not with Dr. Watts's Psalms, but with David's Psalms*. To read Watts's opponents one might think that David himself had placed his imprimatur on the Psalms of Sternhold and Hopkins, the first completed Psalter in English. When Watts's *Logic* was published, he wrote in its preface: "It is for the same reason that the bulk of the common people are superstitiously fond of the Psalms translated by Hopkins and Sternhold, and think them sacred and Divine because they have been now for more than a hundred years bound up in the same covers with our Bibles."[14] Susan Tamke discusses the deep-seated prejudice against hymns among many British Puritans, for whom even owning or using a hymnal in one's private devotions could be considered subversive behavior.[15] Henry Wilder Foote quotes Rev. William Romaine, rector of St. Anne's in Blackfriars, London, in an "Essay on Psalmody" prefixed to the latter's own *Collection out of the Book of Psalms* in which the rector denounced "Watts's Whims." Romaine expressed great concern that he might see (or perhaps was already seeing) "Christian congregations shut out the divinely inspired psalms, and take in Dr. Watts's flights of fancy. . . . Why should Dr. Watts, or any other hymn-maker, not only take precedence over the Holy Ghost, but also thrust him utterly out of the church?"[16] Whether Romaine was more concerned about the Holy Ghost or market competition is unclear.

13. Escott, *Isaac Watts*, 148.

14. Watts, as cited by Thomas Wright, *The Lives of the British Hymn-Writers, Volume III: Isaac Watts and Contemporary Hymn-Writers* (London: C. J. Farncombe, 1914), 132.

15. In 1799, Thomas Tregenna Biddulph, Vicar of St. James' in Bristol, was violently attacked in a pamphlet that accused him of being a Dissenter in disguise. The reason for this charge? He used hymns in public worship. Susan S. Tamke, *Make a Joyful Noise Unto the Lord: Hymns as a Reflection of Victorian Social Attitudes* (Athens, OH: Ohio University, 1978), 22.

16. Henry Wilder Foote, *Three Centuries of American Hymnody* (Cambridge, MA: Harvard University, 1940), 64.

Watts in the Regular Singing Controversy, Revisions, and Tunebooks

In Nonconformist worship during the seventeenth century, a leader read the psalm one line at a time, in alternation with the congregation's singing of each tune phrase. This custom was called "lining out" or "deaconing," after the precentor, clerk, or deacon — often musically unlearned — who had been selected to line out the tunes. Instituted first as a provisional measure for church singing by the English Puritans at the Westminster Assembly of 1644 to assist illiterate worshippers, lining out had been brought to the colonies and become entrenched practice in New England by the 1720s.[17] In the next fifty years, the paradox evolved that psalm-singing declined sharply through the very measure devised to help illiterate singers.

In his preface to *The Psalms of David Imitated,* Watts held forth little hope that the state of congregational singing could change. In fact, he admitted that he expressly tailored his poetic style to a congregational practice he deplored. His solution was to avoid constructing a poetic thought that extended beyond one line, and so to put an end to the absurd exchange of sentence fragments between leader and congregation that often resulted from lining out Psalm paraphrases: "I have seldom permitted a Stop in the middle of a Line, and seldom left the end of a Line without one, to comport a little with the unhappy mixture of Reading and Singing, which cannot presently be reformed."[18] The very reason he had restricted himself to the three most usual Metres — long, common, and short — was to ensure rhythmic clarity. He provided metrical alternative versions to give himself some degree of license while still remaining true to Scrip-

17. "It is the duty of christians *[sic]* to praise God publicly by singing of psalms all together in the congregation and also privately in the family. In the singing of psalms the voice is to be audibly and gravely ordered; but the chief care must be to sing with understanding and with grace in the heart, making melody unto the Lord. That the whole congregation may join therein, every one that can read is to have a psalm-book and all others not disabled by age or otherwise are to be exhorted to learn to read. But for the present where many in the congregation cannot read, it is convenient that the minister or some fit person appointed by him and the other ruling officers do read the psalm line by line, before singing thereof." Cited in Frederic Louis Ritter, *Music in England and Music in America,* Vol. 2: *Music in America* (London: William Reeves, 1884), 51-52.

18. Cited in Music, *Hymnology,* 118.

ture, explaining: "if in one Metre I have given the Loose to a Paraphrase, I have confin'd myself to my Text in the other."[19]

Despite his resignation about the prevailing mode of singing, Watts could not resist giving a few parting instructions. The worship he advocated was first and last grounded in clear understanding of the texts. Underscoring the crucial place of reason and literacy in the worship of God, he wrote: "First, Let as many as can do it bring Psalm-books with them, and look on the Words while they sing . . . to make the Sense compleat. . . . Secondly, Let the Clerk read the whole Psalm over aloud before he begins to parcel out the Lines, that the People may have some notion of what they sing; and not be forced to drag on heavily . . . without any Meaning, till the next Line come to give the Sense of them." Finally, he appealed for a faster tempo, "that we might not dwell so long upon every single Note," and a call for "greater Speed of Pronunciation," which he believed "would be more agreeable to [the Psalmody] of the antient Churches, more intelligible to others, and more delightfull to our selves."

How did Watts's texts reach the colonies? As early as December 1711, the prominent New England divine Cotton Mather recorded in his diary that he had received a copy of the "new Edition" of Watts's *Hymns and Spiritual Songs* (i.e., the second edition of 1709) from the author. Watts's correspondence with Mather and other colonial clergy indicates that the poet wanted to spread his system of worship to the churches in the New World. He even subtitled a few psalms "for New England." According to David Music, British-imprint copies of both Watts's *Hymns and Spiritual Songs* and *Psalms of David Imitated* were available for purchase in New England well before 1729.[20] Nine texts by Watts had been published individually in six Boston collections between 1712 and 1714, including "Hark! From the tombs a doleful sound," "Why do we mourn departing friends," and "When I survey the wondrous cross," apparently the first publication of each of these hymns in America.

Despite the support of Mather and other progressive New England Puritan clergy, Watts's texts met with resistance in the colonies, as they had in England. Even the enthusiastic Mather made clear in his diary that he intended to enjoy Watts's texts only in family worship, or as shared with friends for the same purpose: "Isaac Watts, hath sent me the new Edi-

19. Music, *Hymnology*, 135.

20. David Music, "Isaac Watts in America Before 1729," *The Hymn* 50, no. 1 (Jan. 1999): 30.

tion of his Hymns; wherein the Interests of Piety are most admirably suited. I receive them as . . . a Supply sent from Heaven for the Devotions of my Family. There will I sing them, and endeavor to bring my Family in Love with them . . . and perswade my well-disposed Neighbours to furnish themselves with them; and in this way promote Piety among them."[21] For public worship, however, Mather himself undertook the task of Scripture versification in his *Psalterium Americanum,* which he hoped would be the church psalter of the new nation. This "sterile product," to use Foote's phrase, was in Mather's curious idea of blank verse, and the work never sold.

The most obvious cause of resistance to Watts in New England, however, was what Hugh T. McElrath calls the "stranglehold" on colonial Calvinist worship of the older psalters, notably that of Sternhold and Hopkins. Also popular were its successor of higher poetic quality, the so-called "New Version" of Nahum Tate and Nicholas Brady from England, and the first American-published psalter or book of any kind, the *Bay Psalm Book* of 1640.[22] Later editions of both books included tune supplements. The people's fervent loyalism to these earlier versions was loosened by two main agencies — the singing school movement and revivalism.

The revisions of Watts produced in the colonies during the following decades both reflected and embodied major cultural, religious, and political shifts. Before the Revolution, Watts's *Psalms of David* had become quite widely used in New England churches, replacing almost entirely the *Bay Psalm Book.* Massachusetts schoolmaster and printer John Mycall issued in 1791 a revised Watts psalter in which he had replaced Watts's references to the British Israel with rousingly patriotic sentiments of the Revolution. By 1784, the General Association of Connecticut Congregationalists had commissioned Joel Barlow, a poet of growing reputation who wanted to become the new nation's poet laureate, to prepare an "official" Watts revision for the use of Connecticut congregations. Barlow not only Americanized the national references to Israel, but made stylistic and even discrete theological changes in Watts as well. Barlow's subsequent travels in France and flirtation with liberal political philosophies of the French

21. Diary of Cotton Mather, Massachusetts Historical Society Collection, 7th Series, VIII, 142. Cited in Foote, *Three Centuries,* 65-66.

22. The *Ainsworth Psalter* and *Rous's Version* were also in use to a lesser extent.

Revolution made him immediately suspect on the home front. The Association promptly engaged a new person to complete a second official Watts revision.

The Association's choice was the epitome of orthodoxy: Timothy Dwight, grandson of Jonathan Edwards, a serious Congregational pastor, and Yale graduate who in 1795 assumed the presidency of that school. Dwight both venerated Watts and strove in this project to exceed his model, as is explained in the next chapter by Rochelle Stackhouse.

But for Watts to remain in the control of only New England's established Congregational Church would have been ironic for a Dissenter. Baptists in the colonies, like their Congregational neighbors, had generally used Sternhold and Hopkins; when they finally did relinquish that book, most adopted Tate and Brady. David Music notes that in 1771 the congregation of the First Baptist Church of Boston voted that "Dr. Watts's Psalms together with his Hymns be sung in Public instead of Tate and Brady."[23] Twenty years later, they voted that the "Selection of Hymns by the Revd. Rippon of London, be used at baptisms and communion seasons, as a supplement to Dr. Watts's Hymns." Rippon's collection, as it happens, was itself an arrangement of Watts's texts in a topical format more easily useable during worship. Although the book had been published abroad only four years before, apparently it had an immediate appeal. In 1818 James M. Winchell, the First Baptist Church's pastor, published his own version, *An Arrangement of the Psalms, Hymns, and Spiritual Songs of . . . Watts,* which immediately found wide usefulness among New England Baptists. "Winchell's Watts" contained 687 psalms and hymns by Watts and 327 hymns by other authors. Based on its success, Winchell published a companion tunebook, *Sacred Harmony,* in 1819.

The rise of choirs was linked closely with the adoption of Watts's books. As Benson put it, "The movement to improve singing was inevitably a movement toward the use of Watts or of other hymns."[24] Writing in the 1840s, George Hood recorded that, despite the efforts of reformers, who concentrated on cities (particularly Boston), "there were few country churches with a choir before 1765 or '70. They were generally formed as

23. David W. Music, "Music in the First Baptist Church of Boston, Massachusetts, 1665-1820" in *Singing Baptists: Studies in Hymnody in America,* ed. Harry Eskew, David W. Music, Paul A. Richardson (Nashville: Church Street, 1994), 36.

24. Louis F. Benson, *The English Hymn: Its Development and Use in Worship* (Richmond, VA: John Knox, 1915), 192-193.

the custom of 'lining out' the psalms was done away. Or perhaps they were the means of removing that barbarous and penurious custom. At any rate, choirs and that custom were ever at a war, in which the former have ever proved victorious."[25] The Congregational South Church in Andover voted to add choir seats in the sanctuary in 1779, the same year that they changed books from Tate and Brady to Watts.[26] The First Baptist Church of Boston formed a choir in 1771 when it adopted Watts.[27] Several church records cite the establishment of the choir and the adoption of Watts in a single entry.

By the time the furor of the tract wars and sermonic battles over "Usual Singing" (or the Old Way) versus the new "Regular Singing" had settled, the singing-school movement was launched. The inevitable result of the singing school, targeted as it was at young people, was the establishment of choirs in churches across New England; the precentor surrendered by degrees to the choir. In the course of the conflict, other strongholds fell. Singing schools taught young people of both sexes to read by note, paving the way for mixed or "promiscuous singing" in the worship of God. Lastly, in some city churches, a bass viol was admitted into the gallery to support the psalm-tune and the more musically complex pieces that the choir introduced.

In one sense, then, the shift to Watts's Christianized psalms and hymns meant a move to notated music and choral polyphony, and to a select group that could and sometimes did eventually dominate worship as had the precentor it replaced. On the other hand, the presence of Watts's texts in a church could indicate a congregation's interest in the revival.[28] David Music asserts that Watts made no serious inroads into the churches until the triumph of "Regular Singing" and the beginning of the Great Awakening in the 1740s.

25. George Hood, *A History of Music in New England: With Biographical Sketches of Reformers and Psalmists*, 1846; reprint ed. by Johannes Riedel (New York: Johnson Reprint, 1970), 180-181.

26. Rochelle A. Stackhouse, The *Language of the Psalms in Worship: American Revisions of Watts' Psalter* (Lanham, MD: Scarecrow), 102.

27. Choirs were established at First Baptist in Haverhill, Massachusetts, and Providence, Rhode Island, in 1786 and 1791, respectively.

28. Richard M. Raichelson, "Black Religious Folksong: A Study in Generic and Social Change" (Ph.D. diss., University of Pennsylvania, 1975), 206.

Watts, Theology, and Musical Styles in the Awakenings

Stephen Marini has argued that the Regular Singing controversy was actually "rehearsal for revival" for the first Awakening. "The singing controversy of the 1720's revealed deeper theological, sociological, and cultural tensions in Congregational and Baptist communions that in the revival would become permanent lines of fracture in New England. The Singing Controversy announced the cultural disintegration of Puritanism." In the Awakening, "spiritually heightened singing appeared as a distinguishing mark of regeneration," fostering the development of one important new genre, the camp-meeting hymn or spiritual. Watts's "human composures," writes Marini, kindled a lasting Evangelical tradition of hymns and spiritual songs that at first supplemented and at times overshadowed the Wattsian canon. After 1770, hymn and hymnic psalms of Watts and others acquired an indigenous musical style, appearing in multiple settings by various composers in the wave of tunebook publication accompanying the singing school movement. These musical settings ensured textual longevity through the rise of fixed musical forms. The most distinctive form produced by the singing school movement was the fuguing tune. On the doctrinal front, "the new hymnody acquired theological interpretations accompanying the new synthesis of music and texts and reflecting the Evangelical and Liberal positions that shaped Protestant thought in the new nation." In short, Marini concludes, the universality and publicity of sacred singing made it of all religious media perhaps the most sensitive to the complex changes wrought by the Great Awakening in America.[29]

Watts's texts were important, though in different ways, in the revivals of Edwards, Whitefield, and the camp-meetings. In the mid-1730s, Jonathan Edwards recalled in a letter finding his congregation singing the hymns of Watts only, having cast aside the psalms, when he returned from an extended trip. He wrote: "When I came home I disliked not their making some use of the Hymns: but did not like their setting aside the Psalms." He resolved the situation to everyone's satisfaction, recalling later: "It has been our manner in this congregation, for more than two years past, in the summer time, when we sing three times upon the Sabbath, to sing a Hymn, or

29. Stephen A. Marini, "Rehearsal for Revival: Sacred Singing and the Great Awakening in America," in *Sacred Sound: Music in Religious Thought and Practice,* ed. Joyce Irwin (Chico, CA: Scholars, 1983), 87.

part of a Hymn of Dr. Watts's, the last time, *viz:* at the conclusion of the afternoon exercise . . . the people . . . seem'd to be greatly pleased with it."[30] Clearly modern evangelicals did not invent the "blended" use of worship music! Whitefield was enthusiastic about Watts's texts, and he ultimately produced a collection in 1753 containing Charles Wesley and John Cennick but predominantly Watts. Richard Raichelson has pointed out the paradox that "Whitefield, the great exponent of revivalistic preaching, was more allied with the musical temperament of [tunes set to] Watts than [to] the Wesleys. . . . Ironically, his preaching style was consistent with the Wesleys and contrary to that of Watts." Of the established congregations that had adopted Watts and had come increasingly under Watts's influence after the Revolution, he observes, the revivalistic churches moved to other musical styles — those of the Methodist hymns, of their own folk-hymns, and then the camp-meeting spiritual.[31]

While the Second Awakening of the early nineteenth century had vast reverberations in reshaping conversion theology, redrawing denominational lines, and fueling reforms such as abolition, the revival's clearest effect in lay worship life may have been its legacy of "social religion." Sandra Sizer has analyzed the complex of practices that made up that legacy: lay testimony, exhortation, prayer, and singing by both men and women. Stemming from the new evangelical understanding of conversion and the desire to keep revival fires alive in local churches, the "social meeting" was an evening, lay-led gathering in which Puritan distinctions between public and private worship were set aside, as they had been in the earlier revivals as well.[32]

The limited place of singing in the First Awakening was eclipsed by its central role in the Second Awakening, as documented in dissertations by, among others, Paul Hammond, Richard Hulan, and Ellen Jane Lorenz Porter.[33] The camp-meeting spirituals that emerged from this movement

30. Music, *Hymnology,* 184.

31. Raichelson, "Black Religious Folksong," 207.

32. Sandra S. Sizer, *Gospel Hymns and Social Religion: The Rhetoric of Nineteenth-Century Revivalism* (Philadelphia: Temple University, 1978), 14-15, 50-52.

33. Richard Huffman Hulan, "Campmeeting Spiritual Folksongs: Legacy of the 'Great Revival in the West'" (Ph.D. diss., University of Texas at Austin, 1978); Ellen Jane Lorenz, *Glory Hallelujah: The Story of the Campmeeting Spiritual* (Nashville: Abingdon, 1978); Paul Garnett Hammond, "Music in Urban Revivalism in the Northern United States, 1800-1835" (D.M.A. diss., The Southern Baptist Theological Seminary, 1974).

were of two main types: the improvisatory repetitive, rousing choruses, often added to popular hymn texts of Watts and Wesley, and the freely ornamented, folklike, often modal type. Containing aspects of both was the musically striking setting of Watts's "Alas and did my Saviour bleed" entitled "I Yield," from Hillman's famous collection *The Revivalist*. Watts's first stanza is sung intact. The refrain is a simple, moving poetic utterance in which surrender to Christ at the vision of his crucifixion is framed in language of both intimacy and conquest: "I yield, I yield, I yield, / I can hold out no more; / I sing by dying love compell'd, / And own thee conqueror."[34] The wide-ranging F minor melody reaches its dramatic and melodic peak unexpectedly at the beginning of the refrain, on the leading tone and sustained high F, then catapults downward with anguished cries of surrender in three wrenching grace-note figures. The rest of the refrain, far from the trite rhythms of many camp-meeting choruses, represents a gradual release of both melodic and rhythmic tension as the calm opening tune phrase returns and the soul reaches repose. The fermatas in Hillman's transcription recall the rhythmic freedom and emotional power of early camp-meeting singing that was gradually purged from later notated versions during the following decades.

At Home and School with Watts: Hymns for Children and Hymns in Children's Lives

In Boston in 1715 an obscure 24-page booklet of songs for the use of children appeared, entitled *Honey out of the Rock flowing to little children that they may know to refuse the evil and choose the good. Certain select hymns for the use of such, taken from those of the excellent Mr. Isaac Watts, as more peculiarly adapted for their instruction* (Boston, 1715). The twenty-two hymns in this miniature selection, all taken from Watts's *Hymns and Spiritual Songs,* include no texts still in use. David Music attributes the editorship of this curious collection to Mather, based on typography and the nature of the "Body of Divinity Versify'd" at the end.[35] While it must remain only an intriguing footnote

34. George Pullen Jackson, *Spiritual Folk-Songs of Early America* (Gloucester, MA: Peter Smith, 1937), 240.

35. Music, "Watts in America," 32.

to the narrative of Watts in America, *Honey out of the Rock* is the earliest collection of his work published in the colonies.

Like his poems for adults, Watts's hymns for children were intended above all to be understood and to be useful. He wrote his *Divine and Moral Songs for Children* to be sung in the home or family circle; they were probably not used in worship. The book's profound influence in America was through its adoption as a primer or chapterbook in schools for generations.[36] Escott points out that in these texts Watts celebrates the glories of God's creation. It was for children that he wrote "I sing the mighty power of God," with its colorful detail as well as panoramic view. This hymn first appeared in *Divine and Moral Songs,* and was not adapted congregationally until later. Escott has traced probable influences on Watts from poets including Robert Herrick ("Cloaths for Continuance") and other Puritan authors writing for children, including several from Bunyan's *Book for Boys and Girls,* but Escott also suggests that Watts was the first poet to write from the child's perspective.

Despite what Escott has called "admittedly priggish religious sentiments in some texts," which he blames at least in part on an era "that understood little of child life," that biographer argues that Watts "joyed to stand at the child's level and to look at life and religion from the child's height of mind and soul." It was Isaac Watts who *humanized* children's praises: "they were *divine* songs just because, for the first time, they were human and childlike . . . in 1715, there was nothing even approaching them in content, delightfulness, and versification." Like Watts's adult hymns, importantly, they also "followed a system: the chief occasions of a child's worship were taken into account. . . . In theme and execution, the *Divine songs* run parallel with Watts's work in adult praise." Ironically, John Wesley criticized Watts for this very perspective — or weakness, in his mind — which he set about to reverse in his own texts. The latter, he claimed, when understood by children, would make them "children no longer, only in years and stature."[37]

Childlike as they were, Watts's poems in no way shrank the size of God or of God's demands on every person, however small. The hymn that must have lodged a particularly vivid vision of God's omniscience in children's minds began: "Almighty God, thy piercing eye/Shines through the

36. Benson, *English Hymn,* 120-121.

37. Escott, *Isaac Watts,* 216.

shades of night;/And our most secret actions lie/All open to thy sight." Susan Tamke notes that in the British Victorian children's novel *The Fairfield Family*, "when [the character] little Emily steals a plum, she dreams later 'that a dreadful Eye was looking upon her from above. Wherever she went, she thought this Eye followed her with angry looks, and she could not hide herself from it.'" At this point the novel quotes the Watts hymn to drive home the moral. Moreover, in the *Divine and Moral Songs* Watts also graphically described the punishments of hell. Song 15, entitled "Against Lying," reads:

> The Lord delights in them that speak
> The words of truth; but every liar
> Must have his portion in the lake
> That burns with brimstone and with fire.
>
> Then let me always watch my lips
> Lest I be struck to death and hell,
> Since God a book of reckoning keeps
> For every lie that children tell.[38]

According to writings of the period cited by Tamke, many Victorians even years later as adults, associated hymns with threatening situations because of what they had sung in childhood.[39] Tamke observes that despite this harsh view of the world, or perhaps because of it, Watts's hymns for children continued to be republished throughout the nineteenth century.[40]

The profound effect of Watts's thirty-eight "divine songs" and eight "moral songs" on generations of Americans can only be guessed from the staggering publication history of this slim volume. According to Phyllis Bultmann, over sixty-eight separate editions of this one work were published between 1715 and 1880, not counting a great number of reprints of its individual hymns.[41]

38. Song XV, "Against Lying," stanzas 5 and 6. Isaac Watts, *Divine and Moral Songs for Children* (1715; reprint, Morgan, PA: Soli Deo Gloria, 1998), 55-56.

39. Tamke, *Make a Joyful Noise*, 82-83.

40. Ibid., 77.

41. Phillis Wetherell Bultmann, "Everybody Sing: The Social Significance of the Eighteenth-Century Hymn" (Ph.D. diss., University of California at Los Angeles, 1950), 145. Cited in Tamke, *Make a Joyful Noise*, 80.

Whether children's experiences with hymns were pleasant or troubling, hymn singing and hymn memorization was a shared experience of generations of nineteenth-century children in both England and America. Tamke notes, "The process of memorizing hymns in the family circle and in the schoolrooms created a shared culture among children, at least middle-class children and those children of the lower classes who were educated by middle-class principles." She points out "how widely and deeply embedded this culture was among Victorian adults and children" by recalling Lewis Carroll's two famous parodies of Watts's children's hymns in *Alice in Wonderland.* Carroll satirized "How doth the busy little bee" in his "How doth the little crocodile," and Watts's "'Tis the voice of the sluggard: I heard him complain" became "'Twas the voice of the lobster." As Tamke observes, the spoof was successful only because Carroll's readers were utterly familiar with the hymns.[42]

Although the *Divine Songs* continued to be published and used in America through much of the nineteenth century, in Tamke's phrase, the "complexion of children's hymns as a whole underwent a change." Later Victorian children's hymns became more positive, largely purged of violent language and imagery, with a didacticism that operated now from guilt rather than fear or threat, in Tamke's analysis: "the newer Victorian hymns for children suppressed the overt motive of fear."[43] Swept by literary Romanticism, many of them celebrated the child as God's good creature in the context of nature imagery. Here also Watts the naturalist provided the foundation for later children's hymns.

"Dr. Watts" Singing in the Black Church

The dissemination of Watts's collections to African slaves in the American colonies has been described in a much-quoted letter from 1750 by the Rev. Samuel Davies of Virginia to John Wesley. Davies recounted to Wesley news on the distribution of hymnals and their enthusiastic reception in the slave community: "I have supplied them to the utmost of my ability [with books]. They are exceedingly delighted with Watts' songs. And I cannot but observe that the Negroes, above all of the human species I ever

42. Tamke, *Make a Joyful Noise,* 77.
43. Ibid., 83.

knew, have the nicest ear for music. They have a kind of ecstatic delight in Psalmody; nor are there any books they so soon learn, or take so much pleasure in, as in those used in that heavenly part of divine worship."

Most studies on African-American worship during slavery focus on the ring shout, and pay less attention to the phenomenon that came to be called variously "metered" or "long-meter" singing, "surge singing," lining out, or most often, "Dr. Watts" singing. While this style stemmed from the lining out practice of the white New England churches, it became so transformed and embedded in black musical practice as to have become the root of much African-American musical expression since its inception. The varied use of terminology in sources raises several questions. Was lining the text speaking or singing? Clearly in its British origins, this term meant to read the Psalm line by line, as the Westminster resolution states. We recall Watts's own description of England's "unhappy mixture of reading and singing." The related, distinctively black, practice of "Dr. Watts" or meter singing describes lining by the leader answered by highly ornamented, melismatic, much slower, congregational renditions of the tune phrases.[44]

One early reference, an article from the [New York] *Nation* of 1867, describes lining out as part of the formal African-American worship service, "And at regular intervals one hears the elder 'deaconing' a hymn-book hymn, which is sung two lines at a time, and whose wailing cadences, borne on the night air, are indescribably melancholy. But the benches are pushed back to the wall when the formal meeting is over,"[45] the journalist continues, describing the shout ritual that would customarily follow.

Along the same lines, folklorist Gertrude P. Kurath has noted the influence on hymn singing of West African chants imported by slaves to southern plantations in the eighteeenth century: "They alternated be-

44. It should be noted that this style is distinctly different from the call-and-response technique found in the camp-meeting song and later urban gospel hymn, an immediate echo of a few words between upper and lower voices. Pinkston used the term "lining out" synonymously with "statement and response," but no other source I consulted equates these two terms. Alfred Adolphus Pinkston, "Lined Hymns, Spirituals, and the Associated Lifestyle of Rural Black People in the United States" (Ph.D. diss., University of Miami, 1975), 89.

45. *The Nation,* 30 May 1867. Cited in William Francis Allen, Charles Pickard Ware, and Lucy McKim Garrison, *Slave Songs of the United States* (1867; reprint, Freeport, NY: Books for Libraries, 1971), xiii.

tween solo and chorus, sometimes in overlapping polyphony, always with ornaments and glides."[46]

When in 1975 Alfred Pinkston conducted fieldwork in rural churches in the South, he found long-meter singing still widely practiced in deacon-led "devotional" services commonly meeting before the regular worship service. Pinkston observed that when a hymn is lined, "the words are given melodically" instead of just being recited. "To be effective in lining the hymn, it is necessary to recite the words in a musical fashion."[47] As an example, he cited that "What a friend we have in Jesus" was introduced by one melodic formula for two lines, but a different melodic formula for lines three and four, and neither formula bore any relation to the hymn tune. Congregations sang the melody in unison, but also improvised a second part a fourth below, creating strict organum throughout. The slow but weighty tempo resumed with each congregational response, despite the chanted interruptions. Text declamation, due to tempo and ornamentation, was so unclear as to obscure the sense of the words.

The standard devotional period consisted of one to three lined hymns alternated with as many prayers, and set the tone for the entire worship service. "The deacons feel that this is their main function in the service and to weaken or destroy the devotional period would render them ineffective," Pinkston wrote.[48] He noted that even churches with "college trained ministers" that modernized their services in other respects managed to "[avoid] many conflicts" by retaining this opening devotional period. It was clearly a link to a spiritual and cultural heritage. Even churches that had plenty of hymnals (most of those he visited) did not use the books for meter singing. While lining out, the leader might interpolate testimonies or a story supporting the thought of the hymn stanza. Or prayers by congregation members might erupt, after which congregational singing resumed. After the hymn was sung, it was customary to hum until the pastoral prayer began. (The last stanza of the hymn was usually sung standing, those not able to stand would raise their hands to show support for the call to stand.) Two ministers Pinkston

46. Gertrude P. Korath, "Rhapsodies of Salvation: Negro Responsory Hymns," *Southern Folklore Quarterly* 20, no. 9 (1956): 178.

47. Pinkston, "Lined Hymns," 92-94.

48. Ibid.

interviewed claimed that "the spiritual rewards from reading and singing the hymn from the hymnal are not as inspiring as having someone line the words."

Horace Clarence Boyer has also documented meter singing especially in black Baptist and Methodist congregations in Rochester, New York. Boyer found that the "humming chorus" after the lined hymn was obligatory, and always drew from the last two phrases of the hymn tune.[49] As early as 1961 William Tallmadge analyzed a solo hymn recorded by gospel great Mahalia Jackson, and saw it as a direct adaptation of ornamented, congregational Dr. Watts technique to the solo voice. Tallmadge was one of the first to connect this black tradition to the seventeenth-century pattern of lining out the Psalms; he also saw solo gospel artists as transmitting older congregational practices into new secular styles: "I would venture that the very florid and highly ornamented treatment of melodies by some popular . . . 'rock and roll' singers during the past five years may have derived from the old 'lining-out' style by way of such Gospel solos as Mahalia's 'Amazing Grace.'"[50] More recently, William Dargan has transcribed and analyzed a long-meter rendition of Watts's Psalm 116, "I love the Lord, he heard my voice," noting it as still one of the most sung metered hymns in South Carolina as recently as 1995.[51]

A final aspect of African-American worship must enter this discussion: What possible connection exists between Watts and the black spiritual? In 1883 Frederic Ritter hypothesized in the characteristically condescending white viewpoint that some black hymns "began years ago as compositions of more cultivated minds. . . . This theory accounts for the poetry, for often a negro hymn opens with a stanza or two which would not have discredited Watts" after which later stanzas were added and the original ones eventually dropped. While his theory applies to that subtype of camp-meeting song discussed earlier which used Watts as the basis on which to build choruses, this style survived long afterward in both the African-American and white folk spiritual. Ritter's next observation

49. Horace Clarence Boyer, "An Analysis of Black Church Music with Examples Drawn From Services in Rochester, New York" (Ph.D. diss., Eastman School of Music of the University of Rochester, 1973).

50. William H. Tallmadge, "Dr. Watts and Mahalia Jackson — The Development, Decline, and Survival of a Folk Style in America," *Ethnomusicology* 5 (1961): 95-99.

51. William T. Dargan, "Congregational Singing Traditions in South Carolina," *Black Music Research Journal* 15, no. 1 (Spring 1995): 29-73.

points to another possible connection with Watts: "There is, however, still another set of hymns, the words of which the plantation negro himself composed entirely at the beginning. They are usually short-metred, poetical descriptions of familiar Bible incidents, some of them of incredible length, and bristling with anachronisms. The blacks call this class of hymns 'figurated' from the Bible; and I have heard one which was descriptive of the battle of Christian and Apollyon, and consequently 'figurated' from Bunyan. No word, by the way, is a sweeter morsel on the negro tongue than this original verb, — to 'figurate.' . . . it is used in a dozen senses."[52] Ritter here attributed a unique ability for biblical paraphrase to African-American creativity. But it does not seem to be a very large step from Watts's Psalm "imitations" to the biblical "figurations" of the black spiritual. After all, Watts had been found guilty of an anachronism or two himself. Perhaps African-American worshipers had captured the spirit of Watts, while his more learned revisers such as Barlow and Dwight, in their doctrinally and politically motivated versions, were quibbling over the letter.

The spread of the singing-school movement to the southeast and south after 1800 and the birth of the shape-note singing movement beginning in the 1830s and 40s adds another dimension to the American use of Watts. Richard Crawford, who was among the first musicologists to bring American psalm tunes to scholarly attention, introduced a new research methodology for the study of singing-school and shape-note tunes in his *Core Repertory* study of the 101 most republished tunes in American imprint tune books through 1810.[53] Like Dr. Watts singing, Sacred Harp singing sustains a continuous connection with the eighteenth century, as noted by many scholars, including folklorist John Bealle in a recent study that contextualizes the Sacred Harp tradition in the changing cultural landscapes of southern musical history.[54]

Of the thirty-eight four-shape books published between 1798 and 1855, according to Charles Ellington, "Only *Southern Harmony* and *Sacred Harp* gained sufficient footing to insure their popularity and use well into

52. Frederic Louis Ritter, *Music in America* (New York: Charles Scribner's Sons, 1883), 393.

53. Richard Crawford, *The Core Repertory of Early American Psalmody*, Recent Researches in American Music, Vols. 11 and 12 (Madison, WI: A-R Editions, 1984).

54. John Bealle, *Public Worship, Private Faith: Sacred Harp and American Folksong* (Athens, GA: University of Georgia, 1997).

the second half of the nineteenth century.[55] The 1991 edition of *Sacred Harp* contains eleven settings of the four Watts texts under discussion; *Southern Harmony* contains four. One melody is duplicated between the books, making a total of fourteen tunes.

The 1991 edition of *Sacred Harp,* the book most used from the late nineteenth-century through modern national shape-note revival, presents the clearest picture of the role of Watts in the ongoing American shape-note tradition. In that edition, twenty-one new composers were added, only three of whom had contributed to the previous edition. Their contribution represented 60 new songs, for which 27 are settings of Watts; 136 of the total 560 texts in the 1991 edition are his. As Bealle explains, "contemporary composers 'breathed new life' into the old [Watts] poetry by choosing the texts for their compositions, reengaging the poetic idiom and providing for renewed personal associations with texts that resonated throughout the singing community."[56]

Conclusion

This chapter has examined the use of Isaac Watts's hymn texts in the rich contexts of early American historical, theological, and literary culture. Scholars like Stackhouse, Marini, and Music have shown that Watts came to ascendency in American Protestantism on the crest of two concurrent and often conflicting movements: the rise of Regular Singing and the First Awakening. Watts seemed to thrive both in the move toward order and regulation as well as in a movement toward free-form revival. Watts's efforts produced reform where he did not intend it, and in ways he had not foreseen in musical style and practice. He despaired of the tradition of lining out, yet a beautified, cultural tranformation of African-American lining out came to bear his name, and ultimately to permeate nearly every form of vernacular black musical expression to this day. Perhaps it could be said that the colonies and new nation were the eager Gentile recipients of Watts's musical gospel,

55. Charles Linwood Ellington, "The Sacred Harp Tradition of the South: Its Origin and Evolution" (Ph.D. diss., Florida State University, 1969), 18.

56. Bealle, *Public Worship, Private Faith,* 231. Composers of pieces in *Sacred Harp* and other tune books did not indicate which editions or revisions of Watts they set to music.

in contrast to the British Israel for whom he had first poured out his efforts.

Watts was adopted in America's doctrinal shift from Calvinism to evangelicalism during the Second Awakening; he was modified by republican politics and sanitized in the rise of a new educational philosophy during the nineteenth century. At the time of disestablishment and national independence, when a new language and liturgy were needed, his texts quickly became the congregational staple. Watts became the liturgist for a new nation. As such, his work ensured not only the viability of new hymns in America, but the longevity of at least some Psalms, which his texts carried through the turbulent Psalmody Controversy to the present day.

Watts did for Calvinist worship what Gustav Mahler later did for the symphony, with his myriad quotations from folk song, march, and hymn. Watts made hymnody a microcosm of the world, and peopled it with fish, mountains, rainbows, all manner of creeping things, snatching them all from the Psalms but animating them with rhyme and tune — animation not in the Disneyesque sense but in the sense of the Holy Spirit's *ruach* (or breath), by Whom life constantly, joyously springs forth. Watts brought animals, England, the whole world into divine praise because that is where he believed they belonged — under God's sway and Christ's glorious reign.

Among the ironies in this story is that while Watts's corpus was written as a device for the people, it soon attained its own high authority. John Bealle has observed, "Indeed, today there is surely no Watts revival at hand among prevailing contemporary evangelical Christian movements. Yet *Sacred Harp* and Watts, largely undiluted, have found a curious, if small, niche in contemporary America."[57] I would differ with Bealle, and maintain that Watts has never been revived because evangelical Americans have never lost Watts. They have theologically revised him, politically tweaked his words, and remodeled his tunes, but they have always sung him.

As Bealle has also pointed out, Watts seems an unlikely poetic voice for the postmodern age.[58] However, Donald Davie, whom Bealle calls "possibly Watts's most articulate and enthusiastic supporter in literary

57. Ibid., 230.
58. Ibid.

circles," proposes two possible avenues for approaching Watts: from an antiquarian view and from the perspective of what Davie calls "the axiom." As for the first, Bealle observes, "there is plenty in Watts to satisfy an antiquarian appetite. Davie suggests that it is all too easy to project Watts's sentiments into the past and not apply them to one's own experiences." Until, Bealle points out, the singing community experiences a loss of a beloved member, and suddenly the archaic language, "Why should we start and fear to die?" becomes relevant. Davie explains the second possible approach to Watts, through axiom, as follows: "Religious belief, it has been bluntly said, is irreconcilable with 'the modern mind.' But even if that were so in some general or abstract sense, it is quite clear that even the most modern mind, if . . . it chooses . . . can still enter the imaginative world of Watts, the world of the axiom. One way to make that passage is by relishing the literary (aesthetic) pleasures that only the worlds of the axiom can supply." Precisely because Watts took biblical doctrine as unassailable truth, he took for granted that stones will cry out if mortals do not sing: "Let mortals ne'er refuse to take/Th'Hosanna on their tongues;/Lest rocks and stones should rise, and break/Their silence into songs."[59]

"For Watts," Davie writes, "the stones' supposed behaviour is simply the necessary consequence of the axiom: if God is the Creator, then every one of his creatures — stones as well as men — responds to him and moves at his command." Davie contends that the serious student of Watts's poetic style will, in fact, "break out of the world of 'the aesthetic' into the regions of human experience more liberating, though also more alarming."[60] Elaborating on this thought, Bealle explains what may be part of Watts's power still today: "Watts possesses an encoded resistance to modernity. We moderns may erect mediating schemes for engaging Watts, but these schemes only affirm that a more powerful reading lurks beneath them. Sacred Harp singings, which attract so diverse a spectrum of believers, are ritual encounters in which the mediating schemes that might influence reading — 'vain discourse,' as Watts himself put it — are kept away. Only self-examination stands between singer and text."[61]

In 1998, rising hip-hop artist Lauryn Hill released her first solo re-

59. Donald Davie, "The Language of the Eighteenth-Century Hymn," in *Dissentient Voice* (Notre Dame, IN: University of Notre Dame Press, 1982), 32-33. Cited in Bealle, *Public Worship, Private Faith*, 233-34.

60. Donald Davie, as cited in Bealle, *Public Worship, Private Faith*, 233.

61. Bealle, *Public Worship, Private Faith*, 136.

cording, *The Miseducation of Lauryn Hill.* The fourth piece on the album is Hill's free meditation, or perhaps "imitation," on Mary's Magnificat from Luke 2, written during Hill's pregnancy with her first child. The song is entitled "To Zion." In stanza one, Hill moves seamlessly from telling Mary's story to telling her own — voicing her emotions of joy, awe, and pain at being misunderstood by friends, in which she identifies with Mary. But she journeys through her struggle, arriving triumphantly on the words, "Now the joy of my world is in Zion." As in other songs, Hill draws openly on her Christian faith. She expresses it through her Baptist gospel hymn heritage, in as much as the song ends with polyphonic layering of her theme line and a textual hook from Robert Lowry: "Marching, marching to Zion, Beautiful, beautiful Zion." Granted, this is not Watts pure, but it is Watts once removed, Watts through the voice of Robert Lowry as embraced for over a century in the rich traditions of the African-American church that have nurtured Hill and so many others, Watts as known and loved for generations by countless saints across America in their march to Zion. This, too, is Isaac Watts in America.

CHAPTER THREE

Hymnody and Politics: Isaac Watts's "Our God, Our Help in Ages Past" and Timothy Dwight's "I Love Thy Kingdom, Lord"

Rochelle A. Stackhouse

At the start of the twenty-first century, the issues surrounding the relationship of American politics and American religion remain in many ways as contentious as they have ever been. As some advocates on one hand urge the posting of the Ten Commandments in courts and public schools, and as others on the other hand decry official prayer in those same schools, Americans are still trying to sort out just what place the life of faith should have in the life of the citizen.

American churches also continue to differ on this issue, as they have since at least the eighteenth century. While some congregations take to the streets in political or economic protests, others rebel at the thought of their pastors preaching on any remotely political subject. One major difference between the eighteenth century and today, particularly in churches of New England Puritan ancestry (UCC, Congregational, Presbyterian), is that even if the congregation is politically active and the preacher mentions politics in sermons or prayers, the rest of the liturgical life of the congregation reflects few political or social controversies. Particularly in the hymns most often sung in those church traditions, such issues are absent or so muted as to be easily missed by either casual visitor or faithful worshiper.

By contrast, in the seventeenth and eighteenth centuries in Congregational/Independent churches in both England and New England, believers wove together their worship life, political life, social life, and family life into a complex, if not always seamless, tapestry. A New England Election Day featured special worship services where ministers preached the annual "Election Sermon." Church buildings were used as town meeting houses and even for storing military supplies.[1] Long prayers touched upon all the themes of daily life, including the social and political.

What about music? How could a tradition that allowed for only the singing of the Psalms in worship possibly integrate political or social issues into the musical component of liturgy?

The most obvious answer comes from the Psalms themselves which, in their original contexts, are brim full of political references. Psalms such as 72, 89, and 99, refer to the king, clearly meaning the political ruler of Israel/Judah, and others (74, 83,115, 124, 126, and 137) refer to military battles or prayers for the deliverance of the nation from its enemies. The original writers and singers of the Psalms worshiped a God who ruled every aspect of life and who was intimately involved in the political and social existence of the Hebrew people. It made perfect sense to them that sung prayers should communicate with God and one another about all of life's issues and events. The Psalter as it has come down to us reflects those concerns.

As James Russell Lowell has observed, however, "new occasions teach new duties. Time makes ancient good uncouth." What time also obscures is the original contexts surrounding the writing of each Psalm. Occasionally the Psalter has preserved an introductory sentence that clues us in (as in Psalm 63, "A Psalm of David when he was in the Wilderness of Judah"). But these are rare, and it usually takes a biblical scholar to unearth the longer story. In addition, as the centuries passed and the Christian church adopted the Hebrew Scriptures as its own, many Psalms became interpreted as allegories of the spiritual life — i.e., battles become those between the soul and Satan, and the "King" became Jesus. Politics became spirituality.

That shift may have been especially true for believers who, like the English Puritans/Independents and New England Puritans/Congregationalists/Presbyterians, insisted on singing as exact a translation of the

1. Horton Davies, *The Worship of the American Puritans 1629-1730* (New York: Peter Lang, 1990), 233.

Psalms as possible.[2] The challenge of Psalter-compilers like Sternhold and Hopkins, Tate and Brady, and those who edited the *Bay Psalm Book* in Massachusetts was to fit something close to the King James Psalter into singable meters — meters which had to match a small number of tunes that congregations would know by heart. In this process, the poetic rendering of the Psalm was much less important than how close the paraphrasing came to reproducing either the King James translation or the original Hebrew. In practice, therefore, both the quality of the singing and the ability of singers to understand *what* they were singing were severely compromised.

This situation, however, changed dramatically when the new hymnody emerged in the early eighteenth century, when Americans appropriated that hymnody, and when they added hymns of their own. These transitions, focused on the critical work of Isaac Watts and Timothy Dwight, structure the story that follows.

Isaac Watts

Numerous biographers and hymnologists have written at length on the revolution in song brought about by Isaac Watts.[3] Watts's heritage immersed him in the world of seventeenth-century English Nonconformity. One grandmother was a Huguenot, one grandfather a naval officer under the Cromwellian admiral Blake. His father more than once spent time in jail for his nonconformist beliefs. Watts grew up in a religious and social atmosphere where the Dissenters among whom he lived and worshiped "conceived themselves to be, very exactly, 'a tribe,' a chosen people just as ancient Israelites were chosen, in tension with their neighbors just as an-

2. These descriptive categories can become confusing. Exactly when does a Puritan become an Independent or Congregationalist or Nonconformist? In describing the churches with which Isaac Watts was associated, I will use the common term "Independent," and in describing those of Timothy Dwight, I will use "Congregational." In Dwight's case, Presbyterians might also be included since they widely used his version of Watts's Psalter.

3. See, for example, Bernard Lord Manning, *The Hymns of Wesley and Watts* (London: Epworth Press, 1942); Harry Escott, *Isaac Watts Hymnographer* (London: Independent Press, 1962); David Fountain, *Isaac Watts Remembered* (Worthing: Henry Walter, 1974); J. R. Watson, *The English Hymn* (Oxford: Clarendon, 1997).

cient Israel was."[4] Instead of the university education for which his skills suited him, he attended the Dissenting Academy at Stoke Newington. A poet from an early age, Watts complained from his youth about the texts and quality of the singing in the Independent churches his family attended. After he became a pastor, his family urged him to undertake the project of writing new texts for singing in worship.

Under influences as fresh as the Psalter by John Patrick, who took the first few bold steps away from literal translation, and as ancient as the medieval Sarum Psalter,[5] Watts wrote and in 1707 published *Hymns and Spiritual Songs* and in 1715 *Divine Songs* (a hymnbook for children). In the first book, he sought to offer songs for occasions and theological concepts not covered by the Psalms (e.g., the Christian sacraments), yet he began work with the Psalms themselves.

Watts completed that work in 1719 with *The Psalms of David Imitated.*[6] In a lengthy preface to this book, Watts laid out his intent to "divest David and Asaph, etc. of every other character but that of a Psalmist and a Saint, and *to make them always speak the common sense and language of a Christian.*"[7] He reflected as well on the fact that many of the Psalms were too "personal" to David (or whoever), too individual to be sung by a congregation. Watts went so far as to say he did not think that even Jewish congregations were meant to sing these individualistic songs. Here he was raising the concern that the language of Psalms sung in public worship needed to be kept "within the reach of an unlearned reader."[8] Clearly Watts intended his Psalms not simply to be an ornament in a worship service, but to be clearly understood by the people who sang them.

Watts also defined a major hermeneutical shift in his version of the Psalms as compared to all previous efforts. "How can we assume all his [David's] words in our personal or public addresses to God, when our condition of life, our time, place and religion are so vastly different from

4. Donald Davie, *A Gathered Church* (London: Routledge and Kegan Paul, 1978), 28.

5. For more on Patrick, see Louis Benson, *The English Hymn* (Philadelphia: Presbyterian Board of Publication, 1915), 51; on the influence of Sarum on Watts, see Escott, *Isaac Watts,* 150-151.

6. Watts, *The Imitated Psalms of David* (London: J. Clark, 1719). I have modernized the spelling and capitalization of Watts's preface and Psalms throughout.

7. Watts, *Psalms of David,* xvi, italics in the original.

8. Ibid., xxv.

those of David?"[9] This was the great leap that revolutionized the texts of church music. In the Reformed tradition to this time, the only words seen as fit for worship were the exact words of Scripture. The point of singing was to learn the Scripture; only its words were noble and holy enough to lift to God as an offering in song. Both educationally and devotionally, *sola scriptura* ruled. Whether or not the singer understood the song was beside the point. All that changed with Watts's *Psalms of David Imitated.* "In the older metrical versions there was a concern for a re-presentation of the psalm, but in Watts the concern was for re-interpretation."[10]

This change is critical for understanding not only Watts' Psalms and hymns, but those of his American revisers like Wesley, Barlow, and Dwight. The purpose of hymnody now included helping singers relate the Scripture to their lives through the singing of the Psalms in worship. Reformed and Puritan traditions had long rejected prayer books, at least partially because they felt prayer and preaching needed to come out of the immediate context of the people at worship. Now the music of worship joined this liturgical principle. Louis Benson even argued that Watts's clear intent was to tie the hymn to the sermon, thus making hymns homiletical rather than liturgical.[11] In *Psalms of David,* Watts reveled in contextuality. His themes, displayed both in descriptive titles preceding many individual Psalms and in the texts themselves, included the Gunpowder Plot of Guy Fawkes, the Bloodless Revolution of William of Orange, the accession of George I, and the defeat of the French. The words "English" or "British" occur frequently within his "imitations," making David sing not only as a Christian, but as an Englishman. Watts's obvious intent was to have the worshiping congregation reflect not only on the words of the Scriptures and their own spiritual and moral lives, but on the political and social events occurring around them. Manning has noted that a major difference between Watts and the later hymn writer Charles Wesley is that "Wesley in his hymns concerns himself mainly . . . with God and the soul of man [*sic*]. . . . Watts, too, concerns himself with this drama; but he gives it a cosmic background."[12] I would add that the background is

9. Ibid., x.

10. Robin A. Leaver, "Isaac Watts's Hermeneutical Principles and the Decline of English Metrical Psalmody," *Churchman* 92 (1978): 58.

11. Benson, *English Hymn,* 208.

12. Manning, *Hymns of Wesley and Watts,* 83.

not merely cosmic, but national; not only spiritually broad, but specifically treating the political and social sides of life as well.

Watts's own situation undoubtedly moved him to write in this way. English Independents of the late seventeenth and early eighteenth centuries lived in peace only according to the political vagaries of the day. Toleration depended on who sat on the throne or in political favor. As himself the heir of several generations of Dissenters, Watts also lived through periods when Parliament passed laws that made life more difficult for Nonconformist congregations and for himself with his family. In addition, while his country dealt with enemies outside its borders, English Nonconformists had to deal with enemies within their own land. These political and social realities are critical for understanding both Watts's general hermeneutic and the purpose of his numerous individual Psalm imitations. They also add a note of extreme irony to the subsequent history of some of those Psalms as they were used in both England and America.

Our God, Our Help in Ages Past

In 1714, Parliament passed the Schism Act under the Tory leadership of Lord Bolingbroke. This Act specifically forbade Independents to operate schools (like the one Watts himself had attended), but it implied for Independents an ever greater level of persecution to come. On Sunday, August 1, 1714, the day the Act became operative, Queen Anne died.[13] Amidst the general national anxiety about the succession, the Independents expressed both worry about political upheaval and hope that a more tolerant monarch might come to reign. Many Independents came to regard the day of Anne's death as the "Protestant Passover." In the midst of this turmoil and uncertainty, Watts wrote "Our God, our help in ages past" for his congregation, and later included it in the 1719 *Psalms of David Imitated.* George I repealed the Schism Act in 1719, thus justifying the faith expressed in the hymn. In reflecting on this historical period, an earlier writer waxed eloquent, "As Miriam sang her divine song after the deliverance from Pharaoh, so Watts sang his divine song after the discomfiture of the Jacobites, and impressed upon his own generation and upon posterity

13. Specific information on Watts and the Schism Act is from Thomas Wright, *The Lives of the British Hymn-Writers,* Vol. III (London: C. J. Farncombe and Sons, 1914), 116-121.

that the grace of God — and the grace of God alone — renders man *[sic]* invincible."

"Our God" appears as the second of five imitations of Psalm 90.[14] The first, in Long Meter, carries the subtitle "A mournful Song at a Funeral," and reflects on the mortality of humankind. Verses 4 and 5, however, closely resemble verses in "Our God," though in this imitation they clearly refer to individual human life:

> A thousand of our years amount
> Scarce to a day in thine account;
> Like yesterdays departed light,
> Or the last watch of ending night.
> Death like an overflowing stream
> Sweeps us away; our life's a dream:
> An empty tale, a morning-flower
> Cut down and withered in an hour.

The third version of Psalm 90 (noted as covering verses 8-12 of the Psalm) also concerns death and human frailty, subtitled "Infirmities and Mortality the Effect of Sin; or Life, old Age, and Preparation for Death." The fourth version, covering verses 13 and following, continues that theme to its logical conclusion, subtitled "Breathing after Heaven" (meaning longing for heaven). The last, short meter version covering verses 5, 10 and 12 also concerns the individual human being and points again toward the "Frailty and Shortness of Life."

The focus on the physical body's frailty and the shortness of human life in four of Watts's imitations of this Psalm point up the contrast with the wider, more cosmic, and more political themes of Psalm 90, 1-5, First Part, Common Meter. Consider Psalm 90 in the King James Version of the Bible and then Watts's imitation of the first verses.

Psalm 90, King James Version

1 Lord, thou hast been our dwelling place in all generations.
2 Before the mountains were brought forth, or ever thou hadst formed the earth and the world, even from everlasting to everlasting, thou art God.

14. Watts, *Psalms of David,* 180-186.

3 Thou turnest man to destruction; and sayest, Return ye children of men.
4 For a thousand years in thy sight are but as yesterday when it is past, and as a watch in the night.
5 Thou carriest them away as with a flood; they are as a sleep: in the morning they are like grass which groweth up.
6 In the morning it flourisheth, and groweth up; in the evening it is cut down and withereth.

Psalm 90, Watts

"Man Frail and God Eternal"

1 Our God, our help in ages past,
Our hope for years to come,
Our shelter from the stormy blast,
And our eternal home.

2 Under the shadow of thy throne
Thy saints have dwelt secure;
Sufficient is thine arm alone,
And our defense is sure.

3 Before the hills in order stood,
Or earth received her frame,
From everlasting thou art God,
To endless years the same.

4 Thy word commands our flesh to dust,
Return, ye sons of men:
All nations rose from earth at first,
And turn to earth again.

5 A thousand ages in thy sight
Are like an evening gone;
Short as the watch that ends the night
Before the rising sun.

6 The busy tribes of flesh and blood
With all their lives and cares
Are carried downwards by the flood,
And lost in following years.

7 Time like an ever-rolling stream
Bears all its sons away;
They fly forgotten as a dream
Dies at the opening day.

8 Like flow'ry fields the nations stand
Pleas'd with the morning-light;
The flowers beneath the Mower's hand
Lie withering e'er 'tis night.

9 Our God, our help in ages past,
Our hope for years to come,
Be thou our guard while troubles last,
And our eternal home.

The biblical Psalm clearly describes the universal human condition, and in that context, affirms the eternal reliability and stability of God. Watts begins by affirming that same stability and reliability in the first three verses. One might wonder precisely to whom Watts was referring as "Thy saints": whether all believers from all times, all Christians, or perhaps his Independent kindred, who dwelt secure under *God's* throne while living without security under various English thrones (note that the word "throne" does not appear in the biblical Psalm). Verses four, six and eight, however, move away from both the biblical material (though not in conflict with it) and from the other four versions of this Psalm that Watts presents.

God, indeed, is eternal, and, in verse four, Watts states firmly that nations are not. Not only do human beings return to the dust, so do nations — quite an affirmation to make as the British empire rose to new heights! "The busy tribes of flesh and blood" most certainly also refer to the political configurations of humankind, and again Watts lifts up their transience. To drive the point home, in verse eight, Watts takes the grass image from the Psalm and applies it to nations rather than the general human condition, proclaiming that as "flow'ry fields the nations stand," but "lie withering e'er 'tis night." In verse nine, Watts not only avows God's reliability, but also begs that God be a "guard while troubles last." This last verse gains new breadth in comparison to the first when the "troubles" detailed involve not only the individual human journey toward death, but the turmoil of nations rising and falling, and of those persecuted within them as well. The home — the throne, on which we can depend, he asserts — is God alone.

Clearly, then, in the context of England's political and ecclesiastical situations at the time of its writing and of the congregations of Dissenters for whom the hymn was written, Watts intended its singers to hear, proclaim, and understand a political as well as a theological message. Acts of Parliament will come and go; monarchs will take the throne and will die and be replaced by other transient monarchs. Dissenters need not fear these changes brought by "busy tribes of flesh and blood with all their lives and cares." The hymn in its original version "contrasts [God's] eternal changelessness with the frailty of the civilization that barely tolerated Dissent."[15] The hymn is a bugle call to stay the course, not only in worshipers' personal faith, but also in their relationship to the state and its laws.

What happened to the hymn in the years following its publication, and especially following Watts's death in 1748, makes its original intent powerfully ironic. Watts's psalter came to America shortly after publication in England (published in America first by Benjamin Franklin). It did not gain wide popularity, however, until just before the American Revolution. In the early published versions in New England, Psalm 90, "Our God our help," is intact. John Wesley, however, in his 1737 *Collection of Psalms and Hymns,* and followed in subsequent hymnals, changed not only the first word, but left out or altered several other verses (as he did with other Watts Psalms he used in his compilations).[16] Verses four, six, and eight were eliminated, thus removing "all reference to a tension between Dissenters and society at large that eased once the Hanoverian dynasty had survived."[17] By

15. Lionel Adey, *Class and Idol in the English Hymn* (Vancouver: University of British Columbia Press, 1988), 208.

16. John Julian, *A Dictionary of Hymnology* (New York: Dover Publishing, 1907/1957), 1236. I examined a 1744 edition of Wesley's *Collection of Psalms and Hymns* (London: W. Strahan) and noted that not only did Wesley change "Our" to "O" but also altered verse 6 to read "all their cares and fears" and verse 9 was altered to read "while life shall last" instead of "troubles last." In context, these alterations mean more than they might seem to the casual observer. By the time of his 1779 *Collection of Hymns for the Use of the People Called Methodists,* (London: Hayman Brothers), 44, Wesley had completely divorced the hymn from any grander context of nations and politics by placing it under the subtitle, "Describing Death."

17. Adey, *Class and Idol,* 208. I reviewed selected hymnals and psalters in use between the mid-eighteenth and late-nineteenth centuries in both England and America, and the standard version of this hymn contains the original verses 1, 2, 3, 5, 7, and 9. There are some which include other verses and some which add words not written by Watts. About half of

the early nineteenth century, Watts's hymn had become a popular national hymn sung by all denominations in England and America, including Anglicans.[18]

Lionel Adey explains what happened to this hymn after the mid-nineteenth century: "After the emended text was set by founding editors of *Hymns Ancient and Modern* (1861) to the sturdy tune 'St. Anne,' . . . it became a tribal lay. As such it first appeared under the heading 'National Hymns' about the turn of the [twentieth] century, and became a standard hymn for the Remembrance Day services throughout the Commonwealth that were designed to ensure that fallen soldiers should *not* fly 'forgotten as a dream.'"[19]

Indeed, in countless hymnals in modern Great Britain, Watts's hymn falls in the category of "National Hymns," sung on such occasions as Winston Churchill's funeral and times of national crisis. Although not considered a national hymn in the United States, it is nonetheless commonly sung at funerals or other times of crisis in local churches or communities. How ironic that Watts, on the basis of this hymn, can be described by one commentator, as combining "monarchical patriotism with social concern."[20] That Watts was a British patriot is in no doubt; the many references to Britain as "Zion" throughout his Psalter make that obvious. Yet equating the unpredictable monarchy with the reasons why Watts labeled Britain as "Zion" is quite another matter. The hymn now is understood to say that the nation and throne will stand secure by the grace of God despite what its enemies may do, precisely the opposite of the intent of the hymn in its original context! Watts's words have come to be enlisted for the standing order, despite his intent to underscore the frailty of the standing order and to call for trust in God alone. This process of domestication is certainly not unique in the history of hymnody. Timothy Dwight's hymn, "I love thy kingdom, Lord," would suffer a similar fate in the next century.

---

those I reviewed kept Watts's original word "Our" and the rest adopted Wesley's "O." Most recent hymnals have returned to Watts.

18. In a curious historical/literary sidenote, the hymn appears in the 1849 publication of Charlotte Brontë's novel *Shirley*, set in the early part of that century. In the story, the dying niece of a Church of England rector requests that hymn be sung, and the version printed in the novel includes verses 4 and 8! Charlotte Brontë, *Shirley* (Oxford: Oxford University Press, 1979), 430.

19. Adey, *Class and Idol*, 208.

20. Ibid., 4.

Timothy Dwight

Like their English counterparts, America's descendants of the Puritans (in New England the Congregationalists and later Presbyterians) at first sang only metrical Psalms in worship. The *Bay Psalm Book*, the first book published in the new English world, set the American standard for absolute fidelity to biblical text, and also for disregard of singability or clarity of meaning. Isaac Watts's hymns and Psalm imitations hit the shores of America with the First Great Awakening. Jonathan Edwards championed Watts's work along with a new style of worship. Toward the end of the eighteenth century, as musicians like William Billings sought to improve the quality of singing in New England churches, Watts's texts opened up new possibilities. When the American colonies became independent, however, Watts's Psalter faced a large problem. As indicated above, many of his Psalm imitations contained overt references to Great Britain, and so revisions were clearly needed. John Wesley had begun the project in a small way in some of the Psalms rewritten for his Charleston Hymnbook, but American churchgoers wanted the whole of Watts in a singable fashion.

Numerous revised versions of Watts came out from American publishers between the Revolution and the mid-nineteenth century. The three major early editions came from a Newburyport, Massachusetts, printer, John Mycall (1781), and from "Connecticut Wits," the poet Joel Barlow (1785) and the grandson of Jonathan Edwards and President of Yale, Timothy Dwight (1801).[21] In addition to revising language for many reasons, including Britishisms, Barlow and Dwight also added their own versions of Psalms to Watts, especially for the several Psalms Watts had left out of his version because he deemed them inappropriate for singing in Christian churches.[22]

Timothy Dwight, a poet as well as a theologian, came to revise Watts as a commission from the General Association of Connecticut.[23] Joel

21. For more on the American revisions of Watts, see Louis Benson, "The American Revisions of Watts's 'Psalms,'" *Journal of the Presbyterian Historical Society* 2 (1903-04): 18-34, 75-89; and Rochelle A. Stackhouse, *The Language of the Psalms in Worship* (Lanham, MD: The Scarecrow Press, 1997).

22. Psalms omitted by Watts are: 28, 43, 52, 54, 59, 64, 70, 79, 88, 108, 137, 140.

23. For information on Timothy Dwight, see Charles Cuningham, *Timothy Dwight 1752-1817* (New York: Macmillan, 1942); Kenneth Silverman, *Timothy Dwight* (New York: Twayne Publishers, 1969); Anabelle Wenzke, *Timothy Dwight (1752-1817)* (Lewiston, NY: Edwin Mellen Press, 1989). Most of these barely even mention the Psalter, including, I am

Barlow's reputation as an upstanding Congregationalist had come into question, and many felt he had gone too far from Watts in his earlier revision, so this time the Association chose someone whose orthodoxy could not be doubted. The version which came to be known popularly as "Dwight's Watts" appeared in 1801 and continued to be popular among Congregationalist and Presbyterians into mid-century.[24]

Dwight's historical context, while dramatically different from Watts's in many ways, was similar with respect to the emotional and political position of his church in his time and place. The popular myth of America, and especially New England in the eighteenth century, paints a picture of a deeply devout people who all attended worship more than once a week and gladly allowed their lives to be ruled by religion. Of course, a reading of the literature of the period reveals a more complex reality. Modern historians have shown that especially the Revolutionary period was a time of instability for organized religion. "The advance of organized Christianity after 1680 could not mask the low and erratic levels of church adherence on the eve of the Revolution. Clerics knew well that their hold on the laity was tenuous, and that the colonists were dissolving political allegiances far older than any religious allegiances they then held."[25] Dwight himself, in a sermon preached after a Revolutionary War battle, exhorted the soldiers to remember that nothing stood in the way of the deliverance of America but the sin of its own inhabitants, yet this was a much greater obstruction than British armies. Repeatedly in this period in his writings and speeches Dwight upheld the Christian faith as the only principle which would ensure the success of this new nation.[26] Yet scholars estimate that at the period of the Revolution, "well under 10 percent of the population belonged formally to local congregations."[27]

Still, Dwight and most of his contemporaries in the leadership of the churches repeatedly referred to the emerging United States as Zion. "For

---

sorry to say, a marvelous new biography of Dwight by John Fitzmier, *New England's Moral Legislator* (Bloomington: Indiana University Press, 1998).

24. *The Psalms of David Imitated in the Language of the New Testament and Applied to the Christian Use and Worship by I Watts, DD, A new edition in which the Psalms omitted by Dr. Watts are versified in proper meter by Timothy Dwight, DD* (Hartford: Hudson and Goodwin, 1801).

25. Jon Butler, *Awash in a Sea of Faith* (Cambridge, MA: Harvard University Press, 1990), 194.

26. Cuningham, *Timothy Dwight,* 79.

27. Mark A. Noll, *A History of Christianity in the United States and Canada* (Grand Rapids: Eerdmans, 1992), 166.

Timothy Dwight, the new nation emerging on American soil presented humanity with the unique opportunity to do what it had so far failed to do, to build the kingdom of God."[28] His early visions of the nation were euphoric paeans to possibility.

Soon after the Revolution, however, it became apparent that there was trouble in Zion. Between his triumphalist poem, *America,* in 1780 and the 1794 tribute to his own local church in *Greenfield Hill,* Dwight moved from a man enveloped in the hope of Revolution to one who feared the new world that was coming into existence. Instead he sought to retreat to parochialism, seeing the rural town and church as more expressive of "Zion" than the new nation. In *America,* for example, Dwight had written: "Hail land of light and joy! Thy power shall grow / Far as the seas, which round thy regions flow; / Through earth's wide realms thy glory shall extend, / And savage nations at thy scepter bend. . . . / Then, then an heavenly kingdom shall descend, / And light and glory through the world extend."[29] But by the time of the later poem, his eloquence and energy were focused on the local church rather than the nation. In words reminiscent of his later hymn, he wrote: "For you [meaning the church] my ceaseless toils ye know,/My care, my faithfulness and woe/For you I breathed unnumbered prayers/For you I shed unnumbered tears."[30]

Several factors contributed to this change.[31] Most church leaders had strongly supported the Revolution, believing that the new nation would truly be established, in every sense of that word, as a Christian nation. Ezra Stiles, president at Yale when Dwight was a student, preached a sermon in 1783 which summed up this expectation: "The intent of ancestors on coming to America was not so much . . . to establish religion for the benefit of the state, as civil government for the benefit of religion, and as subservient, and even necessary towards the peaceable enjoyment and unmolested exercise of religion."[32]

28. Wenzke, *Timothy Dwight,* 221.

29. *The Major Poems of Timothy Dwight,* ed. William McTaggart and William Botorff (Gainsville, FL: Scholar's Facsimiles and Reprints, 1969), 11-12.

30. *Major Poems of Timothy Dwight,* 112. This poem does end with a vision of a holy America, but based entirely on the spread of "one faith, one worship and one praise."

31. For a full account of a complex situation, see the Dwight biographies and Butler, *Awash in a Sea of Faith.*

32. Quoted in J. C. D. Clark, *The Language of Liberty 1660-1832* (Cambridge: Cambridge University Press, 1994), 364.

Yet early in the life of the United States, and especially as the Constitution was being formed, it became clear that not everyone in political leadership shared this vision. Leaders like Thomas Jefferson, those who were called Deists (some of whom retained some measure of Christian faith), and others who were hostile or apathetic about the established church worked toward disestablishment in all the states, and on the national level. Rumors from France, in the wake of its Revolution, indicated to some, including Dwight, a vast international conspiracy of "Infidels" seeking to destroy the church. The rise of smaller denominations and religious movements such as the Swedenborgians, Mesmerists, Freemasons, and others also threatened the standing order. Within the established churches themselves theological disputes caused division or schism, such as the Unitarian controversies in New England at the end of the eighteenth century. Dwight, whose vision of America as the city set on a hill propelled his optimism in the wake of the Revolution, soon experienced this optimism "tempered by the realization that some people found other visions more attractive."[33]

Dwight responded to these developments in a variety of ways. He wrote books, articles, sermons, and poems, and published them everywhere. He gave speeches and preached throughout New England. He molded the curriculum and life at Yale College to prepare clergy to fight the "enemies of the church," and he had a hand, though modern scholars disagree on how significant, in launching the Second Great Awakening which, in the end, turned the tide against the onslaughts directed at the churches.[34] One significant reflection on the Second Great Awakening is that, contrary to popular portrayal, what happened was "less a movement to establish a new identity and more an effort to recover or protect old ones."[35] That assessment certainly meshes with Dwight's deep desire to move the nation back to his memory of the values, morals, and lifestyle of rural New England before the Revolution. Until his death in 1817, Dwight crusaded passionately in print and public proclamation for the formerly established churches to

33. Wenzke, *Timothy Dwight*, 227.

34. Again, many scholars have written on the Second Great Awakening. For an early, though interesting, reflection on the Awakening, see Martin Marty, *The Infidel: Free Thought and American Religion* (Cleveland: World Publishing, 1961), especially p. 47 and his reflections on Dwight.

35. Allen C. Guelzo, "God's Designs," in *New Directions in American Religious History*, ed. Harry S. Stout and D. G. Hart (New York: Oxford University Press, 1997), 149, in reference to comments by W. R. Ward in *The Protestant Evangelical Awakening.*

hold a central role in the life of the new nation. He believed strongly that worship, including singing, was key to the success of that crusade.

I Love Thy Kingdom, Lord

Very little has been written about Dwight's hymns and Psalm paraphrases (they usually rate only a footnote in his biographies). Yet they were significant. His version of Watts's *Psalms of David Imitated* appeared as the Second Great Awakening was shaping up, in the very year before his preaching led to a memorable series of conversions at Yale. Indicative of the desire to look back to a previous time, Dwight's *Watts* removed many of Joel Barlow's changes in order to preserve Watts's original language. Yet Dwight was not conservative about adding new Psalm paraphrases of his own; in fact, he added more new texts than Barlow had. One of those texts, paraphrasing a Psalm Watts felt to be unfit for Christians, was "I Love Thy Kingdom, Lord," from Psalm 137. Compare the King James Version of the Psalm with Dwight's paraphrase:

Psalm 137 King James Version

1 By the rivers of Babylon, there we sat down, yea, we wept, when we remembered Zion
2 We hanged our harps upon the willows in the midst thereof.
3 For there they that carried us away captive required of us a song; and they that wasted us required of us mirth, saying, Sing us one of the songs of Zion.
4 How shall we sing the Lord's song in a strange land?
5 If I forget thee, O Jerusalem, let my right hand forget her cunning.
6 If I do not remember thee, let my tongue cleave to the roof of my mouth; if I prefer not Jerusalem above my chief joy.
7 Remember, O Lord, the children of Edom in the day of Jerusalem; who said, Rase it, rase it, even to the foundation thereof.
8 O daughter of Babylon, who are to be destroyed; happy shall he be, that rewardeth thee as thou hast served us.
9 Happy shall he be, that taketh and dasheth thy little ones against the stones.

Timothy Dwight, SM Third Part: "Love to the Church"

1 I love thy kingdom, Lord,
The house of thy abode,
The church our blest Redeemer saved
With his own precious blood.

2 I love thy Church, O God!
Her walls before thee stand,
Dear as the apple of thine eye,
And graven on thy hand.

3 If e'er to bless thy sons
My voice, or hands, deny,
These hands let useful skill forsake,
This voice in silence die.

4 If e'er my heart forget
Her welfare, or her woe,
Let every joy this heart forsake,
And every grief o'erflow.

5 For her my tears shall fall;
For her my prayers ascend;
To her my cares and toils be given,
Till toils and cares shall end.

6 Beyond my highest joy
I prize her heavenly ways,
Her sweet communion, solemn vows,
Her hymns of love and praise.

7 Jesus, thou Friend divine,
Our Saviour and our King,
Thy hand from every snare and foe
Shall great deliverance bring.

8 Sure as thy truth shall last,
To Zion shall be given
The brightest glories earth can yield,
And brighter bliss of heaven.

The most obvious feature of Dwight's hymn in comparison to the biblical Psalm is that they seem to have little to do with each other!

Barlow's version of the same Psalm, "Along the banks where Babel's current flows," one of his most popular pieces, stays very close to the biblical text, yet Dwight, seen as the more conservative of the two, departs substantially from the Bible. Dwight had a theo-political point to make in this hymn, and the biblical Psalm in its lament for Zion gave him the opportunity.

The biblical Psalmist weeps for a nation-state, a city, and a temple; Dwight celebrates an ecclesiastical institution. Here is the major shift in his politics, as well as his theology. In his Valedictory Address to the students at Yale in 1776, Dwight wrote: "From every deduction of reason, as well as from innumerable declarations of inspired truth, we have the best foundation to believe that this continent will be the principle seat of that new, that peculiar kingdom."[36]

One of Dwight's biographers observes, "The task that Dwight set for the nation was no less than the building of the Kingdom of God, and his ministry was an effort to define and to aid that effort."[37] In numerous writings and sermons after 1776, he and many of his contemporaries, including Joel Barlow, repeated the reference to the new United States of America as the coming Kingdom, as Zion.[38] President Ronald Reagan's use of the phrase "city set on a hill" as an allusion to the United States simply repeated what Dwight and his contemporaries were doing immediately after the Revolution. Dwight believed that the means for establishing this kingdom of God in America included "preaching and hearing the word, reading scripture, prayer, correspondence with religious men, religious meditation, and the religious education of children," all of which applied to everyone, regardless of church affiliation or participation. Other means of grace, such as baptism and Holy Communion, belonged only to church members. He foresaw eventually no line between the two.[39] As he participated in new mission programs for the frontier, he imagined not just

36. Timothy Dwight, *A Valedictory Address to the Young Gentlemen who Commenced Bachelor of Arts at Yale College, July 25, 1776* (New Haven: T. & S. Green, 1776), 14.

37. Wenzke, *Timothy Dwight*, 7.

38. See, for example, Joel Barlow's version of Psalm 60. In verse 3, Watts had written, "Great Britain shakes beneath thy stroke," while Barlow writes, "Our Sion trembles at thy stroke," clearly referring to the new nation. Dwight, interestingly enough, writes, "Thy people shake beneath thy stroke, and dread thy threatening hand; Oh heal the *nation* [Watts had written "the island" and Barlow "the people"] thou hast broke, Confirm the wavering land."

39. Wenzke, *Timothy Dwight*, 188.

spreading the gospel, but producing "a whole social order in which religious and civil institutions were mutually supportive."[40] As the eighteenth century drew to a close, however, Dwight modified that view and began to see the visible church as the seat of the Kingdom rather than the nation itself.

In his new paraphrase of Psalm 137, the "kingdom" of verse 1 and "Zion" of verse 8 now most certainly refer to the church, not the nation. His LM paraphrase of the second part of this same Psalm also makes that distinction clear. Verses 1 and 2 read:

> Lord, in these dark and dismal days,
> We mourn the hidings of thy face;
> Proud enemies our path surround,
> To level Zion with the ground.
>
> Her songs, her worship, they deride,
> And hiss thy word with tongues of pride,
> And cry, t'insult our humble prayer,
> "Where is your God, ye Christians, where?"

Indeed, the context of Dwight's two other versions of Psalm 137 are crucial for understanding Dwight's intent in "I love thy kingdom." The LM First Part, subtitled "The sorrows of Israel in the Babylonian captivity," stays very close to the King James Version and is meant as a historical lament. In his LM Second Part, however, Dwight moves into the contemporary world, as he subtitles it "The Church's Complaint." The language, not subtle in the least, condemns those who seek to "level Zion with the ground." Dwight affirms his belief that "Zion [without question in this hymn referring to the Church] her Cyrus soon shall see / Arrayed to set his Israel free." And when that happens, Dwight envisions that "Nations before his [the antecedent is Jesus as Cyrus] altar bend / And peace from realm to realm extend." The language calls forth an emotional framework similar to Watts's "Our God."

Having set the context for complaint, then, Dwight moves in his SM Third Part, "I Love Thy Kingdom," to affirm both God's faithfulness to the Church and the inherent power of the church to withstand whatever "snare and foe" (v. 7) may come its way.

40. Ibid., 49.

By the end of the eighteenth century, Dwight had become the foremost apologist for the church and its strongest defender, often seeing the state as an enemy rather than a partner. His 1794 poem, *Greenfield Hill,* painted the village life of rural Connecticut, with the church at its center geographically, emotionally, politically, and spiritually, as the ideal setting for living out the Kingdom of God on earth. In a sermon from 1798, "The Duty of Americans at the Present Crisis," he said, "For what end shall we be connected with men of whom this [infidelity] is the character and conduct? . . . Is it that our churches may become temples of reason, our Sabbath a decade, and our psalms of praise Marsellois [*sic*] hymns?"[41]

Worship, for Dwight, became a centerpiece in the struggle to establish the Kingdom on American soil, and it was his desire to revitalize worship at Yale that led to his part in the Second Great Awakening.

This hymn raises up the theme of the centrality of worship to the Kingdom, now identified with the church as the mechanism to transform a hostile society. Verse 6 highlights the two sacraments of Holy Communion and Baptism ("her sweet communion, solemn vows" — although an alternate reading might be that "communion" refers to the fellowship of believers united, the "communion of saints," and the "solemn vows" as those of ordination). It also refers specifically to the singing of church members, "her hymns of love and praise." That final point shows that Dwight understood the hymnody of the church to be important and influential.

Finally, the hymn makes clear that the passion Dwight and his contemporaries had felt for the new nation in 1776 now has narrowed to passion for the church as an agent of transformation for that nation. Verses 3, 4, and 5 — those tied most closely to the Biblical Psalm — show a singer whose utmost allegiance is not to a flag, not even directly to God, but to the institution of the Church. Dwight trusts ultimately in God's power and will to deliver that Church out of the hands of its enemies, whether they be Infidels, Deists, Unitarians, or whomever, in order to continue its mission. "Thy hand from every snare and foe shall great deliverance bring." In the end, the "brightest glories earth can yield" will belong not to the new nation, as his earlier poem *America* surely indicated, but to Zion understood as the church. None of Dwight's contemporaries would have missed the

41. Cited in Charles Roy Keller, *The Second Great Awakening in Connecticut* (New Haven: Yale University Press, 1942), 19-20.

clear shift in this hymn's message from his earlier political stance. Like "Our God," Dwight intended this hymn as a clarion call to church members to stay the course and trust in God to redeem not only them, but the nation through them. Their energy, as Dwight's, was to be in service primarily to the Church as bearer of the Kingdom, not the nation. Dwight's core belief, reflected in this hymn, has been well summarized by Anabelle Wenzke: "Although moral government is to be institutionalized through civil government, it is the church which provides the constitution for establishment. . . . The care and maintenance of the church is essential for the establishment of a sound social order."[42]

Conclusion

From an examination of two texts central to the worship of both English and American Christians, this chapter raises two matters for conclusion. The first concerns the methodology of studying hymn texts, the second concerns the "domestication" of hymn texts, particularly in regard to their political content.

Lawrence Hoffman, in his study of Jewish liturgical change, *Beyond the Text,* moved the methodology of liturgical study in new directions by observing that "the very act of worship takes on the function of identifying for the worshipper what it is that he or she stands for, what real life is like, what his or her aspirations are."[43] He insists that any liturgical study must involve exploring content (text), structure, and choreography (enactment of the liturgy). Scholars in ritual studies also emphasize the importance of studying the context in which ritual takes place, not only the structural and choreographic context, but the social, political, emotional, and cultural contexts as well.[44]

These insights are crucial to the study of hymn texts. The words of the texts themselves need to be studied, of course, but with greater attention to alterations that have been made, and continue to be made, as workers of theological, liturgical, political, and ecclesiastical changes in the

42. Wenzke, *Timothy Dwight,* 253.

43. Lawrence Hoffman, *Beyond the Text* (Washington, DC: Pastoral Press, 1984), 69.

44. See, for example, Nancy Jay, *Throughout Your Generations Forever* (Chicago: University of Chicago Press, 1992).

lives of worshipers. The "structure" to be studied needs to include how hymnals are organized and what place hymns have in relation to one another. Full understanding of the meaning and intent of "I love thy kingdom" most certainly requires examining the other texts Dwight set from that same Psalm. Noting that "Our God," at least from the nineteenth century onward, appears in the "National Hymns" section (or its equivalent) in many English hymnals hints at the political nature of the hymn.[45]

Assessing the social, political, and ecclesiastical context of hymns, both for the time when they were written and for later (including their disappearance from worship altogether in whole or part), provides crucial information both for the scholar and for the worshiper. To some extent this sort of contextualizing has been done for worshipers in popular works like Albert Bailey's *The Gospel in Hymns,* which include vignettes from the life of hymn writers, or for hymns with "famous contexts" like "Amazing Grace" or "Silent Night." Yet most worshipers sing hymns without knowing anything at all about the situations of the original writers, and many studies have explicated hymns by focusing purely on the text itself. Yet the work of contextualization is crucial to retaining the power of a hymn's words and for helping them make the transition to the contemporary world. And, it is important to add, this awareness of original context helps to avoid dumbing down the hymn with unnecessary language changes. In the case of the two hymns in this study, the powerful interplay between the biblical text (most modern worshipers probably have no idea that both these hymns were originally Psalm paraphrases) and the political, social, and ecclesiastical context of their writers brings new life to already lively texts. The same awareness opens an opportunity to tie them to modern events in ways not usually done for these two hymns. As Watts envisioned, however, such an exercise could have marvelous results homiletically as well as liturgically.

Delving into the original context of a hymn, and then exploring the subsequent history of its use, can sometimes reveal how that usage, including the very meaning of the text, has changed. The hymns by Watts and Dwight discussed here became domesticated, either by being divorced from their political context and intent (in the case of Dwight) or

45. One example among many would be the *Scottish National Hymnal for the Young* (1910), where "Our God" is placed between the National Anthem and "Scotland for Christ." Adey, *Class and Idol,* 156.

having the political/social/ecclesiastical meaning changed (in the case of Watts). This kind of domestication, particularly in regard to political language, intent, or implication in church music (as also folk music) has a long history. How many school children are taught that the popular folk song, Woody Guthrie's "This Land Is Your Land," was originally a protest against the government's treatment of the poor and the immigrant, written as a response to Irving Berlin's "God Bless America"? Another New England Congregational hymn writer, Washington Gladden, wrote a hymn which suffered a similar fate in the 1870s. "O Master let me walk with thee" is now sung as a hymn of sacrificial discipleship and devotion. It was, however, written in response to protests against his work on behalf of the United States' fledgling labor movement. It originally included the following verse:

> O Master let me walk with thee
> Before the taunting Pharisee;
> Help me to bear the sting of spite,
> The hate of men who hide thy light,
> The sore distrust of souls sincere
> Who cannot read thy judgements clear,
> The dullness of the multitude
> Who dimly guess that thou art good.[46]

In the hymns by both Watts and Dwight this domestication was effected by dropping verses, by separating the texts from the Psalms in which they were rooted, and by the singing of the hymns in entirely new contexts. At least during the nineteenth century, and perhaps before, verses four, six, and eight of "Our God" disappeared — the verses which plainly pointed towards politics. In subsequent usage, the hymn was coopted by the very ruling ecclesiastical and political powers it was originally written to oppose. Most citizens of Great Britain, whether or not they ever set foot in public worship, now know the hymn largely from its use in the Remembrance Day (the equivalent of the U.S. Memorial Day) celebrations, where the hymn is used to strengthen national pride and resolve. Modern singers in either America or Great Britain would never guess that this hymn was a hymn of dissent and protest. Here is a domestication that was accomplished by hymnal editors almost singlehandedly.

46. Albert E. Bailey, *The Gospel in Hymns* (New York: Scribner's, 1950), 563.

In the case of Dwight, the separation of the hymn from the Psalm it allegedly paraphrases, from the other paraphrases he wrote of the same Psalm, and from earlier worshiping situations have transformed a hymn that lifted up the church as fulfillment of God's kingdom (as opposed to the state) and called for allegiance to the church above the state (or anything else) into merely a sentimental paean to white New England steeples or one's own local church.[47] This transformation has only been worsened by many of the recent paraphrases in modern hymnals aimed at modernizing the language.[48] Even the subject headings under which it appears in hymnals influence interpretation. Perhaps the most bizarre might be in *The New Congregational Hymn Book* of the Congregational Union of England and Wales of 1859 which classified this hymn under "Church Meetings." That classification could hardly be more divorced from the original context of the Psalm or Dwight's actual political situation.[49] Here is a hymn whose historical context could suit it for our time, when many see the emotional (as opposed to legal) separation of church and state as an opportunity for the church to move from civil religion to a true, transformational counterculture.

As the history of hymn texts reminds us time and again, language and usage will change. Scholars one hundred years from now will undoubtedly explore how the hymns of Brian Wren, Ruth Duck, and Jeffrey Rowthorn have evolved in what then will be "modern" hymnals. The point of this historical study is not to suggest that anyone try to stop that evolution. What it does suggest, however, is how much of a gift to worshipers understanding the historical contexts of hymns might be as they

47. While verses are usually left out of Dwight's hymn, their disappearance has little impact on the meaning. The standard 5 which appear are the original 1, 2, 5, 6, and 8.

48. See, for example, *The New Century Hymnal* (Cleveland, OH: Pilgrim Press, 1995), 312, which so changes the Dwight hymn as to make it unrecognizable, both poetically and theologically. The first verse, in this version "adapted" by Lavon Baylor, reads, "We love your realm, O God, all places where you reign/We recognize with hope and joy, the world as your domain." While that rendering may be theologically accurate, it distorts Dwight's important understanding of the church as the unique place where God reigns, and as such an institution which has a profound responsibility to transform the world which does not, for the most part, recognize God's rule. To be fair, one of the great gifts of the *NCH* is that it does note the Psalm roots of both Dwight's and Watts's hymns. Of course, if the adapters and editors of this hymnal had looked at the Psalm, they might have rewritten it differently.

49. *The New Congregational Hymn Book* (London: Jackson, Walford and Hodder, 1859), 828.

explore questions such as the relationship of their lives of faith to the political, social, and ecclesiastical contexts in which they find themselves. The messages of both Watts's and Dwight's hymns (as indeed the messages of the Psalter on which they based them) are not only that the church and the lives of the faithful *can* have a response to the political and social realms in which they live, but that *worship* is a proper, indeed a crucial, place in which to proclaim and define that response. The message is that not only the sermons and prayers, but the hymns sung in worship may proclaim and define that response. For Watts and Dwight, texts sung in church had to do with much more than the private faith of worshipers. For them, the singing in worship had broader implications that included politics, both national and ecclesiastical. The psalter or hymnal had a purpose larger than fostering the relationship of the individual to God, or acting solely as a devotional guide (however important devotion was to both writers). The church's song had the power to move people to act as disciples in the world, in all aspects of the world, just as the Psalms had done for Jews through the centuries. This is a gift modern churches could receive anew, if only they knew the histories of their hymns.[50]

50. The author expresses gratitude for the use of the Benson Collection at Princeton Theological Seminary and the Creamer and Methodist Center collections at Drew University; thanks to Dr. Ken Rowe, Dr. Robin A. Leaver, and helpful Drew librarians Alice Copeland and John Califf.

HYMNS AND THE ORDERING OF PROTESTANT LIFE

CHAPTER FOUR

Jesus Shall Reign: Hymns and Foreign Missions, 1800-1870

Robert A. Schneider

The extent and complexity of the historical relationship between "foreign missions" and hymns written and sung by Protestants in the United States can be suggested by several stories from the beginning, middle, and end of the nineteenth century. After telling all three, I will point out some of the significant and intriguing personal, public, and cross-cultural interactions between hymns and missions that they illustrate.

Three Hymn Stories

The first story emerges from several passages in the published memoirs of Harriet Atwood Newell (1793-1812). Newell was one of the first American missionaries sent overseas, the first "martyr" to the cause because she was the first to die while "in the field," and a posthumous celebrity among mission-minded evangelical Christians. In early 1811 this seventeen-year-old Massachusetts Congregationalist mentioned hymns in her diary several times, and named Isaac Watts's "Lord, what a wretched land is this" as her favorite hymn.[1] In April, after missionary candidate Samuel Newell proposed that she marry him and accompany him to India, Atwood

1. Leonard Woods, *Memoirs of Mrs. Harriet Newell, Wife of the Rev. S. Newell, American Missionary to India; Who Died Nov. 30, 1812, Aged 20. Also a Sermon on the Occasion of Her Death* (London: J. Nisbet, 1820), 70-71.

wrote, "The *important decision* is not yet made. I am still wavering. I long to see and converse with my dear mother. So delicate is my situation, that I dare not unbosom my heart to a single person. What shall I do? Could tears direct me to the path of duty, surely I would be directed. — My heart aches. — I know not *what* to do! — 'Guide me, O thou great Jehovah!'"[2]

In August, having accepted Newell's proposal, she quoted a popular missionary hymn and applied the words to herself: "Yes, Christian heroes go — proclaim / Salvation through Immanuel's name; / To India's clime the tidings bear, / And plant the rose of Sharon there. . . . Providence now gives me an opportunity to go myself to the Heathen. . . . Yes, I will go — however weak and unqualified I am, there is an all-sufficient Saviour, ready to support me."[3]

Atwood and Newell were married in February 1812, three days after Newell, Gordon Hall, Adoniram Judson, Samuel Nott, and Luther Rice were ordained as the first American foreign missionaries, and ten days before the Newells sailed from Salem for Calcutta as missionaries of the two-year-old American Board of Commissioners for Foreign Missions. Harriet Newell never actually engaged in mission, dying of tuberculosis on the Isle of France (Mauritius) in the Indian Ocean that November, two months after her nineteenth birthday. Writing to her mother about Harriet's death, Samuel Newell reported that he had asked his wife, "How does your past life appear to you now?" She replied, "Bad enough; but that only makes the grace of Christ appear the more glorious. Jesus thy blood and righteousness/My beauty are, my heav'nly dress;/Midst flaming worlds in these array'd,/With joy I shall lift up my head."[4]

The second story is related in an official publication of the American Board. In 1860, the organization that had sent Harriet Newell to India turned fifty and celebrated its jubilee in Boston's Tremont Temple. The oldest and largest Protestant foreign mission agency in the United States, the Board was a non-denominational evangelical organization endorsed by Congregational, Presbyterian, and Reformed churches and supported by their members. According to an official account, at the final session of the jubilee meeting, the Board, just recovered from unprecedented indebtedness, boldly faced the future by authorizing substantial expenditures

2. Ibid., 74-75.
3. Ibid., 93.
4. Ibid., 222.

for the coming year. Many honorary members and visitors were watching the proceedings.

As soon as the resolution had been adopted by the Board, a wish was expressed that an opportunity might be given for the whole assembly to manifest their feelings. The President, therefore, requested those who desired to express concurrence with the sentiment of that resolution, to do so by rising. The whole great congregation rose at once; one voice unexpectedly struck the note — instantly many caught it — and a multitude of voices, like the noise of many waters, sang the well-known verse, —

> Shall we, whose souls are lighted
> With wisdom from on high, —
> Shall we to men benighted
> The lamp of life deny?
> Salvation! — O, salvation!
> The joyful sound proclaim,
> Till earth's remotest nation
> Has learned Messiah's name.

It was a scene long to be remembered. Many an eye filled with tears, and many a bosom swelled with emotion.[5]

The final story appears in the report of the third convention of the Student Volunteer Movement for Foreign Missions, held in Cleveland, Ohio, in February of 1898. The Reverend James Walter Waugh, a northern Methodist home on leave from his mission in northwestern India, spoke to the student volunteers about "work for the masses."

> Many and many a time have I stood in the crowded bazaars, or melas, to read the Scriptures, and the people would begin to gather slowly, one or two at a time; but when I would sing in their native language one of their native airs I could at once gather a great multitude around me to hear the Word and way of life. (Here Dr. Waugh explained and sung a *bhajan* or hymn in the native language.) Then I would present the truth to them, and the people would tell others what they had

5. American Board of Commissioners for Foreign Missions, *Memorial Volume of the First Fifty Years of the American Board of Commissioners for Foreign Missions* (Boston: ABCFM, 1861), 6. The account was written by the Board's Foreign Corresponding Secretary, Rufus Anderson.

> heard of this wonderful Savior, and thus from the influences going out from our preaching and from our schools the good work began to grow and spread. . . . We make great use of Christian songs in the native tongues and sung to native tunes; and now among the people over there many of our missionaries are known as singing missionaries. We are carrying on the work of God by singing the gospel into human hearts. We believe that by getting in among the people in that way they will be rapidly Christianized.[6]

What do these stories tell us about the relationship between hymns and foreign missions? As an evangelical teenager Harriet Atwood moved in a religious world permeated by Scripture and evangelical theology — and by the words of hymns. One of those hymns, Welsh evangelical William Williams's "Guide me, O thou great Jehovah," first published in 1745, is ranked seventh in the American Protestant Hymns Project list of hymns widely reprinted in American Protestant hymnals.[7] The text Atwood quoted after deciding to go to India, was an American version of an English hymn. "Ye Christian heralds, go proclaim" is not included in the Hymns Project list, but in a recent historical survey it was ranked as the eleventh most-reprinted missionary hymn in sixty popular nineteenth-century hymnals.[8] (See Appendix I.) The pietist hymn in the account of

6. *The Student Missionary Appeal: Addresses at the Third International Convention of the Student Volunteer Movement for Foreign Missions held at Cleveland, Ohio, February 23-27, 1898* (New York: Student Volunteer Movement for Foreign Missions, 1898), 307. Identification of Waugh in *The Encyclopaedia of Missions*, ed. Edwin Munsell Bliss (New York: Funk and Wagnalls, 1891), 2:71.

7. See Appendix I.

8. Richard Steadman Mauney, "The Development of Missionary Hymnody in the United States of America in the Nineteenth Century" (D.M.A. thesis, Southwestern Baptist Theological Seminary, 1993), 148. "Ye Christian heralds" appeared in thirty-one of the sixty Baptist, Congregational, Methodist, and Presbyterian hymnals surveyed. The stanza Atwood quoted was the second of the hymn "Go, much-lov'd brethren, haste and rear" as published in Leonard Bacon's *Hymns and Songs; for the Monthly Concert* (Andover, MA: The Society of Inquiry Respecting Missions, 1823), No. 73. In Wood's *Memoirs* the first line is printed as "heroes I go" rather than the actual "heroes!" of the hymn. It is not clear if Atwood wrote "I," or if Woods or a printer misread the exclamation mark as the letter "I." In any case, her subsequent comments make it clear that she was applying the hymn's words to herself. She must have known the hymn from an English source, as Bacon's is supposed to have been the first publication of the hymn in the United States. In the original English version, "Ye Christian heralds, go proclaim," variously attributed to Baptist Bourne Hall Draper (1775-

Mrs. Newell's final days — it is not clear from her husband's letter if he was reporting that Harriet recited it on her deathbed, or was using it himself to describe her faith — was written by eighteenth-century Moravian leader Nikolaus Ludwig Zinzendorf and translated into English by John Wesley.[9] The story of the hymns in Harriet Atwood Newell's life tells us that hymns played an important role in the personal faith journeys of Americans who involved themselves in the missionary movement.

For the American Board in 1860, the third stanza of a forty-year-old hymn was so closely associated with foreign missions, and so familiar to so many people, that it could be used at a mass meeting as an ostensibly spontaneous and collective gesture of affirmation and commitment. The hymn was "From Greenland's icy mountains," written by Anglican Reginald Heber in 1819 and first published in an American hymn collection in 1823.[10] It was the most reprinted missionary hymn in American hymnals in the nineteenth century, served as the de facto anthem of the foreign missions movement well into the twentieth century, and ranks fifteenth in the Hymns Project list. The Board probably sang it to the tune most often used for it in the United States, MISSIONARY HYMN, written for Heber's text by American composer Lowell Mason in 1824.[11] The American Board's singing of the hymn in 1860 is just one of the many recorded instances in which it was used to express missionary beliefs publicly and proclaim missionary commitment, and the episode reveals the vital role that hymns played in the promotion of the missionary cause.

J. Walter Waugh's account of singing missionaries in India at the end of the century points to another important dimension of the relationship

---

1843) and the little known "Mrs. Voke," this is the first stanza. It reads "Ye Christian heralds, go proclaim," and "to distant climes." Mauney, "Missionary Hymnody," 72, 112; Theron Brown and Hezekiah Butterworth, *The Story of the Hymns and Tunes* (New York: American Tract Society, 1906), 171.

9. Brown and Butterworth, *Story of Hymns and Tunes*, 91-93; Robert Guy McCutchan, *Our Hymnody: A Manual of the Methodist Hymnal* (New York: Abingdon-Cokesbury Press, 1937), 253-254.

10. Mauney, "Missionary Hymnody," 24-25, 58-59.

11. Ibid., 59; Charles Hughes, *American Hymns Old and New: Notes on the Hymns and Biographies of the Authors and Composers* (New York: Columbia University Press, 1980), 165. Heber's hymn was still being included in American hymnals in the 1930s, when Methodist Robert McCutchan declared it "without doubt our greatest missionary hymn" (*Our Hymnody*, 468). By then, however, the verse that had inspired the American Board was being omitted from most hymnals as too self-righteous.

between hymns and missions. Missionaries used hymns in their evangelism, and hymns were integral to the worship life of the new Christians and new churches that resulted from that evangelism. The uses of hymns "in the field" raise important questions about the interaction of American and indigenous religious music, and about the issues of cultural imperialism and cultural accommodation familiar to historians of missions and mission theologies.

Exploring the History of Hymns and Missions

The relationship of "American" hymns and cross-cultural evangelism began with the interaction of European and Native American religions and music, and has continued to the present. My primary focus here is on one relatively brief period of that long relationship, the first fifty or so years of American foreign missions. Both American foreign missions and American hymns changed so substantially in the final third of the nineteenth century that the 1860s are a logical dividing line between the formative period of the foreign missions movement and later periods. My approach is that of a historian of religion in the United States interested in the nineteenth century, in Protestantism, and in the foreign missions movement. It was in the nineteenth century that missions became a significant dimension of American Protestantism. Exploring the various missionary uses of hymns is another avenue, alongside the investigation of ideas, institutions, and individuals, to get "inside" the life and mind of the foreign missions movement. But in the course of my research I came to the realization that if we can move beyond focusing on either missions or hymns, and instead focus on the *interaction* of the two phenomena (hymns and missions), we may be able to uncover important and intriguing historical dynamics in American religious history that otherwise are easily overlooked.

The relationship between hymns and missions has received relatively little attention from historians of either. Historians of American Protestant foreign missions have tended to concentrate on the ideas (the theology or "ideology"), the organizational structures, and the cultural imperialism of the movement. The classic histories of American hymnody mention missionary hymns, but while several recent studies of British hymns address missionary hymns at some length, there have been brief references but no comparable discussions in recent studies of American hymns.[12] The work that comes closest to a comprehensive study of hymns and missions is an unpublished doctoral dissertation by Richard Steadman Mauney, which I have used freely to pursue my own particular concerns.

In short, the scholarship on hymns and missions that does exist, and stories of the sort with which this paper began, together suggest that (1) there were important relationships between hymns and various aspects of the foreign missions movement; (2) evidence of those relationships survives and awaits the researcher; and (3) those relationships are worth exploring further for what they tell us about hymns, about missions, about the place of both, and their interaction, in the history of Protestantism in the United States.

The Foreign Missions Movement

Interest in foreign missions, stimulated among evangelical Protestants in the United States by news of the establishment of English missions to India in the 1790s, took concrete form with the organization of the American Board of Commissioners for Foreign Missions in 1810. The shipboard adoption of Baptist views by three of the Board's first missionaries, Adoniram and Ann Hazeltine Judson and Luther Rice, led to their dismissal from the Board and the creation of the General Missionary Convention of the Baptist Denomination in the United States of America (known as the Triennial Convention, and later reorganized into the American Baptist Missionary Union) to support them and other missionaries. Following the lead of those two organizations, mission activists organized other interdenominational and denominational mission agencies in the middle decades of the century. In 1868 fourteen foreign mission societies together spent $1,726,788 supporting 481 missionaries and 1,895 native

12. Classic American histories include Edward S. Ninde, *The Story of the American Hymn* (New York: The Abingdon Press, 1921), 117, 163, 209-215; Henry Wilder Foote, *Three Centuries of American Hymnody* (Cambridge, MA: Harvard University Press, 1940), 189, 213-214; Albert Christ-Janer, Charles W. Hughes, and Carleton Sprague Smith, *American Hymns Old and New* (New York: Columbia University Press, 1980), 331-332. British studies include Susan S. Tamke, *Make a Joyful Noise Unto the Lord: Hymns as a Reflection of Victorian Social Attitudes* (Athens, OH: Ohio University Press, 1978), 121-138; Lionel Adey, *Class and Idol in the English Hymn* (Vancouver: University of British Columbia Press, 1988), 15, 197-202.

agents in 310 mission stations.[13] The denominations with societies included the American (northern), Free Will and Southern Baptists, Episcopalians, Lutherans, Methodists, several kinds of Presbyterians, and the Dutch Reformed. The New School Presbyterians withdrew from the American Board the following year (as the German Reformed had in 1865), leaving it to become the Congregational foreign mission agency.

The mode of foreign missions that developed in the United States in the first half of the nineteenth century involved the selection, sending, support, and supervision of full-time missionaries, most of them committed for life, by denominational or interdenominational mission boards. Preaching, printing, and education were the primary evangelistic methods, though there was almost constant debate, at least in the American Board and Baptist Convention and Union, about the proper uses of the latter two and the proper balance of the three. Missionaries were usually college-educated, and were ordained ministers of the denominations affiliated with the boards. Because those denominations did not ordain women, only men were officially designated as "missionaries."

From the start, however, women were active in foreign missions. They were the majority of supporters at home, and they went abroad as the wives of missionaries and as teachers in mission schools. After 1860 more women became more involved in more ways, including the organization of women's missionary societies that sent their own female missionaries to engage in "woman's work for woman" around the world. By 1890 "women constituted sixty percent of the American mission force."[14]

In their formative years the mission boards developed procedures and policies for choosing, training, supporting, and overseeing their missionaries. They established fund-raising and promotional methods, worked out relations with their sponsoring churches and denominations, and grew into substantial bureaucratic organizations. Missionaries who returned home were sent on speaking tours to help educate and motivate the churches with regard to missions. Letters from missionaries and other news from the missions, missionary sermons, histories of missions, missionaries' biographies and autobiographies, and treatises on the theory

13. Rufus Anderson, *Foreign Missions: Their Relations and Claims* (New York: Charles Scribner and Company, 1869), 342.

14. Dana L. Robert, *American Women in Mission: A Social History of Their Thought and Practice* (Macon, GA: Mercer University Press, 1996), 130.

and practice of missions created a whole new genre of American religious literature. By the middle of the nineteenth century, the missionary movement had produced institutions and a religious subculture, both of which sought to keep the cause of missions constantly before the broader Protestant community.

Hymns and Foreign Missions

Hymns were intertwined with every aspect of the missionary enterprise. Participants in the movement wrote, published, read, meditated upon, and sang hymns to express their core beliefs, to give voice to their visions of the future, and to strengthen their individual and collective commitment to the cause. They used hymns to communicate their beliefs, visions, and commitment to other Christians, to their society, and to prospective new Christians around the world.

In turn, the missionary movement influenced American and global Christian hymnody in a number of ways. Familiar hymns became associated with foreign missions. New hymns with explicitly missionary themes and images were written. New tunes were composed for familiar missionary texts. Missionaries, as a group, introduced new Christians in other cultures to American hymn texts and musical styles, and they shaped the hymns of the new mission churches. In every way imaginable, the story of missions is the story of hymns.

Hymns about missions (called missionary hymns here) were the most visible product at home of the interaction of missions with hymnody, but they were not the only product nor the only locus of the interaction between hymns and foreign missions. In the missions, hymns were used in cross-cultural evangelism, and consequently they shaped emerging local Christian hymnodies. A third, less easily labeled aspect of the interaction between hymns and missions was the use by people involved in the missionary movement of hymns that had particular meaning for them. These "missionaries' hymns" were not necessarily either about, or the product of, missions. They are included in this discussion because they were important to people active in the cause.

Missionary Hymns

The emergence of an identifiable missionary hymnody — a body of hymns explicitly about missions or containing ideas and images directly associated by mission activists with them — is marked by the publication of two hymn collections in the early 1820s. The first significant collection of hymns explicitly associated with missions, *Hymns and Sacred Songs; for the Monthly Concert and Similar Occasions,* was published in 1823 by a student missionary group at Andover Seminary, the Society of Inquiry Respecting Missions. Andover student and future Congregational leader Leonard Bacon (1802-1881), then twenty-one, compiled the 106 hymns that a Society committee deemed relevant to foreign missions. The year after the Andover publication appeared, prominent Congregational revivalist Asahel Nettleton (1783-1844) published *Village Hymns for Social Worship,* the first major hymnal to dedicate a relatively large portion of its hymns — fifty-four of six hundred — to missions.[15] Nettleton's three sections of missionary hymns for the monthly concert, for missionary meetings, and for collections included — in whole, in part, or rewritten — thirty-five hymns from *Hymns and Sacred Songs.* They were interspersed with nineteen other hymns not in the Andover collection. By 1824, evangelical Congregationalists interested in foreign missions had identified and publicly labeled 125 hymns as in some way directly related to the missionary enterprise and its foundational beliefs.

By identifying hymns in this way, Bacon's and Nettleton's collections contributed to the creation of a de facto "canon" of missionary hymns. They delineated a body of missionary hymns from which editors of later hymnals selected some for reprinting, and to which they added other existing, and, over time, new hymns. In his survey of sixty nineteenth- and early-twentieth-century Baptist, Congregational, Methodist, and Presbyterian hymnals published in the United States, Richard Steadman Mauney found that by the mid-nineteenth century popular denominational hymnals commonly contained sections of between thirty and fifty hymns identified as related to missions.[16] Nettleton's *Village Hymns* set the pattern for such sections, and it was through inclusion in general purpose hymnbooks like his, and not the publication of special interest collections like Bacon's, that missionary hymns were popularized.

15. Ninde, *Story of the American Hymn,* 117; Mauney, "Missionary Hymnody," 25-28.
16. Mauney, "Missionary Hymnody," 20-54.

Not all of the hymns in Bacon's and Nettleton's collections were reprinted often enough to be in Mauney's list, but some that did make the list were among the most popular missionary hymns of the nineteenth century. Mauney ranked mission-related hymns by the frequency of their appearance in his sixty hymnals, and found that 124 hymns had been reprinted in at least five of the hymnals. Forty-one of the 125 hymns in *Hymns and Sacred Songs* and *Village Hymns* were among Mauney's 124.[17] Eighty-three of Mauney's 124 did not appear in either early volume. This means that a third of the hymns in Bacon's and Nettleton's collections became part of the canon of nineteenth-century missionary hymns identified by Mauney, and that they were a third of that canon. Some of the hymns from *Hymns and Sacred Songs* and *Village Hymns* that did make it into Mauney's list were more popular than others. Seventeen hymns from the early collections are among the top thirty hymns in Mauney's list, hymns that appeared in twenty-one or more of his sixty hymnals. Fourteen hymns in Mauney's list (eleven of them in the top thirty) are also in the Hymns Project's list of hymns most frequently reprinted in American Protestant hymnals. More will be said about this core group of missionary hymns later.

On the one hand, then, only a relatively small group of missionary hymns appeared in a large number of hymnals over a significant span of time. On the other hand, a large number of hymns were associated with missions, in one hymnal or another, in the nineteenth century. Beyond Mauney's 124 ranked hymns, over 400 were identified as missionary hymns in the hymnals he surveyed, but were not reprinted often enough to make it into the list.[18] And there were other hymnals and other denominations.

It is not necessary or desirable to identify fixed lists of either all or the most reprinted missionary hymns of the nineteenth century. The numbers and lists we have now tell us the important fact: between 1823 and 1900 significant numbers of hymnal editors came to associate a particular body of hymns with foreign missions. Some denominational preferences existed, but most of the hymns were popular across denominational boundaries. Despite the number of missionary hymns available —

17. Twenty-two of the forty-one were in both Bacon's and Nettleton's collections. Fourteen others were in Bacon's and five others in Nettleton's.

18. Mauney, "Missionary Hymnody," 57.

perhaps more than a thousand by 1900 — in their appearance in hymnals missionary hymns were a minority among hymn types. From eight to ten percent of the hymns in a typical denominational hymnal might be labeled as related to missions. Nevertheless, as the nineteenth century progressed, mission activists had a growing number of hymns with which to express their beliefs and promote their cause, and American Protestants were increasingly likely to encounter the ideas, intentions, and favorite images of the foreign missions movement in hymnbooks and congregational singing as well as in sermons, religious meetings, and religious literature.

Many of the missionary hymns they read and sang were of British origin. The fifteen most-reprinted hymns in the hymnals Mauney surveyed were by English, Irish, Scottish, or Welsh writers, as were twelve of the fourteen missionary hymns in the Hymnody Project list (ten of the twelve were also in Mauney's fifteen). British influence was typical of American hymnody in general in the nineteenth century.[19] In the missionary category, as in others, Isaac Watts was the premier hymn writer, having written sixteen of Mauney's 124 most-reprinted missionary hymns, and four of the fourteen missionary hymns in the Project list. English writers John Newton, Thomas Gibbons, Bourne Hall Draper, William Shrubsole, Benjamin Beddome, and Mrs. Voke, as well as the Scottish James Montgomery and Irish Thomas Kelly, also have multiple hymns in Mauney's list.

As the missionary movement grew, and as more Americans wrote hymns of all kinds, more American hymns about missions appeared in the hymnals. Americans involved with both missions and religious music are now usually associated by historians with one or the other, but in fact they provided a link between the two. They included church musicians Lowell Mason and Thomas Hastings and religious poet William B. Tappan. Among the church leaders who contributed to the growth of missionary hymnody by editing hymnals and, in some cases, writing hymns, were prominent Congregational ministers Timothy Dwight, Samuel Worcester, Samuel M. Worcester, Leonard Bacon, Asahel Nettleton, and David Greene. (Greene was domestic corresponding secretary of the

19. Mary De Jong, "'Theirs the Sweetest Songs': Women Hymn Writers in the Nineteenth-Century United States," in *A Mighty Baptism: Race, Gender, and the Creation of American Protestantism,* ed. Susan Juster and Lisa MacFarlane (Ithaca, NY: Cornell University Press, 1996), 145.

American Board, and coeditor with Lowell Mason of *Church Psalmnody* [1831]).[20] Presbyterian Nathan S. S. Beman, Methodist Nathan Bangs, and Baptists Samuel Francis Smith and Baron Stow, editors of the influential hymnal *The Psalmist* (1843), made similar contributions. Smith, later an editor for the American Baptist Missionary Union, wrote two famous hymns in 1831-32 at the age of twenty-four, while a student at Andover Seminary: "The morning light is breaking," the missionary hymn by an American most widely known and reprinted throughout the nineteenth century, and the famous patriotic hymn, "My country, 'tis of thee."[21]

One way in which hymns and missions were connected was through the participation of the same people in both the foreign missions movement and the movement to reform the use of music in American evangelical churches. From the 1820s on, Lowell Mason, Thomas Hastings, and others sought both to raise the quality of church music and ensure that it served to advance religion and morality rather than merely aesthetic ends. They also rejected the practice of Joshua Leavitt and others of setting hymns to popular secular tunes. Both Mason and Hastings were involved with missionary hymns as well as hymn reform, and many of the church leaders who supported the hymn reform movement were also deeply involved in the missionary movement. Leading evangelicals in Boston cooperated in the mid-1820s to persuade Mason to move to that city. The offices of the American Board and the Baptist Missionary Convention happened to be in Boston, and five Congregationalists associated with the Board and one officer of the Convention served on committees that interacted with Mason. One committee asked him to publish the address on church music he gave in Boston in October of 1826, another invited him to serve as music director of three Congregational churches in the city, and others worked with him in that capacity between 1827 and 1851.[22] The foreign missions movement and the hymn reform movement

20. Mauney, "Missionary Hymnody," 34-55; Carol A. Pemberton, *Lowell Mason: His Life and Work* (Ann Arbor, MI: UMI Research Press, 1985), 50, 72; *Appletons' Cyclopaedia of American Biography*, s.v. "Greene, David"; Rufus Anderson, "Rev. David Greene," *Missionary Herald* 62, no. 8 (August 1866): 225-30.

21. Mauney, "Missionary Hymnody," 41-3, 80-1; Henry S. Burrage, *Baptist Hymn Writers and Their Hymns* (Portland, ME: Brown Thurston and Company, 1888), 329-344; Ninde, *Story of the American Hymn*, 275-285.

22. The five were Lyman Beecher, Rufus Anderson, Daniel Noyes, William Stone, and David Greene, and the Baptist was Heman Lincoln. Pemberton, *Lowell Mason*, 39-59. On Ma-

shared the same moral fervor and single-minded devotion to promoting evangelical faith. Presumably mission activists became music activists because they saw the two as complementary efforts to achieve a single evangelical goal.

The content of missionary hymns seems to reflect quite accurately the beliefs that sustained the missionary movement in its formative period, at least as we know them from both official statements and missionaries' personal accounts. This can be illustrated by a brief look at the missionary hymns in Bacon's *Hymns and Spiritual Songs.*

It is evident, from both the date and texts of those hymns, that the major source of ideas and images in missionary hymns was not firsthand knowledge of what was actually happening in the missions. Workers had been in the field for barely a decade in the oldest missions, and of the hymns in *Hymns and Spiritual Songs* with known authors, only the two by John Lawson — an English Baptist missionary in Calcutta from 1812 — were written by a missionary. These hymn texts reflect the understanding of the missionary enterprise held by supporters at home, not the experiences of either missionaries or their converts. What is expressed in the words of these hymns is a mixture of biblical language and images, literary conventions, and British and American cultural assumptions.

In the missionary hymns of the 1820s several major themes are reflected through the lenses of biblical vocabulary and a fascination with exotic locales. As we look at them now, the most conspicuous aspects of these hymns are their expression of belief in the superiority of Christianity and Christian culture to other religions and cultures, and their use of images of conquest to describe global evangelism. There certainly are enough heathen hymns and battle hymns to justify any charges of cultural imperialism. The combination of Christian exclusivity and Eurocentrism that pervades many of the hymns reveals a real and significant dimension of nineteenth-century European and American Christianity, Protestantism, and evangelicalism.

Heathen imagery and war-and-conquest imagery each appear, with some overlap, in over a third of the hymns in Bacon's collection. A look at

---

son and his crusade, see also Pemberton, "Teaching the People Their Sacred Songs: Lowell Mason and His Work," *The Hymn* 43, no. 1 (January 1992): 17-20, and "Praising God Through Congregational Song: Lowell Mason's Contributions to Church Music," *The Hymn* 44, no. 2 (April 1993): 22-30; and Michael Broyles, *"Music of the Highest Class": Elitism and Populism in Antebellum Boston* (New Haven: Yale University Press, 1992), 62-91.

several of those hymn texts allows us to move beyond a preoccupation with what are now, for many observers including many Protestants, quaint images, offensive terminology, and outmoded understandings of mission. Behind the exotic images lies the central evangelical beliefs that defined and motivated evangelical foreign missions.

Reginald Heber's "From Greenland's icy mountains" was the missionary hymn that appeared most frequently in the hymnals Mauney surveyed — in fifty-three of sixty. It ranks fifteenth in the Hymns Project list. Its appearance in *Hymns and Sacred Songs* was apparently its first publication in a hymn collection in the United States (it had previously been printed in periodicals).

From Greenland's icy mountains,
From India's coral strand;
Where Afric's sunny fountains
Roll down their golden sand;
From many an ancient river,
From many a palmy plain,
They call us to deliver
Their land from error's chain.

What tho' the spicy breezes
Blow soft o'er Ceylon's isle,
Tho' every prospect pleases,
And only man is vile;
In vain with lavish kindness
The gifts of God are strown;
The heathen in his blindness
Bows down to wood and stone.

Shall we, whose souls are lighted
With wisdom from on high,
Shall we to men benighted
The lamp of life deny?
Salvation! O Salvation!
The joyful sound proclaim,
Till earth's remotest nation
Has learn'd Messiah's name.

Waft, waft, ye winds, his story,
And you, ye waters, roll,
Till, like a sea of glory,
It spreads from pole to pole;
Till o'er our ransom'd nature,
The Lamb for sinners slain,
Redeemer, King, Creator,
In bliss returns to reign.[23]

Though the heathen's error and "our" superiority to them appear in this hymn, and the "conquest" of the world by Christianity is implied, both themes occur in a larger theological context. The central theme of Heber's text is the global spread of the gospel and its relationship to the advent of the reign of Christ and God on earth. Historians of missions have long emphasized the centrality in the motivations and consciousness of the early missionary movement of expectations of Christ's thousand-year reign on earth. This hymn and others like it in *Hymns and Sacred Songs* bear that out.[24] In Heber's hymn, Christ's story "spreads from pole to pole" until Christ "in bliss returns to reign."

The images are even more striking in other hymns in the collection. "The star that hail'd Omnipotence," proclaimed William Tappan in his hymn about missions to American Indians, "proclaims the blest millenial morn. . . . The desert blossoms like the rose."[25] "O'er the gloomy hills of darkness, look, my soul, be still and gaze," directed William Williams's hymn of that name, "all the promises do travail with a glorious day of grace. Blessed jubilee, let thy glorious morning dawn!"[26]

Isaac Watts's paraphrase of Psalm 72, published exactly a century

23. Bacon, *Hymns and Sacred Songs*, No. 54. In the seventh line of the third stanza, Heber's original text had "each" instead of "earth's" remotest nation. Foote, *Three Centuries*, 189, mentions the periodicals but repeats the mistake, common in older studies, of crediting Nettleton with the first publication in a hymnal.

24. Clifton Jackson Phillips, *Protestant American and the Pagan World: The First Half Century of the American Board of Commissioners for Foreign Missions, 1810-1860* (Cambridge, MA: East Asian Research Center, Harvard University, 1969), 7-12, 233-234; Charles L. Chaney, *The Birth of Missions in America* (South Pasadena, CA: William Carey Library, 1976), 255-285; William R. Hutchison, *Errand to the World: American Protestant Thought and Foreign Missions* (Chicago: University of Chicago Press, 1987), 51-56, 111-24.

25. "Hark! from yon wilds is heard the strain," *Hymns and Spiritual Songs*, no. 69, p. 70.

26. *Hymns and Spiritual Songs*, no. 28, p. 33.

before Heber wrote his hymn, was the second most widely reprinted missionary hymn in the nineteenth century, and it is ranked twenty-first in the Hymns Project list. This hymn is one of the classic expressions of the millennial fervor that helped fuel the foreign missions movement in its early days, and that pervaded much missionary hymnody throughout the nineteenth century. It appeared, a stanza shorter than the original text and slightly altered, as hymn number 51 in *Hymns and Sacred Songs*.

Jesus shall reign where'er the sun
Does his successive journeys run;
His kingdom stretch from shore to shore,
Till moons shall wax and wane no more.

Behold, the islands with their kings,
And Europe her best tribute brings;
From north to south the princes meet
To pay their homage at his feet.

There Persia, glorious to behold,
There India shines in Eastern gold;
And barbarous nations at his word
Submit, and bow, and own their Lord.

People and realms of every tongue
Dwell on his love with sweetest song;
And infant voices shall proclaim
Their early blessings on his name.

Blessings abound where'er he reigns;
The prisoner leaps to lose his chains,
The weary find eternal rest,
And all the sons of want are blest.

Where he displays his healing power,
Death and the curse are known no more;
In him the tribes of Adam boast
More blessings than their father lost.

Let every creature rise, and bring
Peculiar honors to their King;

Angels descend with songs again,
And earth repeat the loud, Amen![27]

Slightly more than half of the hymns in *Hymns and Sacred Songs* have explicit or implicit millennial terms or images. Just over a third have heathen imagery. Military imagery also appears in little more than a third. By millennial imagery I mean explicit references to the physical reign of God or Christ on earth, or to the second coming of Jesus, as well as the use of biblical images of the kingdom of God on earth or terms associated with that kingdom. The latter include beasts living in peace, deserts blooming, and the advent of the Prince of Peace. Terms referring to it are Jubilee, the latter days, the promised time, the end of time, a new creation, paradise on earth, and the conversion of the Jews.

Other sets of images in the hymns are related to those of God's reign on earth. The most common theme in these hymns, in fact, which appears in a slightly larger number of hymns than do millennial images, is that of the global nature of the spread of the gospel and the coming kingdom. Other sets of images, related to darkness and light, and to nature, including the millennial restoration of nature, appear less often than millennial images but more frequently than heathen images.

It is obvious that in the language of many of the hymns in *Hymns and Sacred Songs,* as in the missionary movement itself, the religious imperative to spread the Christian gospel has merged both with Euro-American assumptions of cultural superiority and with American religious nationalism. But it is the Christian exclusivism and expansionism of the missionary impulse that is most evident. Ironically, the desire to convert the whole world to evangelical Christianity was usually framed in the vocabulary of the Christianized Psalms of Isaac Watts and his imitators. The images in which the ambitions, and the condescension, of American Protestants was expressed were biblical, many of them from Hebrew Scripture: heathens worshiping idols, deserts blooming, kings bowing to the King of Kings, light shining in the darkness. If the missionary message of these

27. *Hymns and Spiritual Songs,* no. 51, p. 53. In addition to numerous changes in punctuation and capitalization from Watts's original, in the third stanza "shines" has replaced "stands," and the original fourth stanza has been omitted: "For him shall endless pray'r be made/And praises throng to crown his head;/His name like sweet perfume shall rise/With every morning sacrifice." The original version is reproduced in *The Book of Hymns,* ed. Ian Bradley (Woodstock, NY: The Overlook Press, 1989), 222-223.

hymns was delivered in images redolent of nineteenth-century Anglo-American arrogance — "shall we, whose souls are lighted with wisdom from on high, shall we to men benighted the lamp of life deny?" — it was nevertheless a religious message, a traditional, evangelical, Christian message. "Salvation! O salvation! The joyful sound proclaim, till earth's remotest nation has learned Messiah's name."

As they thought about what it meant for them to proclaim the joyful sound to earth's remotest nation, to obey in their own era Christ's command to make disciples of all the nations, American evangelicals appropriated existing hymns, and wrote new ones, to express their core beliefs. The modes of expression ranged from Psalm paraphrases ("Jesus shall reign") to "literary hymns" that celebrated the growth of modern missions in biblical-sounding but essentially Romantic lyric poetry ("From Greenland's icy mountains").[28] It was the grand religious vision, expressed in venerable biblical imagery, and not the gritty details of day-to-day cross-cultural evangelism, which missionary hymns attempted to convey. They articulated that vision, moreover, in the cultivated style, formulaic language, and poetic conventions of late-eighteenth- and early-nineteenth-century religious and sentimental verse.[29] Even new hymns about modern missionaries, such as, "Land where the bones of our fathers are sleeping!", one of three Leonard Bacon contributed to *Hymns and Sacred Songs,* were constrained by the standards of biblical language and religious poetry. Witness the fourth stanza's description of what mission entailed: "Dark is our path o'er the dark rolling ocean, — / Dark are our hearts, — but the fire of devotion / Kindles within, — and a far distant nation, / Shall learn from our lips the glad song of salvation."[30]

More study of the theological underpinnings, cultural assumptions, and poetic imagery of Protestant missionary hymns in this early period — in all historical periods — is much needed. The history of the production and reprinting of individual missionary hymns should be

28. On the literary hymn and Heber as a Romantic see William J. Reynolds and Milburn Price, *A Survey of Christian Hymnody,* 4th ed., rev. and enlarged by David W. Music and Milburn Price (Carol Stream, IL: Hope Publishing Company, 1999), 73-74, and Harry Eskew and Hugh T. McElrath, *Sing with Understanding: An Introduction to Christian Hymnody* (Nashville, TN: Church Street Press, 2nd ed., 1995), 146-147.

29. On poetry in the period, see Michael T. Gilmore, "Poetry," *The Cambridge History of American Literature* (New York: Cambridge University Press, 1994), 1:591-597, 607-608.

30. *Hymns and Sacred Songs,* 84.

traced, and the evolving shape and nature of the body of missionary hymnody described. The uses of both missionary hymns and the imagery in them should be analyzed and interpreted, and a number of key questions addressed to both topics. Were there significant differences between denominations in the hymns they used? How did the hymns used, and the hymns themselves, change over time? To what extent were broader theological shifts reflected in the hymn texts, and in the selection of hymns for publication and use? Were changes in the emphasis on various missionary methods reflected in hymns? Did the increasing participation of women in missions, in a wide range of roles, affect missionary hymnody in the late nineteenth and early twentieth centuries? Did hymns play the same roles in the foreign missions of the African-American churches, and other mission efforts not connected with those of the white Protestant mainstream, as they did in the mainstream ones?

The specific mechanisms by which the beliefs proclaimed by leaders of the missionary movement were translated into the lyrics of hymns need to be explored and explained. The role of church musicians and church leaders in the creation of a distinctive American missionary hymnody needs to be examined more closely, as does the actual writing of hymns. Were most writers of missionary hymns professional musicians like Mason and Hastings, professional poets, or quasi-professional (or amateur) writers? Women wrote missionary hymns as well as men — six hymns by the English hymn writer known only as Mrs. Voke and two by American poet Lydia Sigourney are in Mauney's list, and another five by Sigourney appear in *Hymns and Sacred Songs.* There are not immediately obvious differences between their texts and those written by men, but here again careful analysis is needed. Studies of how missionary hymns actually came to be written may help illuminate the process by which missionary convictions, and commitment to missions, were disseminated among nineteenth-century British and American evangelicals.

That missionary hymns were among the means employed to promote and gain support for missions, and to encourage those involved in them, is without doubt. Hymns were sung at ordination, instruction, and farewell ceremonies for missionaries. Some were identified for use at missionary communion services and missionaries' funerals, and may well have been sung at those ceremonies. After he officiated at the wedding of Ann Hasseltine and Adoniram Judson, pastor Jonathan Allen of

Hasseltine's church in Haverhill, Massachusetts, ended a farewell service for the newlyweds with a hymn he had written for the occasion.[31] Missionary hymns were sung at the annual and special anniversary meetings of missionary organizations, as well as when special collections for missions were taken. Into the twentieth century, missionary occasions of any kind provided opportunities for amateur hymn writers of all sorts, from missionaries on furlough to the presidents of women's missionary societies, to follow in Pastor Allen's footsteps and write their own hymns.

The monthly concert of prayer for missions, a practice inherited from eighteenth-century evangelicals, was a staple of missions promotion for most of the nineteenth century, and there were calls for its revival in the 1880s.[32] Bacon's and Nettleton's collections of missionary hymns were intended for use in the monthly concert. Lowell Mason used the monthly events to introduce new tunes and new hymns, and it is evident, as Mauney says, that "hymn singing was a very important element" in the gatherings.[33] Getting a clearer picture of how missionary hymns were actually used in concerts of prayer, and determining what, if any, influence these prayer meetings had on the missionary involvement of evangelical Christians, would contribute greatly to our understanding of hymns about missions.

A better understanding of the actual use of missionary hymns might also help clarify the correlation between the frequent reprinting of a hymn in hymnbooks, and its actual popularity among American Protestants. Without substantial evidence, it would be a mistake to assume that editors' decisions about which hymns to include in their hymnals were directly related to public regard for a hymn, or to the frequency with which that hymn was sung or otherwise used in public or private. The appearance in a large number of hymnbooks of the same small set of missionary hymns could be the result of their inherent quality, their widespread popularity, or the judgment of editors that as the old, familiar standards, they

31. Courtney Anderson, *To the Golden Shore: The Life of Adoniram Judson* (Grand Rapids, MI: Zondervan Publishing House, 1972), 109.

32. *Missionary Review* 10 (July 1887): 443, and 11 (January 1888): 68, quoted in Mauney "Missionary Hymnody," 17. On the monthly concert see R. Pierce Beaver, "The Concert of Prayer for Missions," *The Ecumenical Review* 10, no. 4 (July 1958): 420-427; Mauney, "Missionary Hymnody," 13-19.

33. Mauney, "Missionary Hymnody," 17.

simply had to be included in the missions section of every hymnal. Frequent reprinting gets a hymn into Mauney's and the Hymns Project lists, but we need to have a better sense of what else it does and does not tell us. We simply need to know more about when, why, how, and by whom missionary hymns were used.

Hymns in the Missions

At the opposite end of the spectrum from the hymns about missions sung at home were the songs such as those employed by J. Walter Waugh's "singing missionaries" in the 1890s. The presence and use of hymns in the missions, both as part of the evangelism carried out by missionaries and as an element in the religious life of the new Christian communities produced by that evangelism, are as well if not better documented than the use back home of hymns about missions. Hymns in the missions appear in historical documents — from the personal accounts of individuals to the records of mission stations to standard reference works — and in modern studies of regional music.

For example, articles in late-nineteenth-century reference works on hymns and on missions make it clear that the evangelistic use of hymns and music increased steadily in the missions of a number of Protestant denominations as the century progressed. *The Encyclopaedia of Missions* edited by Edwin Munsell Bliss and published in 1891 introduced a substantial article on "music and missions" with this observation: "Missions touch music at two points: 1. The missionary as an intelligent man studies the poetry and songs of the people among whom he labors. Those investigations are carried on during the earlier period of a mission, and contrary to what some might expect, among savage races, as well as in more civilized communities. 2. After a mission has become successful the newly formed churches must be helped in their worship, especially in the department of Praise, and this we shall see sometimes demands a very deep and thorough knowledge of the foundation principles of music."[34]

Although I am suggesting that missions touched music in more ways than just the two this article mentioned, the *Encyclopaedia* recog-

34. Bliss, *Encyclopaedia of Missions*, 2:251-52.

nized, and its music entry demonstrates, that music was one of the elements of human culture that missionaries encountered "in the field," and attempted to use as they sought effective ways to spread the gospel.

John Julian's landmark *Dictionary of Hymnology* (1892) also recorded the development of hymnody in the missions. In the revised edition of 1907 the entry on "Missions, Foreign" and various related items in the appendices filled over twenty pages. British hymnal editor W. R. Stevenson began the main entry by lamenting the situation which the article was intended to correct.

> The hymnody of Foreign Missions is, as a whole, practically unknown. Most persons have some idea of the great work accomplished by Christian missionaries in the translation of the Holy Scriptures into almost all known languages; but few have ever thought how much has been done by them in the translation and composition of hymns, the preparation of hymn-books, and in general, in the introduction of Christian Hymnody among the various nations to whom they have preached the Gospel.[35]

Stevenson's article is an impressive compendium of information about the hymn writing, translating, and publishing carried on in European and American missions during the previous hundred years. It documents the efforts of missionaries of all denominations to translate into local languages the hymns they knew, to write new hymns in those languages, and to compile and print hymnbooks for use in the missions and mission churches. Indigenous hymn writers in a number of mission fields are named, and issues related to the cross-cultural encounter of musical styles are raised. Remarkably, Stevenson's early-twentieth-century article serves perfectly well as a blueprint for early-twenty-first-century research on aspects of hymns in the missions and indigenous Christian hymnodies that have yet to be carefully examined. New local hymnodies were the ultimate product of the relationship between hymns and American foreign missions, and studies of them will not only delight hymnologists and ethnomusicologists, but also enrich our historical understanding of missionary methods and of the transformations of theology in the crucible of cross-cultural evangelism. They will provide comparative in-

35. John Julian, ed., *A Dictionary of Hymnology*, 2nd ed. (London: John Murray, 1907), 738.

sights into the faith and music — into all the elements of American culture — that were exported through foreign missions.

Missionaries' Hymns

Much less visible than either missionary hymns at home or new hymns for evangelism in the missions, and harder to identify than the subject groupings of hymns in hymnals or the studies of ethnomusicologists, are the hymns that were personally meaningful to people involved in the missionary movement. These hymns may or may not have had any overtly "missionary" content, but they were, for each individual, related in some important way to the faith that moved her or him to act on behalf of global evangelism. There are a wide variety of anecdotes about such hymns in missionary histories, diaries, autobiographies, and biographies. At present, however, it is not clear whether there were any significant patterns in this missionary use of hymns.

One possible pattern that should be investigated further is the apparent spread, as the nineteenth century progressed, of the practice of quoting verses from hymns to make or illustrate a point in a public address or in print. In missionary circles, at least, this seems to have been far more common after 1860 than before. If there was such a trend, it would be interesting to see if we can determine its causes — changes in the nature of the hymns, changing attitudes toward hymns, or just the fact that there were more of them to choose from?

Whatever we discover about hymn citations in publications and speeches, from the start of the movement, as we have already seen with Harriet and Samuel Newell, people involved in missions quoted hymns in diaries and letters. Pioneer Baptist missionaries Ann Hasseltine Judson and Adoniram Judson did so when she told him in an 1823 letter that the words of "Blest be the tie that binds" were "exactly suited" to their case, and when he quoted an unidentified hymn or religious poem in reporting her and their infant daughter's deaths in Burma in 1826 and 1827. Adoniram Judson wrote hymns, not only the first one ever written in Burmese but also three in English with no relation to missions. Two of these were about baptism and one was a paraphrase of the Lord's Prayer. Judson's two later wives wrote religious poetry, some of which was turned into hymn texts by themselves or others. Sarah Boardman Judson wrote fifteen hymns in Burmese, and Emily Chubbuck Judson one. Emily, famous as sentimental fiction writer "Fanny Forster" before her marriage to Judson, also had at least one early poem published, in English in the United States, as a hymn.[36]

One angle to take in studying missionaries' hymns is to ask whether certain hymns tended to be especially meaningful to people drawn to the missionary movement. In 1811 Harriet Atwood asked for God's help with a critical decision in the words of "Guide me, O thou great Jehovah." Sixty-nine years later the hymn was sung at the funeral of Rufus Anderson, long-time administrator of the American Board and a major theologian of foreign missions, because it was one of his favorite hymns.[37] In the 1850s, American Board missionary Maria A. West discovered, as she traveled between Armenian mission stations in Turkey, that "Keble's evening song, — 'Sun of my soul, thou Saviour dear, It is not night, if Thou art near,' — served to solace and beguile the tedium of the lonely way; and never did those sweet words seem sweeter or more appropriate!"[38] That hymn is ranked fiftieth in the Hymns Project list, a position it shares with Rufus Anderson's other favorite hymn sung at his funeral, "Asleep in Jesus, blessed sleep."[39] West comforted a newly widowed Armenian convert to Protestantism by singing with her "How firm a foundation." That hymn was also sung, "as if by a common impulse," at the Baptist Missionary Union's jubilee meeting in 1864, and by missionaries under attack in Tientsin, China, during the Boxer Rebellion of 1900. "The second stanza of this hymn," wrote George H. Trull in 1912, in describing the Chinese incident, "certainly was especially appropriate under such circumstances, and brought great comfort to the missionaries in their distress. Fear not, I am with thee, O be not dismayed; / For I am thy God, and will still give thee

36. Joan Jacobs Brumberg, *Mission for Life: The Story of the Family of Adoniram Judson* (New York: The Free Press, 1980), 60; Francis Wayland, *A Memoir of the Life and Labors of the Rev. Adoniram Judson, D.D.* (Boston: Phillips, Sampson, and Company, 1853), 1:420, 430; Julian, *Dictionary of Hymnology*, 609; Burrage, *Baptist Hymn Writers*, 271-272, 302-306, 396-399, 593-598.

37. A. C. Thompson, *Discourse Commemorative of Rev. Rufus Anderson, D.D., LL.D., Late Corresponding Secretary of the American Board of Commissioners for Foreign Missions. Together with addresses at the funeral* (Boston: ABCFM, 1880), 45.

38. Maria A. West, *The Romance of Missions: or, Inside Views of Life and Labor, in the Land of Ararat* (New York: Anson D. F. Randolph and Company, 1875), 34-5.

39. Thompson, *Discourse*, 45.

aid; / I'll strengthen thee, help thee, and cause thee to stand, / Upheld by my righteous, omnipotent hand."[40] One can easily imagine many other missionaries and missionaries' converts finding solace in those words in a variety of trying situations.

Further investigation of missionaries' hymns should yield greater insight into the role of hymns in the religious lives of people engaged in mission. Was that role substantially different for mission activists than it was for other Protestants? Were particular hymns or kinds of hymns especially appealing to missionaries? Were mission activists, for example, more drawn to hymns of strength and action than those of quiet contemplation? Or did contemplative hymns appeal because they provided a needed counterpoint to the strenuous activism of mission life?

Foreign Missions and American Protestants' Favorite Hymns

It probably is not coincidental that all of the hymns just mentioned as being important to people involved in missions are in the Hymns Project list of hymns most reprinted in Protestant hymnals in the United States. "How firm a foundation" is ranked fourth, "Guide me, O thou great Jehovah" seventh, and "Sun of my soul" and "Asleep in Jesus" both fiftieth. It would be more surprising if the hymns that apparently had wide and enduring appeal for large numbers of American Protestants were not among those that proved most meaningful to missionaries. Along that line, since hymns important to missionaries often became important to those they converted, it would be interesting to confirm common "hymn story" claims about the diffusion of popular hymns. It has been asserted, for example, that "Jesus loves me" "is often one of the first hymns taught to new converts" in missions around the world.[41] No doubt many of the hymns in the Project list have become familiar, in English or in translation, to Chris-

40. West, *Romance of Missions*, 88; ABMU, *The Missionary Jubilee* (New York: Sheldon, 1865), 34; George H. Trull, *Five Missionary Minutes: Brief Missionary Material for Platform Use in the Sunday School for 52 Sundays in the Year* (New York: Missionary Education Movement of the United States and Canada, 1912), 109.

41. Kenneth W. Osbeck, *101 Hymn Stories* (Grand Rapids, MI: Kregel Publications, 1982), 136.

tians in former mission churches. This might be the most extensive influence, at least geographically, of the hymns included in the list.

"We are carrying on the work of God by singing the gospel into human hearts," Rev. Waugh said of his singing missionaries. Missionaries in the first two-thirds of the nineteenth century sang as well as preached the gospel, and they taught the new Christians around them to sing, and write songs, about their faith. Back home, supporters of missions wrote, published, and sang hymns about missions. At the same time, evangelical Christians involved in foreign missions, at home and abroad, were inspired in their work by the hymns that all Protestants found meaningful. An understanding of the significant and shifting relationships of hymns and foreign missions tells us something about hymns and something about missions. It also provides new insights into the dynamics that shaped the beliefs and behavior of American Protestants, because in looking at the relationships of hymns and foreign missions we are looking at the intersection of the personal, the communal, and the societal, and the intersection of religious belief, religious action, music, and national and international cultures.

CHAPTER FIVE

Marketing the Gospel: Music in English-Canadian Protestant Revivalism, 1884-1957

Kevin Kee

A reporter for the Montreal *Standard* described the scene: it was seven o'clock on a Saturday evening in the spring of 1946, and Toronto's Massey Hall was packed. Inside, the show moved briskly from one upbeat musical act to the next. "Outside on the street," the reporter noted, "hundreds of frantic bobby-soxers pushed and scrambled and pounded on the big wooden doors." The burly policeman standing nearby shook his head: "No more room inside. Now run along home. . . . I tell you there's not an empty seat left in the place." The bobby-soxers let him finish, then continued their pounding. "We want in!" they chanted. "We want in!" "What goes on?" the reporter quizzed a blonde youngster nearby. "Frank Sinatra? Oscar Peterson?" "Don't be silly," she replied. "It's Youth for Christ."[1]

While Youth for Christ appeared to some to be a jazz spectacle, the primary purpose of the meetings was evangelistic. Toronto pastor and evangelist Charles Templeton organized and led the rallies to spread a traditional message of conversion to Jesus Christ. Through sermon and gospel songs, Templeton urged young men and women to confess their sins, accept Christ as their Savior, and, with the Holy Spirit's help, live a life pleasing to God.

The use of gospel music to attract audiences to an evangelistic service and to communicate the message of conversion has a rich heritage in English-Canadian evangelism. Late-nineteenth-century Methodist evange-

1. *The Standard Magazine,* 6 April 1946.

lists Hugh Crossley and John Hunter, the most successful Canadian revivalists of their day, drew crowds to their sermons on conversion to Christ with meetings that were patterned after the musical melodramas popular in contemporary theaters. Crossley retired in the 1920s, and moved from the pulpit to the pew, occasionally attending the revival meetings of evangelist Oswald J. Smith. In an era of multiplying entertainment options, Smith drew crowds to his gospel message by featuring free concerts. Charles Templeton, who had attended Smith's church as a teenager, carried on the tradition in the 1940s, drawing on jazz and swing music to interest young people in his gospel message. During the next decade Templeton altered his strategy and adopted a more refined approach, featuring classical music in an attempt to draw Canadian adults to his meetings.

The primary goal of each of these evangelists was to encourage in his audience members a conversion to Christ. By conversion, these evangelists meant bringing men and women face-to-face with the eternal questions of life and death, forcing them to contemplate their obligations to family, church, community, and country. But how could English-speaking Canadians be persuaded to attend revival meetings and hear this message? In an attempt to reach the largest possible audience in the most efficient manner, the evangelists adopted a modern approach to marketing their message. They made religion personally relevant to their audiences, not unlike concerts or other forms of entertainment. Music, both performed on the platform and sung by the audience, was given a central place in their meetings. Each adopted a style that appealed to his specific audience.

The evangelists' use of contemporary musical forms to spread their "old-fashioned" conversion message follows a pattern described by American historian Laurence Moore, who has traced the manner in which religion in the United States has expressed itself in innovative ways and adapted to the needs of the day. In *Selling God: American Religion in the Marketplace of Culture,* Moore contends that in the nineteenth and twentieth centuries, religion had to enter actively into the marketplace of culture in order to hold its place in the lives of Americans. For Moore, the choice was clear, because "either religion keeps up with cultural life or it has no importance."[2] Moore calls this "commodification": the process by which religion changes, and establishes itself in new forms congruent with com-

2. R. Laurence Moore, *Selling God: American Religion in the Marketplace of Culture* (New York: Oxford University Press, 1994), 65.

mercial culture. In an attempt to appeal to all consumers, religion took on the shape of a commodity, using techniques of advertising and publicity employed by merchants. In this way, Moore argues, religion remained vital, and was able to continue to address the needs of people in changing socioeconomic circumstances. Other historians of religion in the United States, such as William McLoughlin, have argued that revivalists have led the way in rearticulating essential Christianity.

The way in which revivalists have used contemporary methods to market their traditional religious messages has received little attention from scholars of Canadian Protestantism.[3] Does the "commodification" of religion hold true for Canada? This chapter attempts to answer that question by focusing on the gospel music used by Crossley and Hunter in the late nineteenth century, Smith in the 1920s and 1930s, and Templeton in the mid-twentieth century. Gospel songs contributed an important ele-

3. To some historians of Protestantism in Canada, the rearticulation of Christianity gives clear evidence of secularization and the decline of religious influence. These historians have argued that revivalists' accommodation to popular culture (such as meetings which resembled jazz concerts) lessened the otherworldly aspect of Christianity and secularized the faith. See Phyllis D. Airhart, *Serving the Present Age: Revivalism, Progressivism, and the Methodist Tradition in Canada* (Kingston: McGill-Queen's University Press, 1992); David Marshall, *Secularizing the Faith: Canadian Protestant Clergy and the Crisis of Belief, 1850-1940* (Toronto: University of Toronto, 1992). Other scholars have offered a different perspective on religious change, and have argued that the use of ostensibly "worldly" techniques by religious leaders does not necessarily mean that their "religious" goals suffer. Sociologist Nancy Ammerman contends that apparently either/or concepts such as "worldly" and "religious" which scholars of religion sometimes use are fundamentally flawed because people live in a "both/and world" (Nancy Ammerman, "Organized Religion in a Voluntaristic Society," 1996 Presidential Address, *Sociology of Religion* 58 [1997]: 213). In the same vein, historian Colleen McDannell challenges what she calls the "binary division" of the sacred and the secular. McDannell observes that "the scrambling of the sacred and the profane is common in American Christianity. Mingling has occurred throughout its history" (Colleen McDannell, *Material Christianity: Religion and Popular Culture in America* [New Haven: Yale University Press, 1995], 8). Others have similarly examined the manner in which this blending has occurred in people's everyday lives. Focusing on late-nineteenth-century small-town Ontario, Lynne Marks points out that personal identity was formed by a number of competing categories, including class, gender, age, marital status, and religious faith. Insisting that these various categories were lived simultaneously, Marks has traced the manner by which Christian belief and action took place within the context of other aspects of experience like class and gender. Religious piety did not exist in isolation; it shaped, and was shaped by, material objects and categories of experience (Lynne Marks, *Revivals and Roller Rinks: Religion, Leisure, and Identity in Late-Nineteenth-Century Small-Town Ontario* [Toronto: University of Toronto Press, 1996], 16).

ment of their meetings, and served two purposes. First, the lyrics preached the revivalists' traditional evangelistic message of repentance, conversion, and godly living. Second, Crossley and Hunter, Smith, and Templeton used gospel music to draw audiences who might have been uninterested in an evangelistic service, but who could be drawn to a free concert. In this way the evangelists commodified religion — they drew on the strategies of the marketplace to present their conversion message in a manner that catered to the expectations of Canadians. As a result, revival meetings took on the form of musical events such as jazz concerts, and the audience response was enthusiastic.

Gospel songs, many of which originated in the United States, have occupied a central place in English-Canadian revivalism since the late eighteenth century. After a powerful conversion in 1775, Henry Alline began preaching and singing a pietistic gospel message that sparked Nova Scotia's "First Great Awakening."[4] Rejecting the conventions of formal church music, Alline wrote gospel songs that coupled religious lyrics with popular folk tunes. According to one scholar, these songs proved to be the most lasting of Alline's legacies and helped spark New England's Second Great Awakening.[5] Leading Methodist evangelists of the Second Great Awakening in the United States, such as Nathan Bangs and William Case, brought the revival spirit to Upper Canadians at the start of the nineteenth century. Central to their services were refrains set to popular melodies that expressed clearly the plan of salvation.[6]

By the mid-nineteenth century, gospel songs featuring simple tunes and a verse-chorus-verse format were an established musical form in both Canada and the United States. American song writers such as Philip Bliss, Fanny van Alstyne (Fanny Crosby), and Ira D. Sankey wrote the lyrics and composed the music for thousands of new pieces, and collections like Sankey's *Gospel Hymns and Sacred Songs* became runaway best-sellers.[7] Mu-

4. George A. Rawlyk, *Ravished by the Spirit: Religious Revivals, Baptists, and Henry Alline* (Kingston: McGill-Queen's University Press, 1984).

5. Ibid., 58.

6. Nancy Christie, "'In These Times of Democratic Rage and Delusion': Popular Religion and the Challenge to the Established Order, 1760-1815," in George A. Rawlyk, ed., *The Canadian Protestant Experience, 1760-1990* (Burlington, ON: Welch Publishing Company, 1990), 32.

7. Barry J. Vaughn, "Gospel Songs and Evangelical Hymnody," *American Organist* 30 (May 1996): 64-65; Sandra S. Sizer, *Gospel Hymns and Social Religion: The Rhetoric of Nineteenth-Century Revivalism* (Philadelphia: Temple University Press, 1978), 20-49. Susan S. Tamke, *Make*

sic leader and soloist for D. L. Moody, the leading revivalist of the late nineteenth century, Sankey made gospel songs a central feature of their evangelistic meetings. Conversions at their services were often attributed to Sankey's "singing of the gospel." At the same time, Sankey's music injected an element of entertainment into the evangelistic meetings. While the subject was serious, the experience was fun. Thanks to Sankey and others, gospel songs became, according to musicologist Erik Routley, the "pop music" of the late 1800s.[8] Hugh Crossley and John Hunter, the foremost Canadian evangelists of this period, were the beneficiaries of this rich inheritance of Canadian and American gospel song.

Crossley and Hunter

Crossley, born in 1850, and Hunter in 1856, had both been raised in nominally Christian homes in the backwoods of central Canada and were converts of camp meetings in their youth. While studying together at Victoria College in Cobourg, Ontario, they conducted revivals for the benefit of students and townsfolk alike. Ordained as Methodist ministers, they responded to calls from widely separated congregations. Then, in 1884, Crossley and Hunter reestablished contact, and reunited in a joint evangelistic mission. Their early successes were impressive, and by the late 1880s requests for their services were booked three years in advance.

The popularity of their meetings may be partially attributed to the evangelists' charisma. Hunter gave the prayers and led the exhortation, while Crossley was responsible for the music and the preaching. Known as the "Singing Evangelist," he frequently delivered his thoughts in the form of a "Song Sermon," underlining the important themes of his message with relevant gospel songs intoned in his mellow baritone voice. The music in Crossley-Hunter services was not a complement to the sermon — frequently it was the sermon itself.

---

a Joyful Noise Unto the Lord: Hymns as a Reflection of Victorian Social Attitudes (Athens, OH: Ohio University Press, 1978), 35. The response to Sankey's songs was so positive that the singing evangelist published a companion volume providing personal stories and background information concerning the songs (Ira D. Sankey, *Sankey's Story of the Gospel Hymns and of Sacred Songs and Solos* [Philadelphia: The Sunday School Times Company, 1906]).

8. Erik Routley, *Twentieth-Century Church Music* (Toronto: Oxford University Press, 1966), 199.

Crossley and Hunter's message, whether spoken or sung, centered on the necessity of conversion. Crossley's songbook, *Songs of Salvation*, reflected this emphasis; "Invitation and Assurance" was the largest section of the collection. Drawing on passages from the Bible, the evangelists attempted to convince their listeners of the need to repent for sin, the possibility of redemption in Christ, and the opportunity for regeneration with the help of the Holy Spirit. Each of their services concluded with an earnest appeal to "accept Christ at once."

Crossley occasionally posed the question directly, singing or leading the choir or congregation in songs like Fanny Crosby's "Will you be saved tonight?": "Jesus is pleading with thy poor soul, Will you be saved tonight? . . . Will you go on the same old way, Or will you be saved tonight?"[9] More often, the evangelist's gospel songs bore witness to the singer's own experience of salvation. "Nineteenth-century commentators," notes hymnody scholar Mary De Jong, "considered hymn-singing a form of testimony and a formative exercise in role playing."[10] "This is what Christ has done for me," the singer seemed to explain, "and he can do it for you too."

Listeners could look forward to eternal life in heaven, if they were among the converted.[11] The section of Crossley's *Songs of Salvation* titled "Heaven" was substantial, and contained numerous crowd favorites such as "Sweet rest at home."[12] Sung to the tune of "Swanee River," the hymn dwelt on the "Dear loved ones who have gone before us, / Waiting for us there; / To loving arms will God restore us, / And in their bliss we'll share. / Then full of faith we'll lay our sorrow / At Jesus' feet;/And in the bright and heavenly morrow / Loved ones — the saved ones meet."[13]

9. Hugh T. Crossley, ed., *Songs of Salvation* (Toronto: William Briggs, 1887), 38. Spelling, punctuation, and capitalization have been left intact in quotations from primary sources.

10. Mary G. DeJong, "'I Want to be Like Jesus': The Self-Defining Power of Evangelical Hymnody," *Journal of the American Academy of Religion* 54 (1986): 463.

11. In this way, Crossley and Hunter followed the lead of D. L. Moody. According to one assessment, Moody marked a shift in revivalists' emphasis from hell to heaven as a way of drawing penitents to conversion. Instead of threatening penitents with images of eternal fire, Moody encouraged sinners to conversion with images drawn from the Bible and middle-class family life. Jonathan Butler, *Softly and Tenderly Jesus Is Calling: Heaven and Hell in American Revivalism, 1870-1920* (Brooklyn, NY: Carlson Publishing, 1991).

12. United Church of Canada [UCC], Victoria University Archives [VUA], John Edwin Hunter Fonds [JEHF], Box 1, Scrapbook, 71, 84.

13. Crossley, *Songs of Salvation*, 141.

Mothers seemed to hold pride of place among the loved ones English-Canadians longed to meet.[14] Crossley and Hunter recognized that the memories of caring mothers might spark the conversion of men and women, and made frequent reference to mothers in heaven. In this way the evangelists tapped into the rising interest in spiritualism, and the widely held notion that those who had passed on could communicate with those on earth. One of the most popular of Crossley's own compositions, "My Mother's Prayer," recounted the evangelist's visit to his childhood home and the discovery of his "trundle bed" which brought back memories of his godly mother. "Yet I am but only dreaming," the evangelist concluded, "Ne'er I'll be a child again; / Many years has that dear mother / In the quiet graveyard lain; / But her blessed, blessed spirit / Daily hovers o'er my head, / Calling me from earth to heaven, / Even from my trundle bed."[15]

Some members of Crossley and Hunter's audiences appear to have been brought closer to conversion by this piece. For example, a convict who in 1889 had attended a Crossley-Hunter revival service in a Kingston, Ontario penitentiary penned a letter to the evangelists, which apparently stated that "My Mother's Prayer" had "brought the writer's dear mother's face before him. Tears came to his eyes as he seemed to hear his mother say 'I am waiting for you my son. I have faith in you, and I love you still my dear boy.'" The letter had been signed "Hope."[16]

Crossley and Hunter also recognized that the loss of a child could bring men and women closer to conversion. In Victorian Canada, the death of a child posed the most difficult of religious problems, as it still does today. But in the late 1800s, the tragedy was faced much more frequently. "During the nineteenth century," a historian notes, "the deaths of children under five comprised as much as 40 percent of the total death rate. For nineteenth-century women, child death was a normal part of the emotional landscape."[17]

Crossley and Hunter saw in this situation a unique religious space for the entry of their message of conversion.[18] Crossley frequently sang

14. See DeJong, "I Want to be Like Jesus," 463.

15. Crossley, *Songs of Salvation,* 147.

16. Kingston *Daily British Whig,* 30 October 1889.

17. Ann-Janine Morey, "In Memory of Cassie: Child Death and Religious Vision in American Women's Novels," *Religion and American Culture* 6 (Winter 1991): 89.

18. UCC, VUA, JEHF, Box 1, Scrapbook, 44. Moody also used stories of children dying to stir the hearts of his English-Canadian listeners. Eric Crouse, "American Revivalists, the

as a solo a father's lament for his deceased child, "Papa, Come this Way:"

A little childish voice is still'd,
Two little lily-white hands are crossed;
Two little eyes forever closed,
The sound of patt'ring feet is lost,
A little form from out our home,
Was borne by loving hands away;
But still I seem to hear a voice,
Within my heart, it says each day,
"Papa, Come this Way."

In the concluding stanza, the father accedes to his child's wishes:

Where'er I go, that voice I hear,
As tho' my darling could not rest,
Until I give my heart to him,
Who died to save and make me blest.
And so it echoes in my heart,
And thro' the chambers of my soul,
I'll not resist that pleading voice,
I'll go to Jesus and be whole.[19]

In the hope that his listeners would respond, Crossley often invoked the death of parents, children, and the listener at the same service. An evangelistic meeting in Kingston in 1889 was typical; a journalist noted that "Rev. Mr. Crossley spoke first to fathers and sang, 'Papa, Come this Way.' Then to those skeptical he sang 'Eternity Where!' and again to sons, referring particularly to the memory of mothers, he sang 'My Mother's Prayer,' and concluded with Christ's invitation to all to come unto Him." The strategy seemed to be successful; according to the newspaper report a "large number" remained after the service to discuss conversion.[20]

That was the point. Gospel songs like "Papa, Come this Way," and "My Mother's Prayer" were written to bring about the conversion of men

---

Press, and Popular Religion in Canada, 1884-1914" (Ph.D. diss., Queen's University, 1996), 60, 61.

19. Crossley, *Songs of Salvation*, 52-53.

20. UCC, VUA, JEHF, Box 1, Scrapbook, 90-92.

and women in the audience. At the same time, however, the performance of these sentimental songs offered late-nineteenth-century English-speaking Canadians a kind of musical theater. Historians have noted that "popular secular songs of the theater" served as one of "the principal models of the music of gospel songs."[21] Crossley went further and made the performance of the song a theatrical experience. In an attempt to draw men and women to their message of conversion, Crossley and Hunter incorporated many of the techniques of the theater into their services. The revivals of Crossley and Hunter were "manufactured" entertainment events, carefully planned in advance, publicized by the press, tailored to the audience, and then repeated at the next town or city six weeks later.

In late-nineteenth-century Ontario, the marketplace of entertainment was becoming increasingly competitive. Increasing urbanization and industrialization provided workers and white-collar employees with disposable income, and leisure time to spend it.[22] In response, entrepreneurs in entertainment opened amusement parks, dance halls, taverns, theaters, and opera houses to the delight of many Canadians. One of the most popular diversions of the time, the theatrical arts, experienced significant expansion in the closing decades of the nineteenth century.[23] According to Robertson Davies, a theater critic and one of Canada's best-known novelists, the theater was "the scene of every kind of entertainment that was not positively circus."[24] Music was frequently offered, in various forms including musical shows and popular opera — "opera for the public taste for melodrama and a sweet tooth for music."[25]

Like other leading Methodists of the day, Crossley and Hunter stood squarely against this form of entertainment. But the evangelists recognized that they needed to do more than simply condemn the theater; they needed to provide a substitute. At the same time they spoke out against the stage, they borrowed from the theater to make their revivals more

21. Quoted in Vaughn, "Gospel Songs and Evangelical Hymnody," 65.

22. Joy Santink, *Timothy Eaton and the Rise of His Department Store* (Toronto: University of Toronto Press, 1990), 249.

23. L. W. Conolly, "The Methodist Church and the Theater in Canada, 1884-1925," in *Drama and Religion,* ed. James Redmond (New York: Cambridge University Press, 1983).

24. Robertson Davies, "The Nineteenth-Century Repertoire" in *Early Stages: Theater in Ontario, 1800-1914,* ed. Ann Saddlemyer (Toronto: University of Toronto Press, 1990), 117.

25. Davies, "The Nineteenth-Century Repertoire," 111, 116-117; Mary M. Brown, "Entertainers of the Road," in Ann Saddlemyer, *Early Stages,* 155.

attractive to Canadians. Crossley's slate of songs for an evening, while consistently conversionist in message, covered the gamut of emotions. If the mood was light, he would include an upbeat tune, or perhaps sing "My Ain Countrie" in Scottish dialect. Somber occasions brought out Negro spirituals and "Papa, Come this Way." It was a highly entertaining spectacle.

Observers were occasionally struck by the similarities between the evangelistic meetings in the Methodist Church and the shows in the local opera house.[26] Fans waited expectantly for the stars' appearance. From opening to closing night, followers arrived hours early, jostled their way to the best available seats, and attempted to attract the attention of one of the ushers selling souvenir songbooks. The hustle and bustle and easy chatter persisted until the choir broke into song and the leading players stepped onto the platform. After a short introduction and more music, the show got into full swing as Hunter launched into his humorous monologue. Soon, however, tears of laughter were replaced by tears of sadness as Hunter invoked the memories of dead loved ones. Crossley followed, interspersing his words with mournful songs. In an era remarkable for its sentimentality, his presentation brought men and women alike to tears. He then ended the evening, too soon for most in the audience. Members of the crowd exited the building, humming one of the melodies they had just heard. At their workplace the next day, they might share the events of the previous evening with their fellow employees, and encourage them to go and view the show for themselves.[27]

Each evening for a six-week run, Crossley and Hunter would do their best to stage the biggest show in town. It was a carefully constructed event, patterned by the evangelists after the most popular entertainment of the late nineteenth century. At the same time, however, the evangelists' meetings remained true to their ultimate purpose. By drawing on forms of commercial culture — specifically the secrets and strategies of the opera house — Crossley and Hunter drew audiences of men and women to their traditional gospel message. Some experienced conversion, and left the revival ready to live a Christian life.

26. Hamilton *Spectator,* 19 December 1889.

27. According to Hunter's son, Ernest Crossley Hunter, "People who liked music went to church. People who liked dramatic entertainment went to church. A good sermon was regarded as a good night out." UCC, VUA, JEHF, Box 1, Crossley Hunter "Old-Time Evangelism," 26.

As the nineteenth century gave way to the twentieth, Crossley and Hunter soldiered on, leading revivals and urging their audiences to convert to Christ. Finally, in 1910, after twenty-six years, Canada's most celebrated revival team disbanded. The Methodist church, Crossley and Hunter's employer, no longer considered evangelistic services as central to its mission. Other churches and evangelists took their place, with new ways to commodify the faith. In 1908, a young man named Oswald J. Smith attended a Crossley-Hunter service in Huntsville, Ontario, and left inspired. Two decades later Crossley sat in the audience while Smith stood on the platform, preaching through sermon and song the message of conversion.[28]

Oswald J. Smith

Born in 1889, Oswald J. Smith was "born again" at age sixteen in a revival meeting in Toronto led by the American evangelist Reuben Torrey.[29] Filled with religious enthusiasm and struck by the spectacle of the evangelistic campaign, Smith dreamed of becoming a celebrity preacher. He attended the Toronto Bible Training School, the Manitoba Presbyterian College in Winnipeg, and finally the McCormack Seminary in Chicago, and was ordained a minister of the Presbyterian Church of Canada in 1918. The day-to-day work of a minister did not interest Smith; he longed instead to lead revivals saturated with gospel music. But in churches like Toronto's Dale Presbyterian, where Smith ministered from 1915 to 1917, his message and methods received a cold reception. When Smith transformed the evening service into an evangelistic meeting, complete with gospel songs in place of the church hymnal, the choir refused to sing. Smith vowed to replace the "worldly faction" which preferred the old hymns with "a sacred choir with a consecrated leader" who would perform upbeat gospel songs. The disagreement between the two parties was not resolved, and after several more conflicts Smith resigned.[30]

28. Oswald J. Smith, *Can Organized Religion Survive?* (Toronto: Toronto Tabernacle Publishers, 1932), 22.

29. Billy Graham Center Archives [BGCA], Oswald J. Smith Papers [OJSP], Collection 322, Box 1, Folder 10.

30. For one sympathetic biographer's account of these events, see Lois Neely, *Fire In His Bones: The Official Biography of Oswald J. Smith* (Wheaton, IL: Tyndale House, 1982), Chapter 13.

Seeing no future for himself in the mainline denominations, he began working with the Christian and Missionary Alliance, but eventually left it as well. In 1928 he finally settled in an evangelistic center of his own creation, the "People's Church." By the 1930s, he had established himself as one of Canada's foremost evangelists. Over the course of his eighty-year career (he lived to be 96) he preached more than 12,000 sermons in 80 countries, and wrote 35 books, the most popular of which were translated into 128 languages.

Smith focused all of his considerable energies on reaching men and women with his message of conversion. To this end he preached a traditional evangelistic message of repentance, spiritual rebirth, and holy living — a gospel message that shared significant points of contact with the message of Crossley and Hunter. Although they would have disagreed on several matters of theology — Crossley and Hunter held to the tenets of the nineteenth-century mainline Protestant establishment, while Smith was a fundamentalist — they shared the same commitment to conversion. Christians should "keep clearly in view our one great objective," Smith told his readers in 1927, "namely, the evangelization of the world, and see to it that everything contributes to that end."[31]

Gospel music, according to Smith, was a central means of bringing about worldwide revival. An avid writer of poetry as well as prose, Smith published 1200 poems, 100 of which were set to music.[32] One admirer referred to Smith as "The World's Greatest Living Hymn Writer";[33] he was without doubt among Canada's premier gospel song lyricists in the first half of the twentieth century. Smith's best-known gospel song, "Then Jesus Came," was typical in its evangelistic emphasis. As in a later recording by George Beverly Shea, the primary soloist for campaigns led by Billy Graham, the song portrayed the healing of a beggar, a demon-possessed man, a leper, and finally the resurrection of Lazarus. In each case, the presence of Christ transformed sorrow and suffering into joy and comfort. The song closed with an evangelistic invitation:

31. Oswald J. Smith, *The Great Physician* (Toronto: The Christian Alliance Publishing Company, 1927), 111.

32. Ontario Bible College Archives [OBCA], Oswald J. Smith Papers [OJSP], Lois Neely, "The Last Interview."

33. OBCA, OJSP, Robert D. Kalis, "The World's Greatest Living Hymn Writer: An Interview with Dr. Oswald J. Smith," 5.

So men today have found the Savior able,
They could not conquer passion, lust and sin;
Their broken hearts had left them sad and lonely,
Then Jesus came and dwelt Himself within.
When Jesus comes, the tears are wiped away,
He takes the gloom and fills the life with glory,
For all is changed when Jesus comes to stay.[34]

"Then Jesus Came" was typical of Smith's songs in its emphasis on conversion. At the same time it was unusual in its use of a third-person narrator; the vast majority of Smith's songs spoke in the first person. For instance, his earliest songwriting success, "Saved!" declared: "Saved! Saved! Saved! — My sins are all forgiv'n; / Christ is mine! I'm on my way to heav'n; / Once a guilty sinner, lost, undone, / Now a child of God, saved thro' his Son."[35] In this gospel song, as in many others, Smith gave testimony to his intense personal relationship with God. "I just wanted to express my own personal experience of my salvation," Smith had remarked.[36] The observation could have been made concerning almost all of his compositions.

Smith's use of gospel songs as a form of testimony echoed the conventions of nineteenth-century evangelical music. Smith looked back with longing to the revivals of Crossley and Hunter, and "the great scenes that were enacted more than a generation ago, when evangelism was at its height."[37] Through his music, Smith tried to recover something of the spirit of that time. Historian Susan Tamke notes that the lyrics of English evangelical gospel songs in the 1800s reflected a yearning for heaven and "an almost gnostic rejection of the world."[38] Similarly, Smith's songs turned inward, away from the concerns of day-to-day life. Often a stanza dwelling on the sorrow of feeling separated from God was followed by a celebration of the glory and happiness of life in Christ. The titles of his most popular songs reflected this emphasis: "Song of the Soul Set Free," "Glory of His Presence," "Then Jesus Came."

34. Oswald J. Smith, *Oswald Smith's Best Songs* (Winona Lake, IN: The Rodeheaver, Hall-Mack Company, 1958), 3.

35. Oswald J. Smith, *The People's Hymns* (Winona Lake, IN: The Rodeheaver Company, 1967), 86.

36. OBCA, OJSP, Kalis, "The World's Greatest Living Hymn Writer," 7.

37. Smith, *Can Organized Religion Survive?*, 22.

38. Tamke, *Make a Joyful Noise Unto the Lord*, 42.

The tone of Smith's lyrics stands in stark contrast to the confrontational manner of some of his well-known fundamentalist contemporaries. According to historian George Marsden, the American fundamentalist movement of the early twentieth century represented "a loose, diverse, and changing federation of co-belligerents united by their fierce opposition to modernist thought."[39] In contrast, historians of fundamentalism in English Canada, while noting commonalities between Canadian and American fundamentalism, have argued that Canadian fundamentalists were more conciliatory than their counterparts to the south.[40] American Billy Sunday, for instance, celebrated the masculine side of Christianity with military marches like "Onward Christian Soldiers."[41] Smith's style was more typical of English-speaking Canadian fundamentalists. Smith tapped into, and represented, a vein of irenic Canadian fundamentalism.

Smith also tapped into his audiences' desire for entertainment. In the bustling city of Toronto, Smith's People's Church operated within a marketplace offering an extraordinary variety of goods and services. Leisure activities were available in abundance, and American movies, radio, and magazines provided popular forms of cheap entertainment. As a leader of a fledgling church, Smith could not take his authority for granted, so he embarked on a course of remarkable religious inventiveness. Drawing on all of the media resources in his environment, Smith succeeded by creating slide shows, movies, radio, magazines, and con-

39. George M. Marsden, *Fundamentalism and American Culture; The Shaping of Twentieth-Century Evangelicalism: 1870-1925* (Toronto: Oxford University Press, 1980), 4-8.

40. For instance, in *Canadian Evangelicalism in the Twentieth Century: An Introduction to its Character,* John Stackhouse argues that militancy was unusual among Canadian fundamentalists. According to Stackhouse, "Canadians, like their British counterparts, became more and more concerned about the general drift of their cultures away from traditional Christianity and responded to that drift in various ways, but they did so generally without militancy and the loss of cultural authority typical of much of American evangelicalism affected by the fundamentalist heritage" ([Toronto: University of Toronto Press, 1993], 198). For similar views see Robert Burkinshaw, *Pilgrims in Lotus Land: Conservative Protestantism in British Columbia, 1917-1981* (Kingston: McGill-Queen's University Press, 1995), 13; and Ian Rennie, "Fundamentalism and the Varieties of North Atlantic Evangelicalism," in *Evangelicalism: Comparative Studies of Popular Protestantism in North America, The British Isles, and Beyond, 1700-1990*, ed. David Bebbington et al. (Toronto: Oxford University Press, 1994), 337.

41. Butler, *Softly and Tenderly,* 63-64; William McLoughlin, *Billy Sunday Was His Real Name* (Chicago: University of Chicago Press, 1955), 179; DeJong, "I Want to be Like Jesus," 476-478.

certs that presented the gospel message in an entertaining format. In these endeavors, Smith showed himself to be what historian Nathan Hatch has called an "entrepreneur in religion," who "perceive[d] a market to be exploited," and pioneered radical innovations, restructuring religion to make it accessible to many.[42] His contemporaries were less generous: one prominent critic and fellow minister publicly criticized Smith for being "a religious show man" who would "do anything at all to get a crowd."[43]

The criticism had little effect. Smith continued to organize upbeat evangelistic meetings similar in style to the services of American revivalists Paul Rader and Billy Sunday. Homer Rodeheaver, Sunday's music director, counseled his choirs of 2000 singers to "go at it like selling goods,"[44] and turned his evangelistic meetings into musical galas.[45] Similarly, Smith took pains to appeal to those who could be drawn to a musical extravaganza, though they would have balked at the prospect of attending an ordinary church service. The evangelist adjusted his music so that it reflected the prevailing style of the "big band era," and watched the number of men and women at his services increase. During the 1930s, when attendance at the People's Church reached its peak, the choir numbered one hundred voices, backed by a forty-piece orchestra, and Sunday evenings featured a "free" one-hour pre-service concert.[46]

Soloists were a central attraction at Smith's evangelistic services. Music was presented as a performance art, and announcements featured the most attractive characteristics of the guest musicians. During Smith's tenure with the Christian and Missionary Alliance, the largest crowds had been drawn by Madame Maria Karinskaya. Before her conversion, the Russian "Prima Donna" had apparently "had it all." Advertisements recounted that "eleven times she sang before the late Czar as well as before the royal families of Persia, China and Japan. In her own country she was

42. Nathan Hatch, *The Democratization of American Christianity* (New Haven: Yale University Press, 1989), 57.

43. Jarvis Street Baptist Church Archives, T. T. Shields to B. A. Whitten, 21 November 1931.

44. William G. McLoughlin, *Modern Revivalism: Charles Grandison Finney to Billy Graham* (New York: Ronald Press Company, 1959), 422.

45. Lyle W. Dorsett, *Billy Sunday and the Redemption of Urban America* (Grand Rapids: Eerdmans, 1991), 101.

46. BGCA, OJSP, Collection 322, Box 11, Folder 3, "Evangelical Services Planned Year Around."

known as the 'Siberian Nightingale' and was twice crowned 'Queen of Song.'"[47] Madame Karinskaya recalled that she "had every material thing the world could offer me."[48] Despite this, she "was dissatisfied with life. I was empty, my heart cold." All of this changed, she observed, when "I gave myself up to the Savior. And now I am absolutely happy."[49] In a manner reminiscent of the musical melodrama of Crossley and Hunter, Madame Karinskaya manifested her decision to live for Christ before Smith's audience. Removing a jeweled headdress that had been a gift from the Czar, she presented it to Smith with the words, "Now I can go into the service of the true King." The presentation ended as she sang a lament for her homeland, "Russia, Dark Russia" to the tune of "Juanita."[50]

Another popular draw to Smith's services were African-American vocal groups such as the Cleveland Colored Quartet. Black music had been popular within Protestant circles for some time. Crossley's renditions of Negro spirituals had been consistent crowd favorites in the 1880s. Smith followed in this tradition by hosting African-American singers. Southern blacks obviously held an exotic appeal for Torontonians, who were drawn to what Smith advertised as the "much-heard-of Negro emotion."[51] Evangelist Charles Templeton recalled that the Cleveland Colored Quartet was frequently "the reason people went to meetings. . . . They were just wonderful . . . laughing a great deal . . . wanting to reach out and be accepted. . . . You went to where they were and you were guaranteed a crowd."[52]

The invention of radio provided Smith with another means of "spreading the gospel." The evangelist created an entertaining format suited to the new medium. Broadcast from the People's Church after the regular Sunday evening service, the program was primarily a religious

47. BGCA, OJSP, Collection 322, Box 1, Folder 21, "Madam Maria Karinskaya."

48. BGCA, OJSP, Collection 322, Box 1, Folder 10, *Our Burden for Russia,* Oswald J. Smith, "Madam Maria Karinskaya."

49. BGCA, OJSP, Collection 322, Box 11, Folder 3, "Russian Prima Donna Will Sing Here."

50. See BGCA, OJSP, Collection 322, Box 10, Folder 8, *The Canadian Alliance* 4:7 (July 1924), "Farewell for Russia."

51. BGCA, OJSP, Collection 322, Box 11, Folder 12, *The Tabernacle News* 9:8 (August 1930).

52. Interview with Charles Templeton, 19 July 1996. I conducted several interviews with Templeton at his home in Toronto, on 19 July 1996, 24 July 1996, and 27 August 1997. The transcripts of these interviews are in my possession.

musical variety show, heavy on entertaining renditions of gospel songs; as a result only fifteen minutes was given to preaching. Eldon Lehman, who organized the program, reminisced that "for six years we had what the manager of radio station CKNC called 'the finest variety hour on Canadian radio.'"[53] At the height of the show's popularity in the 1930s it was broadcast on 46 stations across Canada.[54] Sensitive to the needs of the day, Smith borrowed from and infiltrated popular music, organizing free jazz and ragtime concerts and broadcasting these through new media like the radio. By "commodifying" his methods and message, that is, by using modern forms that were congruent with commercial culture, Smith was able to attract audiences to his services where they could hear his message and perhaps experience conversion.

Charles Templeton

Smith's example inspired many in the city of Toronto. As a result, there emerged other charismatic leaders who used catchy melodies to draw crowds to the "old-fashioned gospel." The popularity of one of these, Charles Templeton, soon eclipsed all others. Younger and more worldly-wise than evangelists like Smith, Templeton drew freely on contemporary commercial culture to reach young people with his message of conversion.

Templeton was born in Toronto on October 7, 1915. A gifted artist, he won a job at the Toronto *Globe* in 1932, drawing a daily cartoon for the sports pages.[55] His work was soon syndicated in newspapers across the country, putting him on a first-name basis with the country's premier athletes and making him a celebrity among his hard-living friends in the newspaper business. Then, in 1936, Templeton "got religion" as he put it, and everything changed.[56] Lured by the news that the Cleveland Colored

53. Douglas Hall, *Not Made for Defeat: The Authorized Biography of Oswald J. Smith* (Grand Rapids, MI: Zondervan Publishing House, 1969), 165.

54. Ibid. For an insightful analysis of fundamentalists' use of radio in Canada in the 1920s and 1930s, see James William Opp, "'Culture of the Soul': Fundamentalism and Evangelism in Canada, 1821-1940" (M.A. Thesis, University of Calgary, 1994), 117-145.

55. Charles Templeton, *Charles Templeton: An Anecdotal Memoir* (Toronto: McClelland and Stewart, 1983), 25-27; interview with Templeton, 19 July 1996.

56. Templeton, *An Anecdotal Memoir*, 31, 33-34; Toronto *Globe and Mail* 21 October 1942; *Maclean's*, 15 May 1947.

Quartet would be performing at Toronto's Parkdale Church of the Nazarene, he attended the service and experienced an emotional conversion. For the next twenty years, he devoted himself to bringing about the same experience in the lives of others. In 1939, while leading an evangelistic campaign for the Church of the Nazarene in Grand Rapids, Michigan, Templeton met Constanci (Connie) Orozco, the soloist for these meetings. Connie had won the "California Hour" vocal contest in 1935, and had been offered a scholarship from Metro-Goldwyn-Mayer, but left the movie studio to sing in revivals. In Grand Rapids in 1939, she struck up a friendship with Charles. He proposed ten days after they met and they married two months later.[57]

The young couple eventually settled in Toronto and created their own church. Templeton also joined forces with his friend and colleague Oswald J. Smith, as well as several American evangelists and church leaders, to form Youth for Christ International (YFC), an organization about which much more is said in the next chapter. Templeton was a standout among the organizers of Youth for Christ — he served as Chair of the Budget and Planning Committee, Regional Vice President for Eastern Canada and New York State, and Executive Committee Promotional Director.[58]

He also led some of the largest weekly Youth for Christ gatherings in North America. From 1944 to 1948, Templeton's evangelistic rallies packed 2,800 young people into the auditorium of Toronto's Massey Hall. Each Saturday evening, the audience heard what one reporter referred to as "old-fashioned repent-and-be-saved gospel preaching."[59] Drawing on traditional evangelical Protestantism, Templeton urged young men and women to confess their sins, accept Christ as their Savior, and, with the Holy Spirit's help, live a life pleasing to God.

The gospel songs favored by Templeton were as conversionist as his preaching. Occasionally, the matter was put forthrightly. "Your sorrows will vanish, / Your night turn to day. / Let go and let God have His way," urged one favorite.[60] More often, the focus was not the singer, but Jesus, whose portrait looked out over the Massey Hall audience. In a manner similar to that of Crossley and Hunter and Oswald J. Smith, Templeton

57. *Maclean's*, 15 May 1947. St. Catharines *Standard*, 7 October 1955.

58. BGCA, Youth for Christ Papers [YFCP], Collection 48, Box 17, File 9, "Welcome to Second Annual Youth for Christ International Convention, July 22-29, 1946."

59. Charles Templeton Papers, Newspaper Clippings File, *New World*, April 1946.

60. Templeton Papers, Music File, "Avenue Road Church Songfest Sheet," 2.

chose pieces that advertised the joy of life in Christ. The congregational songs in Templeton's Youth for Christ services were testimonials; the singers recommended conversion based on their own experience.

Templeton emphasized the excitement and satisfaction of Christian living. He was responding, in part, to widely held concerns regarding the morality of young people that had emerged in the early 1940s. Crowds of young soldiers on leave had wandered aimlessly through the streets of major cities like Toronto, often accompanied by young women out for a "night on the town." Periodicals with a wide readership in English Canada, like *Life* and *Reader's Digest,* had alerted adults to the problem of juvenile delinquency.[61] Youth for Christ leaders organized Saturday night rallies partly out of the conviction that they could help eliminate the problem. A reporter for the Toronto *Globe and Mail* noted in 1946 that "Mr. Templeton gave one of the aims of the Youth for Christ Movement that of getting the young people off the streets on Saturday nights and giving them the straight gospel."[62]

Living for Jesus was the ultimate "thrill," Templeton informed his audiences. He told young men and women that Christ was "the most exciting man who's ever lived . . . the most extraordinary man who's ever lived,"[63] and not just a man, but God Himself. Songs such as "Since Jesus came into my heart" underscored this sense of joy and satisfaction:

> What a wonderful change
> In my life has been wrought
> Since Jesus came into my heart;
> I have light in my soul
> For which long I had sought,
> Since Jesus came into my heart.
> Since Jesus came into my heart,
> Since Jesus came into my heart,
> Floods of joy o'er my soul

61. The 1940s were characterized by what one historian of Canadian religion has called a "moral revolution." John Webster Grant, *The Church in the Canadian Era* (Burlington, ON: Welch Publishing, 1988), 166. From January to June 1943 over 1200 magazine articles had been devoted to the subject of "juvenile delinquency." See Grace Palladino, *Teenagers: An American History* (New York: BasicBooks, 1996), 81.

62. Toronto *Globe and Mail,* 6 May 1946.

63. Interview with Templeton, 19 July 1996.

Like the sea billows roll,
Since Jesus came into my heart.[64]

The tone of his songs was consistently celebratory: "Isn't it grand to be a Christian, isn't it grand?" singers asked one another.

Isn't it grand to be a Christian, isn't it grand?
Isn't it grand to be a Christian, isn't it grand?
Monday, Tuesday, Wednesday, Thursday, Friday,
Saturday and all day Sunday. Isn't it grand?

"It is truly wonderful," another song seemed to reply.

It is truly wonderful what the Lord has done.
It is truly wonderful. It is truly wonderful.
It is truly wonderful what the Lord has done.
Glory to His name.[65]

This kind of repetition was not unusual. The same line could occupy as much as three quarters of the total lyrics, which rarely exceeded nine lines. The short refrains preferred by Templeton reinforced through repetition his basic gospel message. The songs were easy to follow and memorize, and kept the pace moving — audience participants could throw all of their energy and emotion into singing without being hampered by the words.

The same spirited singing was witnessed on stage. Reporters who covered Youth for Christ rallies had to remind themselves that they were at a religious function. That was the point; the meetings, Templeton told a reporter, were "meant to inspire interest rather than reverence."[66] Young people wanted fast-paced entertainment, and they got it; the question was, from whom, and where? There were plenty of options — the early 1940s had witnessed a growing consciousness of the youth market. *Seventeen* magazine had started up in the fall of 1944.[67] The word "teenager" had come into popular use, denoting a demographic group that had developed its own style, typified by the "bobby-soxers." Young people seemed to

64. Templeton Papers, Music File, "Youth for Christ Thanksgiving Rally."
65. Templeton Papers, Music File, Songfest Sheet, 3.
66. *Maclean's*, 15 May 1947.
67. Palladino, *Teenagers: An American History*, 90.

speak their own language, in the form of "jive talk," and developed a particular musical taste — swing music — that dominated radio.[68] When the war ended, these young people had money, and the time and proclivity to spend it. Merchants attuned to this growing market responded with consumer-oriented fashions and fads, music, movies, and soft drinks.[69]

In much the same way, evangelists like Templeton marketed Christianity through Youth for Christ rallies. Using the "devil's means" for God's purposes, Templeton drew on the popular entertainment of the day to draw young people to his meetings. As Joel Carpenter has pointed out, contemporary-styled gospel music was central to the Youth for Christ appeal.[70] A typical Massey Hall rally, noted a reporter for *Maclean's* magazine in 1947, "opened with the National Anthem and swung into a fast-paced musical program."[71] The performances were never boring, shifting briskly among piano solos, vocal solos, male quartets, brass quartets, saxophone trios, cornetists, a male chorus, a female chorus, and specialty acts like the ubiquitous Cleveland Colored Quartet.[72] A Templeton rally at Maple Leaf Gardens, observed a *Maclean's* reporter, featured a "2,000 voice choir, a five-piano team, trumpeters, [and] a band."[73]

Most of these musicians were the same age as the audience members. In 1946, Templeton's Toronto Youth for Christ team included Ted Smith, the pianist and musical director, who was eighteen, and Gus Ambrose, the song leader, who was twenty-three. His brother, Tommy Ambrose, a crowd favorite who delighted audiences with flawless renditions of Negro spirituals, was only four years old.[74] Attractive young women were also a central feature: Connie Templeton sang solos from center stage, sometimes accompanied by the "Youth for Christ Octette." Even the evangelist got into the act, occasionally singing a duet with his wife.

68. Ibid., 50-51.

69. Ibid., 53.

70. Joel Carpenter, *Revive Us Again: The Reawakening of American Fundamentalism* (New York: Oxford University Press, 1997), 165.

71. *Maclean's*, 15 May 1947.

72. Toronto *Star*, 30 December 1944.

73. *Maclean's*, 15 May 1947.

74. Templeton Papers, Newspaper Clippings File, *New World*, April 1946. Interview with Templeton, 19 July 1996. Smith would soon join forces with Billy Graham. In 1998, he was still organizing music for the Graham "missions." Tommy Ambrose went on to have a successful career singing secular music.

Music also dominated Templeton's radio ministry. Like Oswald J. Smith and his other Youth for Christ colleagues, Templeton organized radio programs, essentially gospel music variety shows. On Saturday evenings, part of his Youth for Christ services was broadcast live from Massey Hall on the Toronto CBC station, CJBC.[75] On Sunday afternoons at 1:30, Charles and Connie hosted the "Radio Gospel League," heard by 50,000 Canadians on stations from Charlottetown, Prince Edward Island on the Atlantic coast to Vancouver, British Columbia on the Pacific coast.[76]

From 1944 to 1948, thousands attended Templeton's rallies, and some professed a conversion. The evangelist himself, however, was having second thoughts. Even as he grew more skillful as a public evangelist, he began to question the message he so convincingly communicated. Grave doubts about the central tenets of his "old-fashioned gospel" — especially literal interpretations of biblical events — eventually led him to leave fundamentalist evangelism for liberal mainline Protestantism.[77] The National Council of Churches (NCC), which represented several mainline denominations, had rediscovered mass evangelism following the war — they would declare 1952 "The Year of Evangelism"[78] — and hired Templeton to organize and lead what they referred to as "missions" throughout the United States.[79] From 1952 to 1956 Templeton served first as the Secretary of Evangelism for the National Council, then Director of Evangelism for the Presbyterian Church of the U.S.A. Throughout this period he coordinated and led numerous evangelistic campaigns and hosted a Sunday morning television program for youth, broadcast on CBS, called "Look Up And Live."

The Department of Evangelism of the NCC worked closely with the Board of Evangelism and Social Service of the mainline United Church of Canada, and it was agreed that Templeton would spend four months of

75. Templeton, *An Anecdotal Memoir,* 56; National Archives of Canada, CBC Anniversary Collection, Item 31612, Youth for Christ.

76. *Maclean's,* 15 May 1947.

77. For more on Templeton's move from fundamentalism to the liberal mainline establishment see Kevin B. Kee, "Revivalism: The Marketing of Protestant Religion in English-Speaking Canada, With Particular Reference to Southern Ontario, 1884-1957" (Ph.D. Thesis, Queen's University, 1999), 294-306.

78. Templeton Papers, Advertisements, Programs and Tracts File, "Christ is the Answer! The Greater Evansville Christian Rally, January 27 through February 11, 1952," 10.

79. Templeton, *An Anecdotal Memoir,* 79-80; Toronto *Globe,* 28 July 1951.

each year leading campaigns in Canada for the United Church.[80] Formed in 1925 out of Presbyterian, Congregationalist, and Methodist congregations, the United Church had returned to its evangelistic roots in the years following the Second World War. As an evangelist for the United Church, Templeton continued in the tradition of the late nineteenth-century Methodists, Crossley and Hunter.

Templeton's NCC and United Church services in the 1950s, like his Youth for Christ rallies in the 1940s, made conversion the highest priority.[81] At the same time, Templeton slightly modified his message; conversion was presented not as a final destination, but as a necessary first step towards a life lived in close communion with God. Much of the evangelist's message was geared towards positive Christian living. Templeton's message was attuned to the prevalent notion that religion should be practical. The utility of religion had been central to Canadian Protestant evangelism since the late nineteenth-century revivals of Crossley and Hunter. If religion was to compete in an open marketplace, it had to address directly the hopes and fears of men and women. For this reason Templeton preached what he called a "total gospel" addressed to all aspects of life. The words to Templeton's song, "True Happiness," which was featured on "Look Up and Live," summed up his approach in a nutshell: "In these four things we all may find TRUE HAPPINESS; / Someone to love, a child to hold, a home to build and God."[82]

While Templeton's message changed slightly, the tone of his meetings was altered significantly. During the 1940s Templeton had appealed to young men and women by presenting himself as an upbeat master of ceremonies, presiding over an extravaganza of contemporary-style music that concluded like an old-fashioned revival service. In the 1950s he repackaged his evangelism in a manner that would appeal to more refined sensibilities. Many of the trappings of his Youth for Christ days were discarded — these would have repelled rather than attracted the audiences Templeton was targeting. One journalist described Templeton's approach as "so mannerly and so reasonable";[83] just "the quiet techniques of mod-

80. James Mutchmor, *The Memoirs of James Ralph Mutchmor* (Toronto: The Ryerson Press, 1965), 115-116.

81. For example, see Templeton's evangelistic tract, *Steps to Christian Commitment: How To Become A Christian* (New York: The Division of Evangelism, n.d.).

82. Templeton Papers, Music File, "True Happiness."

83. Templeton Papers, Newspaper File, New York *World-Telegram and Sun*, 10 March 1951.

ern salesmanship," added another.[84] Seeking an explanation for Templeton's evangelistic style, a reporter in the United States credited "the discipline of his Canadian background of reserve and poise."[85] The reporter had made a mistake. Templeton's church sponsors, rather than his country of origin, were ultimately responsible for the tone of the meetings. The mainline establishment had returned to mass evangelism in the 1950s, but on its own terms. These churches preferred meetings with a refined sensibility that reflected their position in respectable society.

Performed music, which remained a central component of Templeton's services, was similarly dignified. Gone were the all-female octet, the brass band, and the four-year-old soloist belting out Negro spirituals. The only instruments heard at his United Church meetings were the piano and organ,[86] and the only voices were those of a local church choir or Connie Templeton. Connie had followed her husband into his new style of evangelism, but now limited herself to classical pieces like Malotte's "The Lord's Prayer."[87] The choir also stuck to highbrow works by composers like Handel and Bach.[88]

Templeton was determined to remain "in tune with the times," and both the times and the target audience were changing. In the 1940s he had appealed to young people by drawing on the style of swing music and radio. In the 1950s he tried to draw mainline churchgoers with a more dignified tone. His audience had grown up, and had developed different tastes. Templeton's services grew up too — jazz and flashy soloists were replaced with classical music and robed choirs. By commodifying religion, first in one way, and then in another, Templeton continued to appeal to English-speaking Canadians in changing socioeconomic circumstances. During his career of twenty years, which ended in 1957 when he left the ministry altogether, the manner in which Templeton marketed the gospel changed significantly. What did not change was Templeton's basic message of conversion. Evangelists continue to employ this strategy — communicating a traditional message with a contemporary sound — in their gospel songs today.

84. Templeton Papers, Newspaper File, *The Daily Journal*, 30 July 1952.

85. Templeton Papers, Newspaper File, *The Irving Presbyterian (Indianapolis)*, March 1953.

86. UCC, VUA, "Manual For a Templeton Christian Mission," 8, 9.

87. For example, see St. Catharine *Standard*, 3 October 1955; *The Vancouver Province*, 31 May 1954.

88. Templeton Papers, Newspaper Clippings File, Charleston *Daily Mail*, 17 May 1954.

Conclusion

A reporter for the Ottawa *Citizen* described the scene: it was eight o'clock on a Saturday evening in June 1998, and Ottawa's Corel Center, a new hockey arena and entertainment complex, was filled to overflowing. What had been billed as the "Concert for the Next Generation — a concert dedicated to youth" had drawn a "record-breaking crowd of 25,000 teenagers." The spectacle "at the Corel Center," according to the journalist, "could have been that at any rock concert anywhere. Teens were leaping and dancing in their seats, and the arena was throbbing with a beat." But this was a concert with a difference: during a break in the music, evangelist Billy Graham stepped forward and, according to the newspaper report, delivered a "sermon based on the temptation of Adam and Eve, as told in the book of Genesis." "You're searching for something, and you're not sure what it is — that something is God," Graham told the young people in the audience. "He'll give you a joy and a peace and a happiness you won't know anywhere else."[89]

While the Saturday evening extravaganza appeared to be like "any rock concert anywhere," the primary purpose of the event was evangelistic. Billy Graham's goal during the Ottawa "Mission" of June 25-28, 1998, was to bring men and women into a relationship with God. To some, his message of conversion was "old-fashioned." The same might have been said of Graham himself: seventy-nine years old, afflicted by Parkinson's disease, and surrounded by a "Mission" team that included a master of ceremonies in his seventies and an eighty-nine-year-old soloist, George Beverly Shea.

Yet the methods with which the aged evangelist and his colleagues communicated their old-fashioned gospel message were unabashedly up-to-date. The "Concert for the Next Generation" had featured top-flight rock musicians. After "Rockin' in the name of the Lord," as the *Citizen* put it, two thousand young people professed a conversion to Christ at the Saturday meeting.[90] When the four-day campaign ended, 107,000 had attended and 9,000 had "come forward" to signal their desire to "accept Christ as their Savior."[91]

89. Ottawa *Citizen*, 28 June 1998.
90. Ibid.
91. Ottawa *Citizen*, 29 June 1998.

Billy Graham's revival message and methods were not unusual. As this chapter has demonstrated, since the late nineteenth century evangelists have used gospel music to draw English-speaking Canadians to their message of repentance, conversion, and renewal. The evangelists have adapted gospel songs to the commercial music of the day in an attempt to make their conversion message appeal to as wide an audience as possible.

Hugh Crossley and John Hunter, Oswald J. Smith, and Charles Templeton believed that the men and women in their audiences wanted to hear how Christianity could make a difference in their day-to-day lives. For this reason, they adjusted the forms and metaphors of their music to reflect their own time and place. They did their best to address contemporary concerns in an attempt to show that Christianity was relevant to Canadians. Because they worked at different times, the forms and metaphors of their gospel songs were not exactly the same. For example, Crossley sang sentimentally of death while Templeton celebrated the excitement of everyday life with Christ.

Despite these differences, the evangelists' use of gospel songs was similar in two ways. First, each evangelist attempted, through music, to bring about in his listeners a conversion to Christ. Crossley and Hunter, Smith and Templeton used gospel songs that posed the question directly — "Will you be saved tonight?" — or that advertised the joy and peace that came after conversion. The nineteenth-century notion of singing as a form of testimony continued into the mid-twentieth century with refrains like "It is truly wonderful what the Lord has done."

Second, through gospel music they "commodified" religion; they packaged what they believed to be a timeless gospel message so that it would be appropriate to their own particular era. Crossley and Hunter, Smith, and Templeton were convinced that if religion was going to be meaningful in the lives of Canadians, it needed to work with other experiences that were meaningful.[92] For this reason they tried to make their revivals personally relevant to their audiences, not unlike forms of entertainment such as concerts. Each adopted a marketing strategy suited to his specific audience. Templeton, for example, attracted young people in the 1940s to his conversion message with a fast-paced jazz program. At times, he was so successful that the reaction of Canadians to his services was

92. This point is argued effectively, with the United States as the context, by Laurence Moore in *Selling God,* 65.

hard to distinguish from their enthusiasm for pop stars' concerts. His shift to older audiences necessitated a change in marketing strategy; in the 1950s he appealed to adults with dignified services featuring classical music.

In an attempt to reach as wide an audience as possible with their message of conversion, evangelists have imaginatively drawn on the strategies of contemporary merchants of commercial culture. This approach to gospel music was central to the success of Crossley and Hunter, Smith, and Templeton. The evangelists used gospel songs, each in the popular musical style of his day, to make Protestant Christianity meaningful to ordinary Canadians. As a result of their efforts, revivals highlighting gospel music have continued as an important expression of Protestantism, and have helped religion engage modernity into our own time.

CHAPTER SIX

"I Found My Thrill": *The Youth for Christ Movement and American Congregational Singing, 1940-1970*

Thomas E. Bergler

The second half of the twentieth century witnessed a revolution in American Protestant church music comparable to the acceptance of hymns in the eighteenth century. A new Christian music tradition emerged which did not exclude or even grudgingly accept popular musical idioms, instrumentation, and performance styles, but instead embraced them. The decade of the 1960s is often cited as the launching point for this revolution, but in fact the key decades of change were the 1940s and 1950s, and among the key agents of change were leaders of the Youth for Christ movement.[1] What Carl Henry and Fuller Theological Seminary did for the small cadre of postwar evangelical intellectuals, Christian popular music did for the rank and file. Evangelical teenagers and sympathetic adults helped fundamentalists emerge from their self-imposed cultural exile, and Protestant worship would never be the same. By providing a setting and a rationale for musical innovation, the Youth for Christ movement played a crucial role in the transformation of musical tastes among American Protestants between 1940 and 1970.

1. Don Cusic, *The Sound of Light: A History of Gospel Music* (Bowling Green, OH: Bowling Green State University Press, 1990), 126-129. See also Milburn Price, "The Impact of Popular Culture on Congregational Song," *The Hymn* 44, no. 1 (January 1993): 13. Michael S. Hamilton, "The Triumph of the Praise Songs," *Christianity Today* (12 July 1999): 29-36.

Youth for Christ, International (YFC) emerged during World War II from a number of local youth rallies that had been taking place from the early 1930s. The organization itself was formally established in 1945 at a Christian campground in Winona Lake, Indiana. Billy Graham was the first full-time evangelist hired by this new organization, and most of the founding members of the Billy Graham Evangelistic Association also enjoyed the Youth for Christ experience. YFC later added high school Bible clubs to the Saturday night rallies, as well as a wide variety of other publishing, social outreach, camping, and international ministries. It was one of the great agents for change in the immediate post-War period.[2]

The musical revolution sparked in part by YFC provoked heated controversy which has not yet died down. Church music experts accuse the innovators of turning worship into a rock concert, while the innovators accuse the traditionalists of turning it into a music appreciation class. Both sides are naive about the cultural complexities of preserving and transmitting the Christian heritage because, in different ways, both assume that taste and theology can be easily distinguished. But Christian music plays a much more complex role in the aesthetic process of individual and collective identity formation. The music used in church is controversial because it mediates between sacred and secular, young and old, emotion and restraint. Caught between old school aesthetes, fundamentalists, and youth culture, the members of Youth for Christ helped legitimate a new pop culture spirituality. Even some of the innovators felt uncomfortable redrawing the boundaries between taste and theology. Because many Christian teenagers did not share the same apprehensions, the revolution in church music must in large measure be attributed to their agency. In the same era that Fats Domino found his "thrill" on "Blueberry Hill," Christian teenagers at Youth for Christ rallies lobbied for a new musical language in which to express and experience the thrill of knowing Jesus.

2. Bruce L. Shelley, "The Rise of Evangelical Youth Movements," *Fides et Historia* 18 (1986): 47-63. Joel A. Carpenter, ed., *The Youth for Christ Movement and Its Pioneers* (New York: Garland, 1988).

Carving Out Space for Musical Innovation

The career of Ralph Carmichael (b. 1927) aptly illustrates key aspects of this musical revolution. As a child, Carmichael often walked by a huge gothic structure on the way to his father's fundamentalist church. He felt drawn to the building and "liked the feeling of it" because it made him "feel so small." One Wednesday night, when the young Carmichael was getting fidgety in church, a kindly man from the congregation took him down the street for an ice cream cone. On the way, they heard choir and organ music coming from the old stone church. Together, they walked up the steps to listen for a moment. Because his fundamentalist family and friends had taught him to be suspicious of such churches, Carmichael remembered feeling that "this sound is evil and mysterious and the place is filled with the devil." Back in his own church, Ralph heard the comforting sounds of the tambourine and his father's trombone.[3]

By 1949, Ralph was a Bible school student in Los Angeles. When Youth for Christ burst on the scene, the leaders of his school condemned it as "worldly" because, "they used spotlights and they sang snappy choruses and dressed in sport coats — bright blues and seal greens and the girls wore bobby sox and saddle shoes." Ralph did not agree with these criticisms, so he became the music leader for the local YFC rally. He put together brass, saxophone, and rhythm accompaniment, but the church hosting the rallies "began to censor it." He also organized a performance ensemble consisting of trumpets, trombones, woodwinds, rhythm, and sixteen voices. Ralph and his group soon got offers from radio and television stations. Carmichael wanted to name his new TV show after the college, but its fundamentalist leaders doubted the moral rectitude of both his musical style and the new medium of television. Ignoring their scruples, Ralph created a show called *The Campus Christian Hour* that later won an Emmy. Seeing his success, the college administrators changed their mind, but Ralph refused to rename his show.[4]

In 1955, Youth for Christ leaders asked Ralph to direct the music at their annual convention in Winona Lake, Indiana. He put together a choir

3. R. Bruce Horner, "The Function of Music in the Youth for Christ Program" (MME thesis, Indiana University, 1970), 218, 227.

4. Interview with Ralph Carmichael, 8 August 1969, in Horner, "Function of Music," 146-155. For the controversy over Carmichael's TV show, see ibid., 219.

of five hundred teenagers, accompanied by sixteen trumpets, twelve trombones, tympani, and other instruments. He used this massive ensemble to perform the popular hymns and gospel songs of revivalism with upbeat arrangements and visual effects. At one point the choir sang "The Old Rugged Cross" and formed a huge cross by holding colored cards. At other times colored spotlights swept the stage. Although Carmichael's style was a hit with YFC directors and teenagers, some adults in the audience complained about this "Hollywood production." "I got sacked after the second year because it was worldly," he remembered.[5]

Meanwhile Carmichael pursued a career that included arranging for artists like Ella Fitzgerald, Nat King Cole, and Roger Williams, as well as for film and television. His arrangements and compositions also became popular with Youth for Christ musical groups and church choirs during the 1950s. But in composing the score for the 1965 Billy Graham Evangelistic Association film *The Restless Ones,* he almost went too far. By introducing syncopated rythyms that came close to a rock beat, Ralph narrowly missed having his score scrapped. Only budget considerations forced the company to use his music. Carmichael proudly reported in 1969 that 4 million people had seen the film, resulting in an "astronomical" number of decisions for Christ. In addition, the hit song "He's Everything to Me" used in the film became the centerpiece for a widely used Youth for Christ songbook. Soon after *The Restless Ones,* Carmichael cowrote a hugely successful Christian folk musical called *Tell It Like It Is,* with Kurt Kaiser, another musician with Youth for Christ experience. *Tell It Like It Is* joined Billy Ray Hearn's *Good News* as a top seller to church choirs. These men promoted their new style at church workshops. They also became important pioneers in the Christian recording industry.[6]

Carmichael's career shows the key role played by YFC musicians in both the transition from fundamentalism to evangelicalism and the transformation of Protestant worship. For a Fundamentalist child like Carmichael, the so-called great music of the church might evoke terror, rather than the intended solemnity and awe. Even after formal musical

5. "Music? 'Even I Felt Like Singing!'" *Youth for Christ Magazine,* September 1955, 13. Interview with Ralph Carmichael, in Horner, "Function of Music," 151.

6. Horner, "Function of Music," 217, 220-221. For the success of folk musicals in the late 1960s and their role in opening the way for Jesus rock, see Charlie Peacock, *At the Crossroads: An Insider's Look at the Past, Present, and Future of Contemporary Christian Music* (Nashville, TN: Broadman Press, 1999), 60-64.

training, many artists like Carmichael remained more committed to evangelism than to the project of elevating Evangelical musical tastes. On the other hand, fundamentalists forced Carmichael and other innovators to take their music outside the four walls of the church. Finally, even evangelistic visionaries, of which there were many in the Billy Graham and Youth for Christ organizations, often held back from each new step in musical innovation. A musical trend that started as an attempt to evangelize teenagers took on a life of its own.

Perhaps one reason critics have pointed to the 1960s as the key decade of change in church music is that by comparison, the innovations brought in earlier decades by Youth for Christ musicians like Carmichael seem relatively tame. Indeed, these musicians drew on an established practice of using popular music styles to achieve evangelistic appeal. Fundamentalists had criticized Billy Sunday's musical director Homer Rodeheaver for using the song "Brighten the Corner," which did not mention God or contain any other explicitly Christian references. Rodeheaver replied that the song was "never intended for a Sunday morning service, nor for a devotional meeting — its purpose was to bridge the gap between the popular song of the day and the great hymns and gospel songs, and to give to men a simple, easy, lilting melody." Similarly, radio evangelists of the 1920s and 1930s like Paul Rader and Percy Crawford used music modeled on the radio orchestra sound to attract young people. These pioneers directly influenced early YFC leaders like Torrey Johnson, Bob Cook, and Jack Wyrtzen. Wyrtzen was also one of several YFC pioneers who had played in a dance band before his conversion.[7]

Given such precedents, it comes as some surprise that the leaders of the Youth for Christ rallies that sprang up all over the country in the 1940s aroused criticism for their entertaining style and upbeat music. Fundamentalist opposition is even more surprising when we note that the movement's first song book, *Singing Youth for Christ,* contained mostly gospel songs and hymns drawn straight from the revival tradition and written by beloved songwriters like Ira Sankey, Fanny Crosby, and Philip Bliss. In their foreword, the editors reminded users of the songbook that "the com-

7. Cusic, *Sound of Light,* 70-74. For the persistence of the distinction between worship and evangelistic music, see Phil Kerr, *Music in Evangelism* (Grand Rapids, MI: Zondervan, 1962), 70-88. For the links between YFC music and popular radio styles, see Joel Carpenter, *Revive Us Again: the Reawakening of American Fundamentalism* (New York: Oxford, 1997), 161-176.

ponents of any spiritual experience are *heart* and *mind*" and that "both are needed."[8] Fundamentalists did not object to the music at early YFC rallies because it employed new lyrics, objectionable melodies, or even a novel theology of religious experience. Instead, they reacted to the "worldly" musical arrangements and performance styles they saw on stage at YFC.

The first two presidents of Youth for Christ, Torrey Johnson and Bob Cook, justified upbeat music because it attracted young people and helped them get converted. They claimed that radio had "spoiled things for the careless gospel musician" because young people could hear "worldly music, *perfectly produced*, any hour of the day or night." They insisted that some young people were shunning Christianity because of its stereotypical image as restrictive and boring. Billy Graham repeatedly told Youth for Christ audiences that "the young people around the world today who are having the best time are the young people who know Jesus Christ."[9] As the explosive growth of Youth for Christ during the war illustrated, many fundamentalists agreed. But evangelistic effectiveness was not enough to convince everyone. Johnson and Cook also had to argue that since Youth for Christ was not a church and its rallies were not church services, they did not violate any standards of propriety or reverence. YFC leaders preferred to conduct their rallies in public auditoriums rather than churches not only because they loved to take over public spaces on the "devil's night" and believed a neutral setting would appeal to non-Christian teens, but also because such settings allowed them the freedom to experiment with a more entertaining style of evangelism.[10]

Young fundamentalists and evangelicals loved this new music that

8. Dr. Frank C. Phillips, Dr. Robert A. Cook, Rev. Cliff Barrows, eds., *Singing Youth For Christ* (Chicago: Youth for Christ International, 1948).

9. Torrey Johnson and Robert Cook, *Reaching Youth for Christ* (Chicago: Moody Press, 1944), 36. Joel A. Carpenter, ed., *The Early Billy Graham: Sermon and Revival Accounts* (New York: Garland, 1988), 30-47, 63-76, 92-94.

10. In their official policy statement, YFC leaders stated that "Y.F.C. is a youth rally, rather than a church service" ("YFC Leaders' Conference," July 1945, 10 [Billy Graham Center Archives, Collection 48, box 13, file 36]). This provision was intended to justify innovation in the rallies. See for example Cedric Sears, "Hour of Destiny," *YFCM* (October 1947): 11. Torrey Johnson insisted that YFC's "vindication" was its success in saving souls. "Pressing On in Youth For Christ" in "Minutes of the 2nd Annual Convention, YFCI, July 22-29, 1946," 3 (BGCA 48-9-4). For similar arguments, see Bob Cook, "President's Report" in "Minutes, YFCI Mid-Winter Hotel Convention, North Park Hotel, Chicago, January 4-6, 1956," 19-21 (BGCA 48-13-3). See also Horner, "Function of Music," 33.

used the popular sounds of the day to express love for Jesus. Gloria Roe, who went on to a professional career in sacred music, remembered that it was through her involvement in Youth for Christ that she had learned that "everything I feel about Him — devotion, joy, commitment, absolutely everything — could be sung about." Another teenage vocalist named Margery Martin described her feelings as she performed at a Youth for Christ rally in 1951, "as I turned to face that group of young people, all my qualms vanished, my knees ceased their noisome knocking, and I was aware only of a keen desire within me to tell those in my presence of the truth which made me free." For Margery, as for so many others, Youth for Christ music was the perfect expression of her religious sentiments, "for within my heart there rang a melody of joy, of peace, of perfect contentment, and of victory."[11]

In addition to repackaging Fundamentalist spirituality as both fun and fulfilling, Youth for Christ leaders provided a key institutional base for musical innovation. In their zeal to attract non-Christian teenagers, Youth for Christ leaders sought out fresh musical talent that could approximate popular styles, much in the way that disc jockeys and record companies recruited new performers. Local Youth for Christ directors recruited and trained teenagers to perform at their rallies. In San Diego, a girl's trio called the Campus Coeds, a mixed choral group called the Kings Korlaires, and a gospel quartet called Men of Note, all performed regularly at YFC rallies. With a network of some nine hundred local Saturday night rallies by 1945, Youth for Christ leaders could also offer an extensive tour circuit to professional Christian performers. Artists like the Palermo brothers, Ted and Gloria Roe, Rudy Atwood, Kurt Kaiser, and Bill Carle became regulars at Youth for Christ rallies. Often they would spend a week in a given city, singing at the local YFC Bible clubs and school assemblies as well as the Saturday night rally. In addition to record sales at the rallies, artists benefited from music reviews in *Youth for Christ Magazine.* They also wrote and performed music for the soundtracks used on evangelistic films shown at the rallies.[12] Albums commissioned and distributed by Youth for Christ pro-

11. Interview with Gloria Roe, 7 July 1968, in Horner, "Function of Music," 192. Margery Sue Martin, "Youth for Christ and My Life," *YFCM* (October 1951): 19.

12. For an example of Christian artists on tour, see "YFC High School Clubs," *YFCM* (December 1959): 4-5; Ken Anderson, "Film Reviews," *YFCM* (December 1954): 30; Carl Bihl, "Record Reviews," *YFCM* (December 1954): 32. For YFC albums, see *Newsletter,* 25 October 1954, 6 (BGCA 48-16-3); "Now Available in Sheet Music," *YFCM* (April 1957): 27; and *YFC Eye*

vided another opportunity for Christian musicians to shine. Youth for Christ even sponsored its own book and record club and developed a fund-raising scheme in which teenagers sold records to help them get to the Capital Teen Convention while earning money for their local YFC program.[13]

The yearly Youth for Christ convention at Winona Lake, Indiana, provided another important venue for the marketing and distribution of new music and the introduction of new musicians. The national office hired top musical talent like Ralph Carmichael and Harold DeCou to put together stunning musical performances. By the late 1950s, even enthusiasts were describing these musical extravaganzas as "broadway shows." Top professionals from the sacred music world also performed. YFC leaders presented these artists to the teenage audiences as model Christians. At the 1959 convention, Tony Fontane sang "Until Then," one of his most often requested songs, using his trademark crooner style with lush piano accompaniment. After his performance, YFC leader Ted Engstrom commented, "What a marvelous trophy of God's grace." In his prayer before the sermon, fellow musician Ted Roe said, "We have already seen and heard a sermon." Although YFC preachers and musicians always tried to distinguish between music "ministry" and entertainment, they also catered to the teenage interest in Christian celebrities. YFC used Christian musicians as "headliners" to promote their rallies and national conventions. One issue of *Youth for Christ Magazine* even included a Christian celebrity quiz that asked readers to identify photos of Christian musicians.[14]

Winona also hosted the yearly finals of YFC's music competitions.

2:8 (November 1961): 17. YFC album titles included *Yours . . . and His, Decade of Destiny, Keyboards and Strings,* and *YFC . . . Men With a Song.* Ted Engstrom, "YFC Book and Record Club Catching On Like Wild Fire," *YFCM* [November 1956]: 14-15; "Inspiration Records: Money in *Your* Pocket!" *Horizons* 2, no. 6 [April 1959], 1-3; BGCA 48-15-34.

13. For movie scores, see "Now Available in Sheet Music: 'If You Know the Lord,'" *YFCM* (April 1957): 27. For teen musical groups in San Diego, see "YFC's Musical Staff: Providing 'Music for Teens' Every Sat. Nite," *Campus* (November 1959): 17.

14. For the "Broadway" characterization, see Mark Senter, "The Youth for Christ Movement as an Educational Agency and Its Impact Upon Protestant Churches: 1931-1979" (Ph.D. diss., Loyola University of Chicago, 1989), 309. For Fontane's performance and comments, see Tape of YFC Conference, Winona Lake, 1959 (BGCA 48-T23). For Christian musicians as YFC headliners, see "Winona Convention Highlights," *News Bulletin* 16 May 1956, 1 (BGCA 48-16-3), and "Bill Carle News Release," November 1957 (BGCA 48-15-3). The Christian celebrity quiz appeared under the title, "Do You Know These Christian Recording Artists?" *YFCM* (March 1963): 17.

Separate categories for song leaders, gospel pianists, vocal soloists, vocal groups, instrumental soloists, and instrumental groups insured that a maximum number of young artists could gain national exposure. These contests began at the local level and progressed through regional competition, giving even more young people a chance to perform. Local rally directors used the competition to recruit and train local teen talent for use in their Saturday night rallies and high school Bible clubs. By the late fifties, Youth for Christ offered national winners other attractive opportunities like recording sessions and tours.[15] Leaders consciously took advantage of the allure of performance to interest young people in the Youth for Christ program.

The music of Youth for Christ could hold its own against its "secular" rivals during the 1950s. For example, in Missoula, Montana in 1951, the Youth for Christ rally and the local high school dance once met at school on the same night. YFC members arranged for their guest speakers, the singing team of Louis and Phil Palermo, to perform at the dance after the rally was over. These Christian teenagers proudly reported to national club director Jack Hamilton that the "spirit of the dance was changed so much" that students only danced to one more song, and the dancing shut down completely after that. But head to head competition with "worldly" music also reshaped the evangelical musical culture. A few YFC leaders promoted their high school Bible club meetings and Saturday night rallies by offering a "Hymn Hit Parade." Others tried "platter parties" to compete with the high school record hops.[16]

Some Protestant leaders found these musical innovations stylistically and institutionally threatening. Guardians of traditional hymnody criticized the music at Youth for Christ rallies and Billy Graham Crusades for being trite and entertaining.[17] Denominational youth leaders felt even

15. Senter, "Youth for Christ Movement," 241-244. For the origins of the contests, see "YFC Clubs," *YFCM* (October 1951): 54-56. For teenage musicians on tour, see Ted W. Engstrom, "Presidential Address," Youth for Christ International 7th Annual Mid-Winter Convention, Minneapolis, Minnesota, January 2-5, 1962 (BGCA 48-13-2), and "Teen Talent Winners Tour," *Monday Memo* 227, 22 July 1968 (BGCA 48-15-43).

16. "30 Towns in Montana Open to YFC Clubs," *YFCM* (January 1952): 64; "Bible Club Leaders Meet: Notes and Ideas" (BGCA 181-1-79); Westminster High School Bible Club Report, 24 February 1956 (BGCA 181-1-80). For "platter parties" see "New Avenues of Teen Activity," YFCI 8th Mid-Winter Convention, March 1963, Denver, Colorado, 1 (BGCA 48-13-14).

17. Typical of this type of criticism was Erik Routley, "On the Billy Graham Song Book," *The Hymn* 6, no. 1 (January 1955): 26, 36.

more threatened. Attending a packed Youth for Christ rally in Kansas City in 1947, Methodist youth leader Hoover Rupert was disappointed with the music even when they sang one of his favorites, "Spirit of the living God, fall afresh on me." Because the song leader prefaced this selection with the question, "How many are having a good time?," Rupert felt that this "rich hymn" had been cheapened into "another sing-songy chorus." Still, he admitted that the young people were singing enthusiastically and seemed to be enjoying themselves. Even the Unitarian minister G. Richard Kuch, who labeled Youth for Christ leaders as fascists, had to admit that "most liberal cynics would find themselves joining in on the chorus of the zestful singing at a YFC meeting." He called on Unitarian and Universalist youth groups to incorporate more singing into their meetings.[18]

Even denominational critics of Youth for Christ often complained that the movement's call for conversion did not lead to Christian social concern. Indeed, the music of Youth for Christ reinforced the centrality of conversion in a way that emphasized personal consolation over calling to active service. One of the most popular YFC choruses of the 1940s and 1950s was "Christ for Me":

> Christ for Me
> Yes it's Christ for me,
> He's my Savior, my Lord and King
> I'm so happy I shout and sing;
> Every day as I go my way it is Christ for me.[19]

In contrast, national Methodist youth leaders repeatedly used hymns like "Are Ye Able?" "Young and Fearless Prophet" and "For the Living of These Days" to prod young people toward social activism. Where evangelicals saw teenagers as ideal candidates for conversion, liberal Protestants idealized them as natural social activists. As the opening stanza of "Are Ye Able?" put it,

18. Hoover Rupert, "Field Report: 'Youth for Christ' Rally, Grand Avenue Methodist Temple, Kansas City, Missouri, January 11, 1947" (Methodist Center for Archives and History, General Board of Discipleship Records 1184-3-2:02). Rev. G. Richard Kuch, "Youth for Christ: a Challenge to Liberal Youth," *American Unitarian Youth,* December 1945, 8-9, 11 (MCAH, GBD 1184-3-2:02).

19. *Singing Youth for Christ,* 88. This gospel chorus became a virtual YFC theme song. See Horner, "Function of Music," 83, note a.

"Are ye able," said the Master,
"To be crucified with me?"
"Yea," the sturdy dreamers answered,
"To the death we follow thee."

Indeed, it would take "sturdy dreamers" to sustain the Social Gospel agenda during the politically conservative 1950s. In contrast to YFC leaders, Methodist Youth Department officials used popular music only in national convention pageants designed to shake teenagers out of their middle-class complacency and revivalist spirituality.[20]

Denominational youth experts who attended Youth for Christ rallies noted the hellfire preaching and the emotional music, but did not realize how effectively they complemented one another. In addition to criticizing "sing-songy choruses," denominational officials also commonly complained about the extended use of songs like "Just as I am" and "Almost Persuaded" while the preacher was urging teenagers to come forward and receive salvation. It was no accident that revivalists called this point in the meeting the "invitation." Rather than challenging teenagers to go out and do something, YFC preachers invited them to receive something. In evaluating this mix, critics of revivalism often assumed that such preaching and the resulting conversion or rededication experiences were spiritual dead ends.[21]

Yet the sermons at Youth for Christ meetings were often very challenging. At the Winona convention in 1952, YFC President Bob Cook told his teenage audience that in light of the fact that the world could end at any moment, they should be ready to pay the ultimate price in order to preach the gospel to the whole world. "ARE YOU WILLING TO DIE FOR CHRIST?" he asked.[22] Critics missed the fact that challenge and comfort fit

20. *The Methodist Hymnal* (Nashville, TN: Board of Publication of the Methodist Church, 1964), 413. For an example of the use of such hymns at a conference, see Alfred D. Moore, ed., *For the Living of These Days: Report of the First National Convocation of the Methodist Youth Fellowship, Oxford, Ohio September 1-5, 1942* (Nashville, TN: National Convocation of the Methodist Youth Fellowship, 1942). For the use of jazz to shake up Methodist teenagers, see "National Convocation of Methodist Youth, Minutes of the Directing Committee, November 24, 1958" (MCAH, GBD), and *The Program* (Nashville, TN: National Convocation of Methodist Youth, 1959) (MCAH, GBD 1124-4-2:05).

21. See Hoover Rupert, "Report on 'Youth for Christ' Rally," Nashville, TN, 8 December 1945, and Hoover Rupert "Field Report: 'Youth for Christ' Rally," Kansas City, Missouri, 11 January 1947 (MCAH, GBD 1184-3-2:02).

22. Dr. Robert A. Cook, "Willing . . . to Die?" *YFCM* (September 1952): 12-21.

together seamlessly in evangelical spirituality. It was not that YFC leaders failed to issue a challenge to young people. The key difference was that unlike mainline youth leaders, they did not use music as a primary vehicle for those challenges. Instead, music provided the enjoyment and comfort that balanced the harsher messages about heaven and hell, worldliness and holiness, complacency and martyrdom.

In their criticisms of Youth for Christ, Methodists and other denominational youth experts seemed to forget that for some time they too had been trying to tailor their music and worship styles to appeal to youth. During the 1930s and 1940s denominational presses turned out a flood of worship handbooks like *Worship Services for Youth* and songbooks like *Sing it Again, Lift Every Voice,* and *Hymns & Songs of Christian Comradeship.* Typically, the authors and editors of these resources hoped to educate and elevate musical tastes, often expressing confidence that properly guided young people would naturally choose the beautiful and sublime over the "cheap and tawdry" in worship. But at summer camps, picnics, and conferences, Methodist youth leaders liked to warm up the crowd with folk songs and catchy gospel numbers before moving on to more serious musical fare. In part to protect their aesthetic ideal of worship, Methodist youth experts coined the term "fellowship singing" to refer to this type of activity.[23]

Nevertheless, music that met adult ideals of beauty and taste did not always appeal to young people. At a staff meeting in 1953, Methodist youth expert Howard Ellis urged his fellow staff members to find a hymnal that could "express the growing evangelistic spirit in youth gatherings" and yet "get away from the Youth for Christ songs." Staff members agreed that no such resource was available and that *The Methodist Hymnal* was not working for youth meetings. Hoping to evade the hard choices involved, they decided to urge youth leaders to use the "great hymns of the church" but also to look for a more youth-friendly hymnal.[24] Although they pursued

23. Alice Bays, *Worship Services for Youth* (New York: Abingdon-Cokesbury, 1946). Such worship manuals were common among mainline Protestants in the 1930s and 1940s. See, for example, Laura Athearn, *Christian Worship for American Youth* (New York: The Century Co., 1931), and Sue Randolph Griffis, *Lamps for Worship: A Year of Worship Programs for Young People* (Cincinnati, OH: Standard Publishing Co., 1937). Presbyterians produced *The Hymnal for Youth* (Philadelphia: Westminster Press, 1941), which went through fifteen printings by 1952. For the use of lighter music among Methodists, see "Program: Summer Activities," *The Planner* (July/August/September 1944).

24. "Joint Staff on Youth and Student Work Dec 4, 1953" (MCAH, GBD 1124-2-3:06).

an aesthetic traditionalism and hoped to establish transgenerational tastes centered around a single denominational hymnal, Protestant youth leaders found themselves pushed by their youthful constituents toward more popular musical fare.

While denominational youth leaders wavered, Youth for Christ leaders set aside their musical scruples even if they could not escape generational conflict. Many YFC leaders hoped that teenagers could be educated to appreciate the full range of the church's musical heritage. But they believed that since this music would not appeal to the non-Christian teens who made up their target audience, they would have to leave such music education to the churches. At the same time, the argument that the YFC musical style was just a concession to non-Christian tastes could often wear thin in practice. As early as 1948, Bob Cook exhorted leaders to "Stop merely inviting Christian youth to come and listen to a charming program!" He admitted that "the minority at any rally are unchurched" and few if any came from "the so-called 'seamy' side of town." YFC musician Shirley Wendt observed that "often a person who comes to one of these rallies is coming for an outlet because they don't enjoy singing anthems in church." As if it was not hard enough to balance the appeal to Christian and non-Christian teenagers, YFC leaders also had to contend with a large number of fundamentalist adults at their meetings. These adults were drawn to the reassuring spectacle of teenagers embracing the revivalist faith, but over time some rally directors chafed under the restrictions imposed by conservative adults in the audience.[25] The musicians at Youth for Christ meetings provoked periodic controversies because they tampered with the musical heritage of revivalism that had done so much to create a sense of transgenerational identity. At first, their musical innovations were mild enough that most of the older generation of fundamentalists could still recognize a kindred spirituality in the young. But as the "old-time religion" converged with what would later be called "that old-time rock and roll," a generational earthquake loomed.

25. For YFC leaders' hopes of elevating teenage music tastes, see Horner, "Function of Music," 72. Bob Cook, "What Happens Next?" *YFCM* (July 1949): 4-8. "What's Cookin? A monthly chat with Bob Cook," *YFCM* (April 1949): 25, 75. One early critic complained that two-fifths of the crowd at a Nashville rally were adults. Rupert, "Field Report: 'Youth for Christ' Rally," 1. For the dilemma of trying to appeal to youth without alienating adults, see Horner, "Function of Music," 87-88.

Between Rock and a Hard Place

Success in appealing to youth brought a new set of challenges to Youth for Christ. Its leaders became arbiters between fundamentalist sensibilities and commercial youth culture. They continued the old fundamentalist strategy of condemning worldly practices like smoking, drinking, dancing, and card playing. Perhaps because of a strong consensus regarding these standards, music emerged as the most dynamic frontier of cultural change within the movement. When secular musicians performed religious songs and Christian performers experimented with "jazzy" gospel numbers, Youth for Christ members struggled to draw clear boundaries between secular and sacred music.

Rock 'n roll proved an especially traumatic test of these boundaries because it seemed to counterfeit the excitement and fulfillment of the Christian life. But because YFC music had taught Christian teenagers to experience their relationship with Jesus as thrilling and fun, the early adult prohibitions against rock 'n' roll could not endure. YFC leaders chose to see Christian movies and television programs as legitimate cultural conquests, but they mistrusted religious entertainment produced by outsiders. For example, Bob Cook argued that even the religious films produced in Hollywood, like *The Robe* or *A Man Called Peter,* were spiritually harmful not only because they presented a "watered-down version of the Gospel" but because they seduced young Christians into breaking their rule about going to the theater. In contrast, Cook and other YFC leaders praised Christian films produced by Christian studios and shown at Youth for Christ rallies or in churches.[26] Media like radio, film, and television could be emptied of their worldly content and refilled with Christian content, but worldly social settings could not be so easily redeemed.

Popular music proved to be a more difficult case because it crossed supposedly impermeable boundaries between sacred and secular realms. In the second half of the 1950s, performers and record companies began to cash in on popular religious sentiments with songs like "I Believe" and "Church Twice on Sunday." In 1955, "Angels in the Sky" by the Crew Cuts, "The Bible Tells Me So" by Don Cornell, and two versions of "He," one by Al Hibbler and the other by the McGuire Sisters, reached the top 15 on *Bill-*

26. Robert A. Cook, "What About Hollywood Movies?" *YFCM* (April 1957): 15-16. See also Mel Larson, "Hollywood Heartwash," *YFCM* (September 1960): 32-33.

board's pop charts.[27] Responding to such music, YFC evangelist Carl Bihl insisted that *"the god of the juke box evidently is not the God of the Bible!"* He complained that "juke box hymns" communicated bad theology and omitted the name of Jesus in order to sell more records. Even though most of these songs were ballads, he argued that their "strong sensuous beat" led "the thoughts and emotions away from, rather than to, the things the Lord would have us love and cherish." He deplored the fact that some "Gospel meetings" mistakenly used such music, and expressed outrage that the song "What Lola Wants" was on the flip side of the hit single "Church Twice on Sunday."[28]

Although Bihl rightly assumed that what Lola wanted was something other than to attend church twice on Sunday, many teenagers who did go to church shrank from issuing a blanket condemnation of juke box hymns. Even a panel of Christian teens handpicked by the editors of *Youth for Christ Magazine* were divided on the question, "Do juke box hymns cheapen the Gospel?" Two of the panelists, Dave Carter and Theresa Overstreet, insisted that "it depends greatly on what the hymns say and who sings them." They approved of such songs if recorded by Christian performers who intended the music as a witness to unbelievers. The panelists who did condemn these songs interpreted the biblical call for "separation" from the world in spatial terms. Jerry Oas warned that such music "may draw Christians into a place where they would not go and to do things to ruin or cheapen their testimony." Connie Markakis agreed, and asked "How can the Lord's song be sung in a strange place, like the juke box, and still bring someone to the Lord?" Yet other articles celebrated YFC leaders who got the local high school hangout to include some sacred platters in its juke box or created their own teen centers complete with "sacred" juke boxes.[29] As a metaphor for bodily and spiritual purity, spatial separation from the world had its limits. It did not provide clear criteria for distinguishing between aesthetic perceptions and moral or theological judgments. As Theresa Overstreet pointed out in defense of juke box hymns, any "true Christian" would be able to recognize which songs were "sung for Jesus' glory and to win souls for Him."[30]

27. Cusic, *Sound of Light*, 112.

28. Carl J. Bihl, "Blessing? Or Blasphemy?" *YFCM* (July 1957): 11.

29. "Sacred Records in Erie, Pa., Juke Boxes," *YFCM* (June 1953): 38. Jack Cousins, "Hey Gang! Look!" *YFCM* (December 1952): 38-39, 42.

30. "Youth Speaks Up!" *YFCM* (November 1955): 22.

Such problems of interpretation reveal one reason why social setting was so crucial for Evangelical conceptions of the sacred. In a pagan setting, only the inner attitude or intention of the performer could determine whether the music was legitimately sacred. But such inner states were less accessible to the observer, provoking more anxiety that the performance might not be safe. When "the world" accepted religious music, some evangelicals had to condemn it because it suggested an unthinkable affinity between pagan tastes and Christian spirituality.

Although "juke box hymns" provoked controversy, it proved even harder to evaluate the "jazzy" gospel choruses and performance pieces used in some YFC rallies. In 1956, the editors of *Youth for Christ Magazine* convened another youth panel to discuss the question, "Are Gospel choruses too jazzy?" Echoing what she had learned in Youth for Christ, Margaret Brown said that "if a few lively choruses are sung at the beginning of a meeting it creates a welcome spirit and the unsaved present will realize that the Christian life is not dull." Ruth Voskuyl noted that "'jazziness' is a relative thing" and that the evaluation of a given song depended on individual taste, the "spirit or method" in which it was sung, and the setting. She thought that "jumpy, noisy, gay music is not appropriate for a worship service because it does not inspire a spirit of reverence and worship towards God." Still, she thought that on a hay ride, such music "expresses as no other music could, the happiness and thrill which one experiences in knowing the Lord Jesus Christ as Savior."[31] By moving Christian music into more "neutral" settings, YFC members found the freedom to express religious sentiments still unacceptable in church. Although they all expressed reservations, none of these carefully screened teenagers condemned lively gospel choruses. Young evangelicals reared on Youth for Christ music were already pushing beyond their elders.

In contrast, some adults insisted that a sacred location or even a pure intention could not redeem a secular style. Gunnar Urang, head of the music department at Trinity Seminary in Chicago and former Youth for Christ music director, found much to criticize in the style of some supposedly sacred musicians. He asked pointedly, "Why is it that Jo Stafford, the crooner, sings gospel songs 'straight,' and Blanche Thebom, the Metropolitan star, sings 'Open My Eyes that I May See' with appealing simplicity and quiet devotion, while many of our Christian 'stars' either croon or go

31. "Youth Speaks Up!" *YFCM* (August 1956): 12.

over-dramatic in their singing?" He agreed that music played a crucial role in evangelism, but worried that "sensual harmonies and frenetic rhythms" would suggest to the listener "the fleshly amusements and entertainment of the world." He compared such music to the unthinkable case of a preacher telling a "smutty story" in the name of speaking the language of the people. Becoming revealingly concrete, he posed the case of "a girl singer" who "impresses us as trying to imitate a 'torchy crooner,' making a song about the love of Christ sound like an expression of fleshy love." He complained of one gospel record, "the words were overpowered by jazzy and 'swingy' instrumental support, and the solo itself was sung like a 'blues' number." As far as Urang was concerned, the use of musical "gimmicks" like "slides and slurs, meaningless high notes, or a crooning style" all but proved that the artist was not singing under the control and inspiration of the Holy Spirit, and might not even be a true Christian.[32]

As a musical professional employed by evangelical institutions, it was easy for Urang to draw sharp distinctions between Christian performers whose style was inspired by the Holy Spirit and those who used "worldly" stylings as a substitute for spiritual authenticity. Urang and others clung to such criteria in the face of teenage tastes because they found the possibility that insiders might corrupt sacred music to be even more threatening than the fact that a few outsiders were stealing some success with "juke box hymns." A good many performers agreed. After his conversion, Tony Fontane turned his back on a popular music career which included the hit "Cold Cold Heart" that had sold 1.2 million copies, as well as appearances on the Ed Sullivan and Steve Allen shows. He assumed that secular and sacred music careers could not be combined, and leaders of Youth for Christ applauded his choice. Similarly, gospel organist Les Barnett played with Frank Sinatra, Peggy Lee, and Rudy Vallee before his conversion, but later devoted himself to his sacred music career.[33]

Other evangelical musicians straddled this supposedly unbridgeable chasm between sacred and secular musical identities. Gospel musicians regularly performed on "secular" radio stations in the 1930s and 1940s. A southern gospel quartet called The Blackwood Brothers won the Arthur Godfrey talent show on CBS in 1954. Gospel quartets like the

32. Gunnar Urang, "Singing in the Holy Spirit," *YFCM* (April 1957): 26-27.

33. "A New Song," *Campus* (February 1959). Otis Skillings, "Top Notch Tunes," *Campus* (April 1959): 29.

Blackwoods and the Stamps sang back up on Elvis Presley's records and even performed as opening acts for some of his live shows.[34] Ralph Carmichael wrote and arranged music in both popular and religious genres. Even more dramatically, the impeccably clean-cut Pat Boone achieved huge commercial success singing bowdlerized covers of rhythm and blues songs like "Tutti Frutti" and "Long Tall Sally."[35] Sensing that Boone was violating the spirit of the law, Norman King complained in *Youth for Christ Magazine* that a "man from the South, who's never been kissed except by his pretty wife, comes along and mixes a genteel sort of Rock 'n' Roll with Bible verses, and everybody figures the problem is solved."[36] King refrained from naming Boone, perhaps because the young crooner rivaled Elvis in his popularity with teenagers. Not only did his singles sell enormously well, even beating out Elvis's "All Shook Up" in head-to-head competition in 1957, but his advice manual to teenagers, *'Twixt Twelve and Twenty,* topped the nonfiction best-seller list in 1959 with 260,000 copies.[37]

A full decade before the emergence of "Jesus rock," teenage tastes seemed to be thwarting evangelical attempts to maintain clear boundaries between sacred and secular music and performers. Indeed, one reason Boone probably got by with so little criticism was that most evangelicals were preoccupied with the evils of rock 'n' roll. In the first article on the subject to appear in *Youth for Christ Magazine,* radio preacher William Ward Ayer argued that rock music contributed to juvenile crime and cited examples of violence and vandalism at rock concerts. He believed that rock music provoked "sex-crazed, irrational, irresponsible actions" because, like its voodoo precedents, it induced demon possession. Revealingly, he cited an anthropologist who claimed that the drum beat induced a trance state that allowed the spirits to "mount" their victims. For observers like Ayer, demonic influence seemed to be a plausible explanation for the erotic frenzy that overtook teenage girls at Elvis's concerts. Ayer insisted that this music was "alien to our culture" and would destroy America. He bemoaned the

34. Cusic, *Sound of Light,* 100-107, 116-119.

35. Brian Ward, *Just My Soul Responding: Rhythm and Blues, Black Consciousness, and Race Relations* (Berkeley: University of California Press, 1998), 44, 49-50, 136, 140.

36. Norman King, "Teen-Age Idol Worship," *YFCM* (March 1959): 6-7.

37. *This Fabulous Century, Vol. VI: 1950-1960* (New York: Time Life Books, 1970), 152-153, 197. The same source claims Boone was "one of the few to survive the transition from pop to rock."

fact that while Communist radio stations played the classics, Radio Free Europe broadcast the music of "confusion, savagery and hopelessness." But he did not comment on the absence of those same "classics" at Youth for Christ rallies. Ayer also denounced the commercial exploitation of young people by leaders of the expanding teen music industry. Warnings from many secular critics of rock music also contained the themes of racial prejudice, sexual danger, lawlessness, commercial exploitation, and Cold War competition.[38] But YFC leaders and other Evangelicals certainly had a hand in creating and popularizing such arguments.

It would be a mistake, however, to accept at face value the evangelicals' claim that rock 'n' roll was alien to their culture. In fact, it was precisely because it was so close to their culture, and yet produced such threatening effects, that it evoked such heated denunciations. Condemnations of the "jungle beat" did indicate a racist fear of the supposed emotional and sexual licentiousness of black culture. Yet white evangelicals betrayed a subtle ambivalence toward bodily and emotional ecstasy and the Africans who symbolized it. One anecdote that circulated widely in anti-rock presentations told of a missionary who had played first classical, then rock music records for a group of African tribesmen. They flew into a frenzy when they heard the rock beat and begged the missionary not to play this evil music any more. The moral of the story was that even black "savages" could be more "civilized" than white teenagers. Even more than they feared racial degeneracy, white Evangelicals feared that the ecstatic release found in rock music might successfully compete with religious emotion. Ayer concluded his tirade against rock with the warning that it might "even provide a carnal substitute for the joys and exaltations of the Holy Spirit's indwelling presence."[39]

38. William Ward Ayer, "Jungle Madness in American Music," *YFCM* (November 1956): 19-21. For similar arguments, see Marlin "Butch" Hardman, "Rock 'n' Roll: Music or Madness," *YFCM* (October 1958): 10-12; Marlin "Butch" Hardman, "The Real Scoop on Rock 'n' Roll," *YFCM* (October 1959): 10-12; and Ron Wilson, "Who *Did* Invent the Twist?" *YFCM* (July 1962): 7-8. For an insightful reading of the critics of rock, see George Lipsitz, "Land of a Thousand Dances: Youth, Minorities, and the Rise of Rock and Roll," in *Recasting America: Culture and Politics in the Age of Cold War*, ed. Lary May (Chicago: University of Chicago Press, 1989), 267-284.

39. For the missionary anecdote, see Bob Larson, *Rock and Roll: The Devil's Diversion* (McCook, NE: Bob Larson, 1970), 66, and Jay R. Howard and John M. Streck, *Apostles of Rock: The Splintered World of Contemporary Christian Music* (Lexington: University Press of Kentucky, 1999), 35. Ayer, "Jungle Madness," 21.

Although Ayer no doubt believed that this was a competition between opposites, the evidence suggests otherwise. The religious upbringings of performers like Elvis Presley and Jerry Lee Lewis are well known. That Lewis was the cousin of Pentecostal evangelist and gospel singer Jimmy Swaggart, who would later become a vigorous critic of "Christian rock," is a fact that symbolically illustrates the close personal and cultural connections between white gospel music and early rock 'n' roll. As a young performer, Elvis tried out for the Songfellows, a gospel quartet, but its leader Jim Hamill turned him down because of his inability to harmonize. Even after his commercial success, Elvis preferred to listen to southern gospel music. He also recorded gospel singles and albums and maintained warm personal friendships with some gospel performers. He confided to one such friend that he had originally modeled his appearance and performance style on southern gospel star Jake Hess of the Statesmen. J. D. Sumner, a member of two different quartets that had sung with Elvis later recalled, "southern gospel singers always wore flashy clothes, even back in the early 50s. And we had real long hair combed back before long hair ever came in style."[40] It is well known that the rock 'n' roll performed by Elvis and Lewis had its roots in both "rhythm and blues" and "hillbilly" styles. While music historians can define meaningful distinctions between black gospel and the blues and between southern gospel and "hillbilly" music, some religious audiences felt threatened by the stylistic similarities. It was probably for this reason that evangelical critics seized on the "jungle beat" of rock music as the locus of its evil nature. They needed such a clear stylistic marker to distinguish their increasingly pop influenced music from rock 'n' roll. Thus the performance styles and musical idioms of early rock music aroused a visceral reaction in evangelical Christians because they semi-consciously recognized it as the Mr. Hyde to their Dr. Jekyll musical culture.

Although they could not directly confront this family resemblance between rock 'n' roll and Christian youth music, evangelicals did consistently contrast the appeal of rock music with that of salvation and the lure of teenage "idols" with devotion to Jesus Christ. YFC teenagers were aware of Elvis's Christian background, and hoped he could be converted. Youth for Christ member Larry Nelson thought teens thronged to Elvis because he seemed to fulfill their desires for "a thrill," "a buddy," and "security."

40. Cusic, *Sound of Light*, 117-118.

Only Jesus could truly meet such needs, he argued. Marg Jones said of Elvis: "Watching gals 'moon' over a picture of his swinging body reminds me of their lost condition and my mind compares the picture with the heathen dances of darkest Africa." One anonymous teenager wrote of her disillusionment with Elvis, "The fact of the matter is, I've found something else that has given me more of a thrill than a hundred Presley's ever could! It's a new friendship with the most wonderful Person I've ever met, a Man who has given me happiness and thrills and something worth living for." Adults promoted such comparisons as well. Norman King wrote, the "teen-age 'idol' craze" is "never a problem to those who have really fallen in love with the Lord Jesus Christ!"[41] No doubt "mooning" over Elvis was a poor substitute for falling in love with Jesus, but the parallel revealed similarities as well as differences.

The repeated denunciations of rock 'n' roll suggest that not all Christian teenagers agreed. On rare occasions, teenage endorsements of rock even made it into YFC periodicals. In 1959, the monthly magazine of San Diego Youth for Christ printed a letter from teenage member LuAnn Gower, who wrote in response to an article that recommended activities for dates. As far as LuAnn was concerned, "a rock and roll dance is tops for dating." Yet as of 1969, Allentown, Pennsylvania YFC director John Blake was one of the few to admit that "many of the Christian young people here just love rock . . . and they can't wait to get home from church to turn it on."[42]

Reluctant Revolutionaries

In 1960, a full decade before they endorsed "Jesus rock," YFC leaders recognized that they needed new strategies to bolster the appeal of their rallies. Since the number of rallies had not grown since the mid 1950s, leaders be-

41. "Special Panel: What About Elvis Presley?" *YFCM* (November 1956): 18-19; "The Last Time I Saw Elvis," *YFCM* (March 1960): 4; Norman King, "Teen-Age Idol Worship," *YFCM* (March 1959): 6-7. For similar parallels between evangelical spirituality and the appeal of rock and rock stars, see Thurlow Spurr, "How to Build an Idol," *YFCM* (September 1960): 14-15; "Should Christians Be Fan Clubbers?" *YFCM* (June 1959): 18-19; Hardman "The Real Scoop on Rock 'n' Roll," 10-12; and "Is Rock 'n' Roll on the Way Out?" *YFCM* (March 1960): 14-15.

42. "Prefers Rock 'n' Roll," *Campus* (November 1959): 18. Interview with John Blake, 11 July 1969, in Horner, "Function of Music," 141-146.

came less apologetic about the appeal of entertainment. At a 1961 convention, Tedd Bryson told rally directors frankly, "don't be afraid to 'entertain' and give teens what they want."[43] The national office hired Thurlow Spurr to promote better music in the rallies. Spurr created a subscription service that provided monthly musical arrangements for brass and choir. Together with Carl Bihl he also issued a new songbook, *Youth for Christ Songs and Choruses.* This book included a slightly higher proportion of choruses than the 1948 songbook, and shortened many of the hymns to two verses or less. Bihl and Spurr did include a few recent songs by artists like Gloria Roe. But for the most part, they simply supplemented the older revival music that had dominated the 1948 songbook with a few gospel songs and choruses written in the 1940s and 1950s. This new songbook marked not the beginning, but the end of a musical era. Vocalist Flo Price, who performed at many Youth for Christ rallies, observed in 1969, "I've seen kids yawning halfway through 'Christ for Me' all across the country."[44]

In response, the most innovative rally directors and musicians began to experiment with folk and folk-rock styles and instrumentation. In Fresno, California, YFC director Larry Ballenger made some drastic changes around 1963. He sought out musical performers who could approximate the sound of The Association or Simon and Garfunkel. He realized that the "warm up music" used at the beginning of his rallies was for entertainment and audience participation, not for spiritual impact. He doubted that it was necessary or even appropriate to use Christian music for such purposes. "Let 'em sing 'Georgy Girl,'" he suggested. Significantly, he warned that "identification with music in the long run is going to slow us up in the communication of the message." For innovators like Ballenger, musical style and the message it could communicate were almost completely separable.[45] Thurlow Spurr agreed that in order to "win

43. For decline in the number of rallies, see Senter, "Youth for Christ Movement," 249 and "A Statistical Report of YFCI" in "Minutes, YFCI 9th Annual Mid-Winter Convention, January 7-10, 1964, Miami, Florida" (BGCA 48-13-17). For the call to be entertaining, see "YFCI 6th Annual Mid-Winter Hotel Convention, Los Angeles, California, January 1961," 18-19, 22-23 (BGCA 48-13-9).

44. "YFC Music Master — Thurlow Spurr," *YFC Eye* 1, no. 4 (April 1960): 1. "It Will Make Your Music Program Spin!" *YFC Eye* 1, no. 6 (September 1960): 17. Horner, "Function of Music," 212.

45. Interview with Larry Ballenger, 9 July 1969, in Horner, "Function of Music," 136-141.

the right to be heard" YFC musicians should use musical styles "popular today on records, television, commercials, motion pictures." He insisted that musical styles were "amoral" and that evangelicals had arbitrarily and incorrectly decided that God liked only one style of music. But Spurr did not start writing rock and roll tunes.[46] Still, the weight of opinion among YFC leaders seemed to be shifting.

A 1969 survey of leaders and musicians revealed that most of them endorsed folk and folk-rock styles as the most appealing to teenagers. While YFC directors most often used the hymns and gospel songs of revivalism, 88% of them also used folk music. The most innovative musical groups of the 1960s even performed non-Christian "problem" songs like the theme song from the film *The Valley of the Dolls* or "Who Will Answer" by Ed Ames. Ray Nickel and his folk group The New Creation performed the latter song and followed it with their own original song "God Will Answer."[47] Others like Paul Walberg formed traveling musical groups modeled on Up With People that presented a wholesome pop sound. Even when they could get away with using guitars and amplification, such groups often had to be careful about drums and rhythmic movement on stage. Walberg used strings to cover the rock beat of his songs as a way to please both old and young evangelicals. His group also alternated driving rock selections with quiet, meditative ballads in order to hold audience interest.[48] In Denver, YFC club and music director Ralph Fry used "up-tempo and heavy beat type music" in high school assemblies that he would never try in churches.[49]

In 1967, Ralph Carmichael addressed a national meeting of YFC leaders, warning them that "yesterday's progressive is usually the greatest deterrent to today's progress." He called on youth leaders to do some "market research" and insisted that any musical style could be adopted if it communicated the message clearly and was performed sincerely. Like some other musicians of his generation, he claimed to dislike folk and rock music. But he noted that "even the adult taste in music has become top-40 oriented." Transgressing his own distinction between evangelistic and worship music, he admitted that "the music that was used at the time

46. Interview with Thurlow Spurr, 15 July 1969, in Horner, "Function of Music," 194.

47. Horner, "Function of Music," 77-109, 176, 210.

48. Interview with Paul Walberg, 5 July 1969, in Horner, "Function of Music," 197-201.

49. Interview with Ralph Fry, 8 July 1969, in Horner, "Function of Music," 161.

of a person's conversion is ordinarily the music that he'll want to stay with and worship with unless there are some drastic changes." Thus he predicted that teenagers reached with the new folk-rock sound would eventually "want to worship to" that sound. As distressing as some might find that prospect, Carmichael took it philosophically. "It would shock the britches off the good saints of two or three hundred years ago if they got into one of our YFC meetings and heard us ripping through a couple of fast choruses of 'Do Lord,' 'Safe am I' [and] 'Happy Now'," he said.[50]

Two years later, at the national YFC convention, Walberg's World Action Singers had to cut their broadway and pop medlies from the program. YFC leaders defended their decision by saying that this was a meeting of Christians, not an evangelistic gathering. "If there's not going to be any non-Christian kids in the meeting, why do they have invitations?" Walberg asked.[51] The distinction between evangelistic meetings and church worship, which had never been sharp, was disintegrating. Such resistance marked a rearguard action against the musical tastes that Youth for Christ leaders had themselves helped to create. As early as 1970, the national YFC office began sponsoring traveling folk-rock groups with names like Under New Management, Random Sample, Young and Free, and Soul Concern.[52]

Ralph Carmichael's 1969 songbook, *He's Everything to Me Plus 53* reflected and furthered these trends. Unlike even *Youth for Christ Songs and Choruses* of 1960, Carmichael's book included almost no revival music classics. Instead, contemporary compositions by Kurt Kaiser, Flo Price, and Carmichael predominated, with a smattering of spirituals and a handful of classic hymns like "Amazing Grace" and "Be Thou My Vision" thrown in. Very few of the songs or hymns contained more than two verses, most were just choruses. Less a classic collection than a way to distribute the latest songs, this book pointed to a future in which "contemporary" would be an increasingly common adjective used to describe Christian worship music.

The title song "He's Everything to Me" and another by Carmichael entitled "I Looked for Love" became especially popular with Youth for

50. Horner, "Function of Music," 222-226.

51. "Paul Walberg on Psychological Pacing and Commentary on the Modified Concert Performance for Youth for Christ International," 5 July 1969, in Horner, "Function of Music," 201-202.

52. Promotional materials for these groups can be found in BGCA 48-19-22.

Christ audiences. These and similar songs subtly shifted the way in which young people expressed their loving relationship with Jesus. Revival hymns and gospel songs had often spoken of loving intimacy with the Savior, using texts like this one from "In the Garden":

> And He walks with me,
> And He talks with me,
> And He tells me I am His own,
> And the Joy we share as we tarry there,
> None other has ever known.

In Carmichael's "I Looked for Love," the believer's encounter with Jesus paralleled the teenager's search for a boyfriend or girlfriend. After recounting her search for love in nature, in "a friendly face" and in "a creed I once knew," the singer concludes:

> And then one day I heard the story of love like I'd never known,
> How God gave His Son to save me and wanted me for His own,
> His own, His very own.
> And now I know what it means to belong,
> Not lost in a crowd swept along by the throng,
> But to Him who gave His life
> Every longing to fulfill
> And I know that He loves me and He always will.[53]

Similarly, at the 1968 YFC convention, one male crooner sang a song with a chorus that included the line "I'm in love with Jesus."[54] Such music paved the way for the love songs to Jesus that would appear in later decades. Teenagers found such songs appealing in part because they resonated with the established musical language of romantic love found in popular culture.

53. Ralph Carmichael, ed., *He's Everything to Me Plus 53* (Waco, TX: Lexicon Music, Inc., 1969).

54. Tape recording of Youth for Christ Convention, 1968 (BGCA 48-T17).

Conclusion: It's Got a Nice Beat, Easy to Worship to, I Give it an Eight

Sometimes presented as the commercial vulgarization of Protestant hymnody, the transformation outlined in this chapter also reflected a powerful stream of popular religious sentiment. Just as the Catholic papacy endorsed devotional practices in the nineteenth century as a way to bolster church loyalty, some twentieth-century Protestants set aside their personal distaste for pop music in order to attract the young. Similarly, a few recent authors have challenged the received interpretation of 1960s "soul" music that dismissed it as a sell out to white commercial interests. Without denying the process of commercial exploitation, these authors argue that soul music also functioned as a resource for collective racial and political identity formation within the black community.[55] In each of these cases, intellectual and artistic elites have typically dismissed popular tastes as theologically, socially, or politically enervating.

Yet if soul music may be read as a crucible of popular resistance that paralleled the ideas and activities of civil rights leaders, then perhaps gospel pop may also have something significant to tell us about popular religious sentiments among the white middle class. The fact of the matter is that the "great hymns of the church" had never dominated the worship of American Protestantism, particularly its revivalist branch. Church music experts fought to elevate the musical tastes of rank and file American Protestants, but like their counterparts in other "highbrow" vs. "lowbrow" battles, they only succeeded in creating a cultural enclave of their own. Despite their protestations of theological purity and sophistication, such traditionalists also functioned within a matrix of influences that included commerce, class, and musical trends. The highbrow modern hymn "God of Outer Space" has not endured any better than "He's Everything to Me."

In fact, to settle for the common aesthetic objection that only "great" music endures is to miss some of the deeper changes wrought by gospel pop. Much like earlier revivalists, the musical innovators of Youth for Christ updated their musical language to communicate more effectively to their

55. For the Catholic case, see Ann Taves, *Household of Faith: Roman Catholic Devotions in Mid-Nineteenth-Century America* (Notre Dame, IN: University of Notre Dame Press, 1986). For soul music, see Mark Anthony Neal, *What the Music Said: Black Popular Music and Black Public Culture* (New York: Routledge, 1999).

audience. Instead of the familial metaphors that predominated in the revival hymns popularized by Moody and Sankey, the new music of revivalism used the erotic metaphors of the teenage dating culture. Instead of calling the sinner to "come home" the new music described the delights of falling in love with Jesus.[56] In both cases, these metaphors worked because they resonated both with the revival tradition *and* with popular culture. Even where the lyrics remained similar to those of earlier revival favorites, the new musical idiom helped recontextualize the experience of Jesus' love for those who sang these songs. But the new revivalism went further than its predecessors in abandoning the classical criteria for "great" worship music. To accuse the new music of being short-lived is to miss the point. Gospel pop songs do not need to endure, because for their enthusiasts, the best music is always the latest. Instead of changing every fifty to one hundred years, the popular musical tastes of revivalism now change by the decade, if not faster.

The rise of gospel pop also revealed a popular redefinition of the emotions deemed proper in worship. Reverence, contrition, and perhaps a subdued sense of exaltation had been the only approved emotions in Protestant worship. Even fundamentalists and evangelicals, whose actual experiences of worship could be quite different, firmly held to this ideal in theory, often resorting to the artificial distinction between worship and evangelism in order to protect it. But the new music demonstrated that exuberant excitement and other "thrills" could be a legitimate part of worship. While traditionalists tried to induce reverence by making church music as different from popular fare as possible, evangelical teenagers tried to make worship more fun than a school dance. Just as Elvis popularized elements of black culture among white middle-class teenagers, gospel pop functioned as an emotional "cover" that allowed the ecstatic release found in black, Pentecostal, and holiness spiritualities to reenter the world of white evangelical restraint. Theological judgments will necessarily vary regarding how faithfully this music communicated the essence of the Christian faith. All such judgments, however, should take into account the possibility that on a human level, the sentimental idealization of romantic relationships, the erotic frenzy provoked by Elvis and the Beatles, and the "thrill" of singing gospel pop all met similar important needs for millions of young Americans that other aspects of their lives did not satisfy.

56. Sandra S. Sizer, *Gospel Hymns and Social Religion: The Rhetoric of Nineteenth-Century Revivalism* (Philadelphia: Temple University Press, 1978).

CHAPTER SEVEN

Protestant Hymnody in Contemporary Roman Catholic Worship

Felicia Piscitelli

This chapter assesses the prevalence of Protestant hymns in Roman Catholic publications printed between 1959 — the year in which Pope John XXIII issued a mandate for the Second Vatican Council — to the present; and then examines the use of these hymns in Catholic contexts. The term "Protestant" refers to non-Roman Catholic churches within Western Christianity, with the understanding that this broad definition encompasses denominations whose doctrines and liturgy come very close to those of Catholicism, as well as traditions whose beliefs and practices are quite different from it.

Historical Background

The *Armed Forces Hymnal* which was published in the late 1950s or early 1960s, offers a telling glimpse about relations between Protestants and Catholics and their respective hymnodies at that time.[1] The book is divided into three distinct sections, Catholic, Jewish, and Protestant. The Protestant section is the largest by far, with roughly three hundred musical numbers — hymns, service music, and Anglican chants. The small

1. *Armed Forces Hymnal,* published under supervision of the Armed Forces Chaplains Board (Washington, DC: U.S. Government Printing Office, [no date]). The other hymnals mentioned in the text are cited in Appendix II.

Catholic section contains a simple plainchant setting of the Mass[2] plus thirty-six hymns. The Mass (the *Missa de Angelis,* or Mass of the Angels) and nine of the hymns are in Latin; three hymns are bilingual (English and Latin), and the rest are in English. (The Jewish section is also relatively small; its texts and hymns in Hebrew are written in the English alphabet with phonetic spellings.) The compilers did not anticipate much crossover between the two Christian traditions, for each has its own rendition of "O come, O come, Emmanuel," "O sacred head, surrounded/O sacred head, now wounded," and "Ye sons and daughters of the Lord/O sons and daughters, let us sing." The tunes of the first and third of these hymns are notated as chants in their Catholic versions, while they appear in modern time signatures and four-part harmony in their Protestant forms. "Faith of our fathers," "Silent night" and "Angels we have heard on high" appear in both sections. Another Christmas hymn is given in Latin in the Catholic section ("Adeste fideles") and in English in the Protestant one ("O come, all ye faithful"). Four decades ago, hardly anyone would have expected to find "A mighty fortress is our God" in any Roman Catholic hymnal. Yet even then a few other Protestant hymns, such as "Praise to the Lord, the Almighty," "Now thank we all our God," and "Holy, holy, holy! Lord God Almighty," were gaining popularity among Catholics.

Today Martin Luther's rousing composition appears quite regularly in Catholic publications, though usually with some alterations. The other three hymns just named are so widely adopted that they are often thought of as "traditional Catholic hymns," in much the same category as "Holy God, we praise thy name" and "Faith of our fathers," which are Catholic in origin. Due to its popularity and to the similarity of its text to the Sanctus, "Holy, holy, holy! Lord God Almighty" has been fashioned into a piece of service music.[3] Another Protestant hymn, "Abide with me," was Mother Teresa's favorite; it was sung at her funeral a few years ago.[4] Some contemporary non-Catholic hymn writers also enjoy considerable popularity in Catholic circles, including Fred Pratt Green, Timothy Dudley-Smith, Fred

2. Many present-day writers leave the word "Mass" uncapitalized. I prefer to capitalize the term for the Roman Catholic and Anglican Eucharistic service in order to distinguish it from non-religious meanings (i.e., mass media, atomic mass, etc.).

3. Owen Alstott, "Holy, Holy," from *Heritage Mass* (Portland, OR: OCP Publications, 1978).

4. George William Rutler, *Brightest and Best: Stories of Hymns* (San Francisco: Ignatius Press, 1998), 165.

Kaan, Brian Wren, and Marty Haugen. Even the recent *Adoremus Hymnal*, whose editors seek to restore and uphold Catholic traditions, includes texts by Isaac Watts, Charles Wesley, and other Protestant authors. By the same token, current Protestant hymnals are likely to include material written by Catholic authors and composers.

What caused this about-face? Despite appearances, the inclusion of Protestant hymns in Catholic collections, and vice versa, is not really a new phenomenon. In 1537 — during the Reformation itself — Michael Vehe put Lutheran compositions into his Catholic songbook.[5] The earliest music collection for English-speaking Roman Catholics in what is now the United States contained pieces by Protestants George Frideric Handel, Nahum Tate and Nicholas Brady, and Francis Hopkinson.[6] Borrowing occurred from the opposite direction, too. A sizable number of hymns in German and English are, in fact, translations or paraphrases of Latin texts (compare "Komm, Gott schöpfer, heiliger Geist" with "Veni, creator spiritus," or "Savior of the nations come" with "Veni, Redemptor gentium"). The Oxford or "High Church" Movement, which sought to restore elements of early Christianity to the Church of England in the nineteenth century, was particularly important in producing and disseminating such translations. John Mason Neale, Thomas Helmore, and Edward Caswall were a few of the hymn writers and translators associated with this movement. What the different situations sketched in the previous paragraphs show is the tremendous growth of congregational hymnody in vernacular languages and the spirit of ecumenical cooperation that have come about in response to the Second Vatican Council (Vatican II), which met from 1962 to 1965.

The Council brought to fruition reforms that many Catholics had sought for decades. These reforms include the increased involvement of all the faithful in the life of the church; a renewed emphasis on Scripture; an invigorated sense of the church's mission in the world; more active congregational participation; worship in languages other than Latin; and

5. Friedrich Blume, *Protestant Church Music: A History* (New York: W. W. Norton, 1974), 21, 47.

6. John Aitken, *A Compilation of the Litanies and Vespers, Hymns and Anthems As They Are Sung in the Catholic Church Adapted to the Voice or Organ* (Philadelphia: J. Aitken, 1787-1788; available as microfiche). For an analysis of this collection, see Robert R. Grimes, "John Aitken and Catholic Music in Federal Philadelphia," *American Music* 16, no. 3 (1998): 289-310. A small collection tacked onto the end of a prayerbook, *A Manual of Catholic Prayers* (Philadelphia: Robert Bell, 1774), contains the words (no music) to twenty-four pieces that appeared later in Aitken.

greater dialogue with Christians of other traditions. Vatican II did not originate all of these renovations, as many believe; rather, it served as a catalyst bringing together numerous developments and movements toward church reform that were already underway.

The implementation of everyday living languages in Roman Catholic worship was astonishingly rapid and pervasive. Within only a few years, Latin became a rarity, even though the Second Vatican Council's *Constitution on the Sacred Liturgy* called for the retention of Latin at the same time it permitted the use of the vernacular.[7] In contrast, the switch from Latin to German in the Lutheran liturgy during the Reformation was much slower. At first, German was used only in songs; Latin continued to be used for strictly liturgical texts, in varying degrees, until well into the eighteenth century.[8] The drive to adopt vernacular languages after Vatican II created an immediate need for new texts and, thus, for new music. In tandem with these developments, an explosion of new compositions based on biblical and liturgical texts, frequently written in popular music styles, began in the 1960s and continues to the present.

The fact that Protestants already possessed hundreds of texts in English, set to music that is easy for congregations to sing and mostly in the public domain, proved to be a boon to Catholicism. In addition to their singability, many Protestant hymns express beliefs and doctrines shared by all Christians — Catholics, Eastern Orthodox, and Protestants alike. One Catholic hymn writer, Omer Westendorf, wrote, "a great portion of the Protestant hymns were more Catholic in doctrine than were the Catholic hymns in current use at the time."[9] This is especially true of hymns

7. *Constitution on the Sacred Liturgy* (1963), articles 36, 54, 63, 101. This document is available in *Vatican II: The Conciliar and Postconciliar Documents,* ed. Austin Flannery (Collegeville, MN: Liturgical Press, 1983); *The Liturgy Documents: A Parish Resource,* 3rd ed. (Chicago: Liturgy Training Publications, 1991); and on the World Wide Web. Contrary to popular belief, it is not the Latin language itself but, rather, the use of the Tridentine rite according to the 1962 Missal — as opposed to the current revised rite promulgated in 1970, celebrated in Latin — that requires special indult (permission) from the local bishop. However, many people confuse the "Latin Mass" with the older rite by equating the two.

8. Blume, *Protestant Church Music,* 167.

9. Omer Westendorf, *Music Lessons for the Man in the Pew* (Cincinnati, OH: World Library of Sacred Music, 1965), 66. Sometimes using the pen names Mark Evans, Paul Francis, or J. Clifford Evers, Westendorf wrote several useful hymns, including "Where charity and love prevail," "You satisfy the hungry heart with (gift of finest wheat)," and "God's blessing send us forth."

from communions such as Anglicanism (including the Church of England and the Episcopal Church) and Lutheranism which, like Catholicism, have strong liturgical and sacramental emphases.

Although the compilers and editors of Catholic hymnals include quite a few hymns from non-liturgical and evangelical traditions, they tend to be more cautious with them due to differences either in doctrine itself or in its interpretation, or even the way in which a teaching is promulgated. To illustrate the latter point, all Christians believe both in having a personal relationship with Christ and in worshiping as a community. Evangelicalism, however, places particular stress on the one-on-one relationship. To judge from its hymnody, this personal emphasis appears even in public worship. Catholicism, on the other hand, is apt to place greater stress on the communal aspect of worship. When the faithful come together at Mass, they join not only with each other but also with the communion of saints and even the choirs of angels in prayer and praise. One's personal friendship with Christ is further cultivated and enriched outside of Mass through private prayer, Bible study, service to the community, inspirational reading, and such devotional exercises as the recitation of the rosary or Adoration of the Blessed Sacrament. Therefore, highly subjective evangelical hymns like "I Come to the Garden Alone" are rare in Catholic publications. Where they do occur, they seem to have more of a devotional character rather than a liturgical one. Catholicism also differs from certain non-liturgical churches in their respective views on the Second Coming; hymns that spoke of the rapture of the church or that had a strong dispensationalist focus would not be used in Catholic services. (A similar process is at work when Protestant hymnal compilers avoid Catholic hymns emphasizing the Real Presence of Christ in the Eucharist or the Mass as a sacrifice, or those honoring Mary or other saints.)

In 1955 Omer Westendorf, who then owned the World Library of Sacred Music in Cincinnati (the firm is now part of the Chicago-based J. S. Paluch Company), brought out *The People's Hymnal,* which included a number of Protestant (and Catholic) hymns that subsequently became widely used by Catholics. In 1964, while Vatican II was still in session, a new edition of this hymnal was issued as *People's Mass Book;* it incorporated "A mighty fortress" (justified by Westendorf as a paraphrase of Psalm 45 [46])[10] and a few African-American pieces. Inspired by the growth of ecu-

10. Westendorf, *Music Lessons,* 68-69.

menism, Clifford A. Bennett and Paul Hume put out the *Hymnal of Christian Unity* that same year. (Hume, a noted music critic and radio personality, was a convert to Catholicism.) Most of the major Catholic hymnals and missals[11] issued since Vatican II, excluding publications devoted mainly to contemporary liturgical songs, but including the conservative *Adoremus Hymnal,* make use of a large number of hymns of Protestant origin.

At various times throughout history, Catholics have sought what could be called an "evangelical" approach to their faith through more personal relationships with Christ, more informal yet intimate worship services, the formation of lay Christian communities, and greater emphasis on proclaiming the gospel to the world. This approach, which has intensified in recent years, is illustrated in various publications[12] and in the Cursillo and the charismatic or Neo-Pentecostal movements. The ecumenical charismatic movement in particular places a high value on lively congregational singing, and it has contributed a small body of contemporary worship songs. John Bell, Betty Pulkingham, Mimi Farra, and Kathleen Thomerson are a few non-Catholic hymn writers influencing current Catholic hymn singing. There also seems to be increasing interest among Catholics in music having an evangelical background or orientation, including "contemporary Christian" songs (as distinguished from compositions intended for strictly liturgical use, such as settings of the Mass, in contemporary popular styles). *Gathering to Praise* (see Appendix II) was an early attempt to bring evangelical "contemporary Christian" music to a Catholic audience, but it enjoyed only partial success. "Contemporary Christian" music is more popular today than it was in the early 1980s, and publications geared toward youth are making

11. A missal is a "Mass book," containing the order of service, biblical readings, and prayers, arranged in order of the liturgical calendar, for the main service of the Roman Catholic church. Small, easy-to-follow missals, often containing commentary, additional prayers for private devotion, and even illustrations, were issued a few decades before the Second Vatican Council to help worshipers follow the Mass, at that time still in Latin. During the years of rapid liturgical change, cheaply printed "missalettes" became popular. These are intended to be used for a specific period of time (a month, liturgical season, or even a year), and then discarded. Since Vatican II many missals and missalettes have also included hymns, with or without music.

12. See, for example, Albert Boudreau, *The Born-again Catholic* (Locust Valley, NY: Living Flame Books, 1980); Keith Fournier, *A House United: Evangelicals and Catholics Together* (Colorado Springs: NavPress, 1994); and "Evangelicals and Catholics Together: The Christian Mission in the Third Millenium," *First Things* 43 (1994): 15-22.

more use of it (for instance, *Spirit and Song*, a new publication cited in Appendix II).

The Uses of Hymns in Roman Catholic Worship

Roman Catholicism has an enormous repertoire of hymns, sequences, antiphons, and other compositions in Latin spanning nearly two millennia. Hymns were, and are, important in the Divine Office, often called the Liturgy of the Hours, a daily cycle of prayer and psalmody at specified times of the day. These Hours are observed especially in religious communities (i.e., monasteries, convents, abbeys, etc.) and in cathedral churches (a cathedral being a church where a bishop has his headquarters). The best known and most elaborate of the Hours are Lauds (Morning Prayer) and Vespers (Evening Prayer). A large number of English hymns translated from the Latin originated as Office hymns, "O come, O come, Emmanuel" being one famous example. In recent years the church has promoted Morning and Evening Prayer even at parish (neighborhood) churches; and the editors and publishers of hymnals usually include orders of service for this purpose. Both a modern Office book, *Christian Prayer* (see Appendix II) and the *Hymnal of the Hours* (edited by Andrew Ciferni [Chicago: G.I.A. Publications, 1989]), contain hymns, both Catholic and Protestant in origin, for use in the Liturgy of the Hours.

Traditionally, hymnody plays a secondary role in the Mass, the main public worship service of the Catholic Church. To be sure, a televised broadcast of a Mass from the Vatican will present a good deal of singing, some of it even coming from the congregation — chants, psalms, antiphons, responses, the Pater Noster ("Our Father" — the Lord's Prayer), and special pieces for the choir. However, relatively few of these songs correspond to what English-speaking people would call hymns. During the first half of the twentieth century, when proponents of liturgical reform advocated increased congregational participation, they generally envisioned that the faithful would join in singing responses — e.g., "Et cum spiritu tuo" ("And also with you)" in response to the priest's "Dominum vobiscum" ("The Lord be with you"); also Amens at the ends of prayers. They also promoted the congregational singing of the standard texts that are used in all Masses, collectively called the Ordinary: the Kyrie (Lord, Have Mercy), Gloria (Glory to God in the highest), Credo (the Nicene

Creed, also called the Profession of Faith), Sanctus (Holy, Holy, Holy), and Agnus Dei (Lamb of God). Even now, liturgical experts emphasize that Catholic congregations should sing *the* Mass, not sing *at* Mass. Today they urge worshipers to sing especially acclamations, such as the Alleluia before the reading of the Gospel; the antiphons or refrains of responsorial psalms, and the shorter texts of the Ordinary, particularly the Sanctus. The people may sing other parts of the Mass like the Gloria, Agnus Dei, Lord's Prayer, etc., if desired.

Hymns or hymn-like vocal forms in vernacular languages, such as carols, Italian *laudi spirituali,* German Lieder, etc., have existed since the late Middle Ages. These vernacular songs were generally used outside the liturgy, in processions, mystery plays, para-liturgical devotions, even in the home and at Catholic schools. For instance, "At the cross her station keeping" (the *Stabat Mater*), a traditional Catholic hymn, is customarily sung at Stations of the Cross, a devotional service especially popular during Lent and Holy Week; usually one verse is sung per station. Participants might open the service with "O sacred head, surrounded" or "Were you there when they crucified my Lord?" The latter illustrates how a Protestant hymn can be adopted for Catholic devotional use.

Even though hymns in general, especially hymns in languages other than Latin, were usually outside the scope of the preconciliar Mass, traditions of vernacular hymn singing at Mass existed long before the Second Vatican Council, particularly in certain German- and Slavic-speaking areas. One German tradition that came to America with Catholic immigrants in the nineteenth century was the *Singmesse* or *Betsingmesse* ("pray-sing-Mass"), at which the priest quietly recited the Latin texts while the congregation sang short, catchy hymns in the vernacular paraphrasing or commenting on the action taking place in the service. To what extent the *Singmesse* may have influenced later liturgical development is a topic for further research.

A more recent custom directly affecting present-day Catholic musical practice is the insertion of hymns at certain points during a "low Mass" (i.e., a Mass at which most or all of the texts are spoken, as opposed to the sung or "high" Mass), when there is relatively little action at the altar. These points, the Introit, Offertory, and Communion antiphons, are part of the Propers, that is, the parts of the Mass that change from one celebration to the next. The Roman Missal specifies appropriate antiphons, typically verses taken from the Psalms or other biblical texts, for each Mass of the liturgical calendar. In practice, the singing of hymns at these times has taken the place of singing or reciting the antiphons (however, the antiphons are recited at Masses having no music, such as those celebrated on weekdays). It has become common in many (if not most) American parishes for the congregation to sing a recessional hymn as people leave the church. The liturgy formally closes with the dismissal ("The Mass is ended. Go in peace," or "Ite, missa est"), and the recessional follows. Technically, then, the recessional hymn is outside the liturgy proper. The singing of hymns at the Entrance, Offertory, Communion, and Recessional constitutes what liturgists often disparage as the "four-hymn syndrome," particularly when hymns are sung instead of the preferred acclamations and other liturgical texts of the Mass. Nonetheless, this pattern of singing three or four hymns, perhaps with some of the Mass parts named in a previous paragraph, is widespread. Quite a few of the hymns sung come from Protestantism.

Even though hymns are secondary to the Scriptures and texts of the liturgy itself in importance, they should nevertheless be appropriate to the liturgy in which they are used. When choosing hymns, a liturgically astute music director takes into account the liturgical calendar, the scriptural readings for that particular service, where in the service a certain hymn stands in relation to liturgical action, and, in a more general way, the "themes" of both the liturgy and the hymns under consideration. A hymn may be selected because its text is suitable for a particular season of the liturgical year — Advent, Christmas (which includes the feast of the Epiphany), Lent, Easter Triduum (consisting of Holy Thursday, Good Friday, and Holy Saturday), Easter Season, and Ordinary Time. Thus, "Come, thou long-expected Jesus," with its tone of expectation and hope, is used during Advent, while the penitential character of "Have mercy, Lord, on me" matches that of Lent. Music could also be chosen for a specific feast or fast day, for instance, "Hail the day that sees Him rise" for the Feast of the Ascension. Frequently hymns correspond to particular parts of the service. "Holy, holy, holy! Lord, God Almighty" is a favorite entrance hymn for the long season of Ordinary Time (as well as for Trinity Sunday), while "Now thank we all our God" is a classic recessional. Also, liturgical musicians try to match the texts of hymns with the Scripture readings even for "regular" Masses, for this effort helps in achieving harmony within the liturgy among the readings, the homily (which is based on the readings), and the music.

Unlike other denominations, Roman Catholics in the United States have never had an official, standard hymnal mandated by the United States Conference of Catholic Bishops, which has the authority to establish such a national musical repertoire, either before or after the Second Vatican Council. To some degree this is due to the secondary function of hymns in the Mass. Another reason is that church music, including hymnody, is under less ecclesiastical control than the texts of the liturgy itself, and even translations of the Bible; these latter are subject to the bishops' approval and regulation. *Music in Catholic Worship,* the most important document issued by the American bishops concerning church music in the postconciliar era, makes recommendations for good liturgical practices. Yet, it is worded very broadly in order to accommodate the highly divergent needs of an enormous church. At the time of this writing an American Catholic parish may select from nearly two dozen hymnals, music issues, or missalettes from several different publishers. It also has the option of compiling its own collection of music if people are available who are willing to undertake such a project.

Protestant Hymn Tunes in Catholic Hymnals

So far this discussion has focused on texts. It is worth at least mentioning the importance of Protestant hymn tunes — perhaps with new texts — in today's Catholic hymnody. Tunes from early American or Southern shape-note collections like HOLY MANNA, RESIGNATION, CONSOLATION, NETTLETON, and BEACH SPRING crop up quite frequently. "God of day and God of darkness" by Marty Haugen, sung to BEACH SPRING, is a well-known example of a new text with an old tune. At least one Catholic composer, the relatively little known Henry Bryan Hays (b. 1920), had his Southern Protestant background in mind when he wrote the tunes in his collection, *The Swayed Pines Songbook*. The melodies have much of the angular strength of shape-note tunes.[13] The Shaker tune SIMPLE GIFTS and the erroneously named QUAKER HYMN are surprisingly popular among Catholics.

13. Henry Bryan Hays, *The Swayed Pines Songbook* (Collegeville, MN: Liturgical Press, 1981). Part of the contents of this book is incorporated in the *Collegeville Hymnal,* listed in Appendix II.

The ecumenical but mainly Protestant monastic community in Taizé, France has evolved a style of simple, austere, yet beautiful music for worship consisting of short refrains, ostinatos, or rounds that are repeated numerous times. Either small or large groups may sing this music. Some of the texts are in Latin: because thousands of pilgrims visit Taizé from all over the world, it was felt that a politically neutral language like Latin would help in unifying prayer among speakers of different languages. Several current Catholic hymnals include examples of music from Taizé.

Methodology

In order to determine how many of the hymns appearing in contemporary Roman Catholic hymnals are Protestant in origin, I created a database in which I indexed the contents of sixty-seven Roman Catholic hymn collections, including hymnals, songbooks, prayer books, and missals, representing a broad spectrum of musical styles and publishers. (These books are cited in Appendix II.) Hymn sections in missals and prayer books are particularly interesting, since these usually represent a "core" repertoire of familiar pieces. Most of these publications were selected from a bibliography I have prepared of Catholic hymnals published during and after the Second Vatican Council.[14] However, I included two from the immediate preconciliar period (*Our Parish Prays and Sings*, 1959 and *People's Hymnal*, 2nd ed., 1961), since these two collections were quite influential in shaping the subsequent development of Catholic church music. I also incorporated the contents of a few collections published since my bibliography came out, and a recent book of hymn stories intended for Catholic readers, written by a former Episcopalian, which reflects the author's memory of the *Hymnal 1940*.[15] To avoid unnecessary duplication, some editions of certain hymnals were not indexed. Collections devoted to one author, composer, or performing group, or intended for use by specific parishes or religious communities were omitted. Likewise omitted were collections whose content is solely or primarily in languages other than English. However,

14. Felicia Piscitelli, "Thirty-Five Years of Catholic Hymnals in the United States (1962-1997): A Chronological Listing," *The Hymn* 49 (Oct. 1998): 21-34.

15. Rutler, *Brightest and Best*.

certain hymns in Latin do appear in otherwise English-language publications. These are significant in Catholic worship and were, therefore, counted the same as titles in English.

For this chapter, I extracted a list of titles from my database and compared it to the list of the most-published Protestant hymns provided by Stephen Marini for the Institute for the Study of American Evangelicalism (ISAE) (Appendix I) and to another list of Hymns and Tunes Recommended for Ecumenical Use, prepared by the Consultation on Ecumenical Hymnody (CEH) (Appendix II).[16] In my initial thinking, I postulated that there would be a strong overlap between my Catholic database and the Ecumenical list, and a weaker correspondence between the Catholic database and the ISAE-Marini list. My reasoning was based on the knowledge that the hymnals consulted for the compilation of the Ecumenical list included at least one Roman Catholic hymnal *(Worship II)* as well as hymnals from liturgically-oriented and "mainline" Protestant churches. Such a list was more likely to suit Roman Catholic worship than a list of predominantly Evangelical hymnody. My hunch about the different levels of correspondence between my Catholic database and the Ecumenical list, versus that between the Catholic database and the ISAE-Marini list, was correct. The percentages proved wrong, however. In my first estimate, I guessed that 50% of the ecumenical titles and 20% of the evangelical ones would show on my list. In reality, the percentage of hymns from the Ecumenical list appearing in my database is greater than I had anticipated. I also expected a somewhat higher percentage of evangelical hymns to appear in collections geared toward Catholics having a bent toward evangelical forms of piety or expression, such as African-Americans and charismatics. As a matter of fact, several of the titles on the ISAE-Marini list that appeared only once or twice in the Catholic database were in *Lead Me, Guide Me: The African-American Catholic Hymnal.* By the same token, other titles on the ISAE-Marini list appeared solely in other hymnals, like *The Catholic Hymnal* (1974) and consciously ecumenical *Collegeville Hymnal, Vatican II Hymnal,* or *Worship: The Third Edition.* The extent of evangelical/charis-

16. This list taken from James R. Sydnor, *Hymns: A Congregational Study,* student ed. (Carol Stream, IL: Agape, 1983), 70-74. It is also published in the October 1977 issue of *The Hymn.* For a recent critique of this list of ecumenical hymns, see C. Michael Hawn, "The Consultation on Ecumenical Hymnody: An Evaluation of its Influence in Selected English Language Hymnals Published in the United States and Canada Since 1976," *The Hymn* 47, no. 2 (April 1996): 26-37.

matic interaction cannot be determined from the database, largely because much of the charismatic repertory itself is recent, and because it seems to adopt mainly newly composed material.

The Most Frequently Published Hymns in Catholic Hymnals

Since I had selected sixty-seven titles to index, I determined that hymns having seven or more "hits" in my database would make up a list of the Most Frequently Published Hymns in Catholic Hymnals (see Appendix I and III) corresponding to the top 10 percent of my database. Seven is a good number because it avoids placing too much weight on, say, four or five very recent publications. The result is a list that spans four decades. I went through the list, consulting reference sources and companion books to several denominational hymnals (as well as my previous knowledge) and determined which of these titles are by non-Catholic authors and translators; these I have indicated with an asterisk in Appendix III.

Readers should note that the popularity of a given hymn or the extent of its usage might or might not correspond to the frequency of its publication or appearance in hymnals. For instance, since my "most frequently published" Catholic list spans nearly four decades, a much-used contemporary song may not even appear on it. Some of the publications indexed consist solely of pieces composed after the Second Vatican Council; as a result, none of the hymns in either list appeared more than fifty times in the database. Also, because of the church's strong emphasis on matching hymns to the liturgical year and to particular liturgical uses, a given hymn may appear in most Catholic hymnals and thus receive a high ranking on the "most published" list, but its actual use mostly corresponds to certain times of the year or even to specific days (i.e., "Lord, who throughout these forty days" for the season of Lent; "As with gladness men of old" for the feast of the Epiphany; etc.). Patriotic numbers such as "The Star-spangled Banner," "My country, 'tis of thee," and "O beautiful, for spacious skies" are another category of pieces whose limited use contrasts with their rather high rankings in Appendix III.

Conclusion

My initial conviction that some Protestant hymns will appear repeatedly in Catholic hymnals, to the extent that they can be considered "regular Catholic hymns" whether or not they are of Catholic origin, turns out in fact to be correct. Yet even the hymns in the Marini list, issued by the ISAE, though less prevalent in Catholic hymnals on the whole, nevertheless show that today's Roman Catholics are greatly indebted to their fellow Christians in Protestant churches for a substantial portion of the hymns they sing.

CHAPTER EIGHT

White Folks "Get Happy": Mainstream America Discovers the Black Gospel Tradition

Virginia Lieson Brereton

Studs Terkel's memoir, *Talking to Myself,* includes a section called "Mahalia," in which he recalls his friendship with the great gospel singer, Mahalia Jackson. Terkel was an early fan of Jackson's, and in fact her appearances on his show increased her visibility in Chicago and contributed to the creation of her international reputation. Later, at her request, he was to serve as writer for a program she produced on Chicago television. Like most white observers who admired gospel singers, Terkel was exceedingly conscious of her physical presence, and perceived it to be a crucial part of her musical and religious expression. On one occasion especially he found himself watching her hands: "Her hands are clasped on the table. They are delicate, graceful hands. Not dainty, not soft. The calluses are eloquently there. She has scrubbed floors of other people's parlors." She told him, he recalled: "You got to work with your hands. All artists should work with their hands. How can you sing of Amazing Grace, how can you sing prayerfully of heaven and earth and all God's wonders without using your hands? My hands demonstrate what I feel like inside. My hands, my feet. I throw my whole body to say all that is within me. The mind and the voice by themselves are not sufficient." This is prelude to the part of Terkel's account that really fascinates me. One day, he recalled, Jackson talked about how much she had loved Bessie Smith as a girl and how she had imitated her — "before I was saved," as she put it, with a teasing glance at Terkel. Terkel goes on:

> Uh oh, I know what's coming. And she knows I know. "An' I'm gonna save you, too, Studs." It isn't the first time she offers this challenge; nor is it the last. It is to become our Chautauqua debate: believer versus atheist. The studio audience at her radio programs, during the warm-up, have come to delight in this theological dispute, knowing quite well who will come off the laughing winner. I always lose. Don't misunderstand. I have never in my life thrown a match of this nature. I am, in this instance, pitifully overmatched. All my [atheist] Bob Ingersoll arguments are demolished in her soaring song. And her humor.[1]

What is going on here? This is hardly a simple encounter, or a one-time occurrence. Terkel pays Jackson homage for her faith and for the impressive art that arises from that faith. He finds her message — or at least the form in which it comes — utterly convincing. He also values her life history — her early poverty and hard work, her experience with racism, her at-oneness with her body — as sources of wisdom. But wait: Terkel, we well know, is never going to be saved, by Jackson or anyone else, at least not in Jackson's sense of the word. He may feel his arguments have been demolished, but he is not really ready to yield. It is not clear even how much he wants to yield, or what yielding would mean. And yet he willingly entered into dialogue about faith with Jackson, and it is a dialogue he obviously delights in. What do we make of his apparent ambivalence — his affirmations and his resistance to what Jackson offers?

I would argue that Terkel's experiences as expressed here is paradigmatic. This account tells us much about the responses of many white listeners to black gospel — indeed of all listeners, white and black, who are doubters and skeptics but are deeply moved by the music of gospel singers like Jackson. Terkel's story also offers a way to get to a core question of this chapter: what difference does it make to white listeners that black gospel music is explicitly and assertively religious?

Like most white music lovers I was a latecomer to black gospel; I had been listening to white gospel — groups like the Carters, the Stonemans,

1. Studs Terkel, *Talking to Myself: A Memoir of My Times* (1973; New York: New Press, 1995), 260, 261.

and bluegrass, but did not come across black gospel, at least not consciously, until some ten or fifteen years ago. Even those whites who made it their business to know what was going on in jazz and blues knew very little about it until around 1950, when it was already at least two decades old.[2] It had grown up in the black churches, beginning with the "sanctified" ones and gradually winning wider acceptance in Baptist and Methodist circles and even eventually in Episcopalian and Catholic institutions. Beginning in the late 1920s, Thomas Dorsey, a former bluesman and pianist for singer Ma Rainey, swore off secular blues and began to compose what he called "gospel blues." By 1931 he and his associate Sallie Martin had formed the National Convention of Gospel Choirs and Choruses. Gospel, largely confined to the black churches, remained mostly unheard by white listeners until Mahalia Jackson emerged on the scene in the early 1950s. Through the good offices of jazz aficionados like John Hammond and Studs Terkel, the white world "discovered" a voice that Chicago blacks had been hearing since the thirties. A convenient date for Jackson's rise to stardom was her concert in Carnegie Hall in 1950. She switched from the small independent label Apollo to Columbia Records in 1954, a move that made her much more accessible to white audiences.

Even Jackson's rise to acclaim in the white world did not necessarily alert those admirers to the existence of a whole field of other singers worthy of their attention. In fact, it is not clear that white audiences perceived a genre of music called "black gospel," perhaps in part because in her Columbia recordings and in her "white" concerts (e.g., in her appearance at the Newport Folk Festival in 1958) she expanded beyond the usual gospel repertoire, singing traditional hymns and many of the spirituals long familiar to white audiences. Personally, I remember thinking of Jackson, however inaccurately, as something of a folk singer. After Jackson died in 1972, the world of black gospel music receded for most whites. (Not coincidentally, the folk music revival of the fifties and sixties was ebbing then as well.)

Shortly before Jackson's death, however, Anthony Heilbut published *The Gospel Sound* (1971).[3] Heilbut, who is white, was an English professor at

2. John Hammond includes two black gospel groups, the Golden Gate Quartet and Mitchell's Christian Singers, in his historical recording, "From Spirituals to Swing," 1937-38.

3. Anthony Heilbut, *The Gospel Sound: Good News and Bad Times* (1971; New York: Limelight Editions, 1985).

the time. His enthusiastic account of the rise of black gospel had steady if not dramatic sales and was reissued in 1986, with revisions, and has been in print since then. In addition, Heilbut's liner notes for records and, more recently, compact discs (he is a producer for the Spirit Feel label) have been educating gospel listeners for several decades.

Fortunately, in the last fifteen years or so a number of books and dissertations on gospel have appeared, many of them by black scholars. These works have examined parts of the gospel scene that Heilbut had sketched out as a whole. Best known is Michael Harris' book on Thomas Dorsey and Bernice Reagon's series on National Public Radio called "Wade in the Water," but we have also been blessed with other books and dissertations.[4]

Paralleling this growing body of information and analysis of gospel music is the rise of a knowledgeable white audience for gospel. In recent years European and American tourists have regularly stopped off to hear the famous gospel choirs in Harlem; it's not unusual for folk music programs to include a segment of gospel from the "golden age"; crowds flock to the Sunday morning "gospel breakfasts" at the Houses of Blues; CDs of the best-known gospel singers and groups are readily available at the kind of record store that also carries jazz and the blues.

So, we have available a growing body of information and analysis of gospel music, singers, composers, and performance styles. Even though much remains to be studied, the "facts" of gospel music are increasingly accessible. What I hope to do in this chapter moves in another direction; I

4. Bernice Johnson Reagon, ed., *We'll Understand It Better By and By: Pioneering African American Gospel Composers* (Washington, DC: Smithsonian Institution Press, 1992); Michael W. Harris, *The Rise of the Gospel Blues: The Music of Thomas Andrew Dorsey in the Urban Church* (New York: Oxford University Press, 1992); Kip Lomell, *"Happy in the Service of the Lord": Afro-American Gospel Quartets in New York City* (Philadelphia: University of Pennsylvania Press, 1991); Glenn Douglas Hinson, "When the Words Roll and the Fire Flows: Spirit, Style and Experience in African-American Gospel Performance" (Ph.D. diss., University of Pennsylvania, 1988); Jenna A. Jackson, "Testifying at the Cross: Thomas Andrew Dorsey, Sister Rosetta Tharpe, and the Politics of African-American Sacred and Secular Music" (Ph.D. diss., Rutgers University, 1995); Deborah Verdice Smith Bamey, "The Gospel Announcer and the Black Gospel Music Tradition" (Ph.D. diss., Michigan State University, 1994); Anita Berade McAllister, "The Musical Legacy of Dorothy Love Coates, African American Female Gospel Singer, with Implications for Education and Theater Education" (Ph.D. diss., Kansas State University, 1995). See also numerous articles in *Black Music Research Journal*, some of which are alluded to elsewhere in this essay.

want to explore black gospel's white audiences with the rather immodest goal of learning something about the religious "soul" of white America as we enter the third millennium. In other words, I want to examine what the cultural critics call the "white gaze," in this case the white gaze on black music. Or rather maybe I should invoke the "white ear." I want to address some of the following questions: why do whites apparently "privilege" black gospel among all the kinds of religious/sacred music available to them (besides the fact it's wonderful music!)? For example, I suspect that many whites may feel more comfortable with black gospel than white, since white gospel still carries connotations of simplistic redneck hedge hopping. Or, to take another example, do whites find a bracing "embodiedness," an earthiness in black gospel that they don't find in Bach cantatas or Tallis motets? What difference does it make to whites that the content of black gospel, both its musical forms and of course its words, is explicitly and outspokenly religious? Is their appreciation of black gospel different from their appreciation of the compositions of Scott Joplin or Miles Davis or Duke Ellington? I may not be able to do more than refine and play with these difficult questions, but they seem to me to be important ones, for they are one way to understand the condition of American religion in the early 2000s.

Before going much further I should try to say what I mean by black gospel's white audiences. Whose "white gaze" or "white ear"? On the most obvious level, of course, I mean those who go to concerts, churches, and festivals where black gospel is being performed, those who buy recordings and listen on radio and TV. But those faceless crowds don't usually record their experiences for public consumption. Thus, more concretely I mean the middle- or upper-middle-class educated white appreciators who have put their responses to gospel in print or on tape — Anthony Heilbut, John Hammond, Studs Terkel, and Jackson's "official" biographer, Laurraine Goreau.[5] By extension I'm also thinking of those writers on jazz who think about what it means to be a white listener who is deeply moved by a traditionally black art form.[6] I'm also thinking of whites who don't iden-

5. For John Hammond, see his autobiography, *John Hammond on Record* (New York: Summit Books, 1977); Laurraine Goreau, *Just Mahalia, Baby* (Waco, TX: Word Books, 1975). See also Jules Schwerin, *Got to Tell It: Mahalia Jackson, Queen of Gospel* (New York: Oxford University Press, 1992).

6. John Lincoln Collier, *The Reception of Jazz in America: A New View* (Brooklyn, NY: Institute for Studies in American Music, 1988); Collier, "Face to Face: The White Biographer of

tify as believing Christians, or at least aren't accustomed to worship in the style of the black churches.

In one sense there was ample precedent for white appreciation of black gospel; whites had been "discovering" and appropriating black music since at least the time of the nineteenth-century minstrel shows.[7] At the end of the nineteenth century, whites enjoyed the Negro jubilee singers (Fisk College singers being the most famous, and still singing today), who raised thousands of dollars for their colleges and reduced Queen Victoria to tears with their renditions of the old spirituals. Whites flocked to the ragtime piano playing of black musicians and composers like Scott Joplin. They helped create a "dance craze," swinging to the jazz of the teens and twenties. By the end of World War I, white students were now attending college in sufficient numbers to supply a substantial audience for the hottest of the hot jazz players. Later white audiences greeted the rise of rhythm and blues; finally, during the folk revival of the fifties and sixties, they searched for — and sometimes found — the surviving old Delta blues singers like John Hurt, Muddy Waters, and Howling Wolf. In each of these periods white musicians often did more than listen joyously or reverently or intently; they emulated the black singers they admired, or at least incorporated substantial "black" musical elements into their own playing styles.

It is important to note that black music benefited in the eyes of many whites by being categorized as part of the music of the "folk"; white folk melodies and instrumentation have been subject to the same sort of appropriation by middle-class people, although in less intense form. White urban middle-class musicians and audiences have been listening to, collecting, and imitating the music of classic country, bluegrass, sacred harp singing, and white gospel. In fact, with the proliferation of recordings of world music recently, the productions of all folk around the globe are up for grabs.

Overall, though, black music has been most prized and sought for in the United States. What did white folks see in it? On one level, of course, it was simply great music. But it also offered particular valuable elements.

Black Subjects," *Black Music Research Journal* (1985): 33-42; Gary Tomlinson, "Cultural Dialogics and Jazz: A White Historian Signifies," *Black Music Research Journal* 11 (1991): 229-264.

7. Robert C. Toll, *Blacking Up: The Minstrel Show in Nineteenth-Century America* (New York: Oxford University Press, 1974).

For whites, as often for blacks, black music was typically a vehicle of rebellion or at least of dissent from the culture of the white middle class. It had the power to shock and it expressed many of the longings of white folks (probably of most folks): freedom, emotionality, and spontaneity amidst the routines of factories, corporations, and bureaucracies; country ways in the city; communities and extended families amidst strangers; sexual expression in distinction to Victorianism and latter-day Puritanism; egalitarianism and justice in an unequal, racist society; poverty and even suffering as an antidote to too much comfort and abundance; wild abandon as against restraint; passion as against boredom; poetry in a world of too much prose. As early as 1845 an essayist in *Knickerbocker* magazine rhapsodized about the culture of black slaves: "Where must we look for our truly original and American poets? What class is most secluded from foreign influences, receives the narrowest education, travels the shortest distance from home, has the least amount of spare cash, and mixes the least with any class above itself — our negro slaves, to be sure! That is the class in which we must expect to find our original poets, and there we do find them. From that class come the Jim Crows, the Zip Coons, and the Dandy Jims, who have electrified the world."[8] Though we rightly scoff at that kind of attitude now, and certainly at the implied insults, I'd argue that we've never entirely shed that tone of wonder and admiration at the musical and poetic creations of this oppressed race in our midst.

Gospel added a crucial element to admire in black culture which the 1845 speaker didn't mention: intense, emotional, assured religiosity, at a time when many critics felt these things had gone out of white American life — not least the life within the churches. Earlier musical forms had contained a definite religiosity — for instance, the spirituals and some jazz (like Ellington's sacred compositions) — but none as avowedly and assertively religious as gospel.

As the foregoing comment probably suggests, I'm inclined to argue that in fact it does make a difference to white listeners that they are hearing a music deeply embedded in the piety of the black church, and, further, that they understand the performers of the music to be thoroughly consecrated Christians. They value the religiosity of black gospel and its purveyors not because they are evangelicals necessarily, or have any ex-

8. Robert Cantwell, *When We Were Good: The Folk Revival* (Cambridge, MA: Harvard University Press), 55.

pectations of ever coming to subscribe to the messages of the songs. But they find the spirit of the music intensely gratifying and satisfying.

For one thing, I would contend, the music addresses some of the most troubling binaries of Western culture: those of secular and sacred, body and spirit, emotion and intellect that many of us postmoderns have come to question and to regret.[9]

The body-soul dichotomy is a prime instance. On the one hand, gospel acknowledged and indeed seemed to celebrate the human body, not least the female body. Singers clad in colorful and glittering costumes "danced" to the rollicking rhythms of gospel. At the very least they *moved,* often rocking down the aisles of the church. They shouted and moaned so as to be heard. On the other hand, there was nothing more empyrean than a Mahalia Jackson or Mason Williams drawing out one of those long melodic lines of a Watts hymn, some of them in minor keys. And yet at their most spiritual, these gospel singers sounded full-bodied, and they were known to swing those long melodic lines.

They inspired their black hearers to participate in the same complex mix of rhythmic movement, loud ecstasy, and rapt worship. Singers hadn't done their job unless they "wrecked the house," unless the congregation "fell out." Some worshipers collapsed in the aisles, "slain in the spirit"; others echoed the shouting and moaning of the singer. Nurses and deacons watched over the more excited, to see that they didn't harm themselves or others in their transported state.

Gospel singers were there in the body in another sense: they usually achieved impressive girths. Mahalia Jackson for one was legendary for her wonderful Southern cooking and her love of eating, but there is no indication that she saw her gustatory appetites as incongruous with her role as God's instrument. By the time I interviewed Delois Barrett Campbell she was very large as well as beautiful. Some of the singers brought a gusto to other aspects of their lives; Jackson had three sometimes tempestuous marriages and a fondness for lavender Cadillacs and mink coats.

Gospel singers, then, were decidedly present in body as well as spirit.

9. One need hardly look beyond the booming business in books about spirituality, e.g., the work of Thomas Moore (especially *Care of the Soul*), or Phyllis Tickle, *Re-discovering the Sacred: Spirituality in America* (New York: Crossroad, 1995). A more academic attempt to expand our notions of "knowing" is Douglas Sloan, *Insight-Imagination: The Emancipation of Thought and the Modern World* (Westport, CT: Greenwood, 1983), or see the arguments in Colleen McDannell, *Material Christianity* (New Haven: Yale University Press, 1995).

For the more conventionally and traditionally-minded, black and white, this was disturbing, especially early on, for worship was supposed to highlight the spirit rather than the body. After all, it was the desires of the body that kept tempting humanity away from holiness. Physical pleasure had a bad name among the saints. But contrasting ideas were abroad too. There had always been a healthy degree of embodiedness in black Southern worship. Under the influence of Freud and a new interest in the primitive, whites had been coming around to thinking that body and mind were unalterably entangled, and that maybe the culture should accept this circumstance gracefully and even gladly, even in church. Accordingly, during the 1920s Protestant ministers here and there had experimented with dance (albeit of the decorous kind) in the liturgy. And music that invited physical movement increased in prestige, as jazz came more and more to be viewed as an art form. Not surprisingly, jazz too moved into the liturgy of some churches.

Yet these currents had been making only tentative inroads into sacred worship. In the view of those who have lately urged the incorporation of the body in our thinking about music and worship (and especially in the music of worship), much remains to be done. Black music, as Susan McClary and Robert Walser have written, invites us to "theorize the body," to lessen our preoccupation with pitch, form, and written musical texts in order to pay more attention to rhythm, improvisation, and performance. Though McClary and Walser do not address the issue of black gospel directly, it seems to me that in no form of black music is it more necessary to "theorize the body." To go a step further, the implication of the work of McClary and Walser is that we would do well to explore the meaning of the body not only in the music but also the religious experience of black Christians. And, to bring the issue back to the white audience, through an understanding of gospel, white people might better understand and enrich the religious embodiedness in their own traditions — an embodiedness that they have so often ignored or denied.

McClary and Walser caution against a reductive approach to the body in music (and by implication in religion). At its worst such reductiveness ascribes most of the "body" to black music and most of the intellect to white music. Or "body" is simplistically interpreted as tantamount to "sexuality." To counter our tendencies to fall back on the familiar racialized categories (black female body, white male mind), these writers plead for recognition among music scholars of the fact that physicality and sexuality are tremendously complex discursive fields. That is, to discuss the erotic or bodily aspects of cultural texts or performances is not to reduce them, for, as in cultural criticism more generally, we need to produce accounts of historical social interaction that are rich and nuanced enough to support critical readings.[10] McClary and Walser draw on the epistemological work of Mark Johnson, who argues that understanding of our embodiedness (especially in our choice of metaphors about our world) is absolutely fundamental to understanding of what we think of as our most *disembodied* intellectual processes.[11]

That the warning about reductionism is well founded is demonstrated by a contradictory impulse of white writers on gospel: to reassert and restore the binaries of body and soul by attributing certain kinds of purity to the motivations and activities of the gospel singers they admire. When all is said and done, writers on gospel like to think that singers "live the life" they "sing about."[12] For one thing, white writers on black gospel musicians — even the most savvy and professional among them — have tended to absolve their subjects of the taint of commercialism or entertainment. They have insisted that their subjects were not interested in money, even those singers who earned piles of it. When the performers have displayed a pleasure in material things (the furs and Cadillacs mentioned earlier), it's portrayed as a childlike interest, borne of severe deprivation in earlier years. Thus, the fact that the Cadillac is lavender (as Jackson's was) bespeaks whimsy rather than bad taste or a sellout to the marketplace. Or writers enjoy the ease with which musicians let go of possessions for the sake of the grand gesture. Heilbut recalls the way gospel singer Clara Ward sang at Mahalia Jackson's funeral, then hurled her mink wrap toward the casket: "She had already suffered two strokes and was to die a year later. Clara's flamboyant gesture called attention to her wealth and her song. It was in keeping with the Wards' record of showmanship, but it seemed a more private statement from

10. Susan McClary and Robert Walser, "Theorizing the Body in African-American Music," *Black Music Research Journal* 14 (1994): 80. See a fuller development of some of McClary's themes in *Feminine Endings: Music, Gender, and Sexuality* (Minneapolis, MN: University of Minnesota Press, 1991).

11. Mark Johnson, *The Body in the Mind: The Bodily Basis of Meaning, Imagination, and Reason* (Chicago: University of Chicago Press, 1987).

12. Thomas Dorsey's song "I'm Gonna Live the Life I Sing About in My Song." See Heilbut, *Gospel Sound*, 33.

Clara to Mahalia, beyond words but fully comprehensible to those who knew them."[13]

Another way white students of gospel attempt to establish this unworldliness of the musicians has been to look away from the stars of gospel to the musicians who haven't made any money to speak of, who pursue a blue-collar job Monday through Friday and travel a regional, gospel highway with great devotion on the weekends. Thus, scholars have displayed an interest in using painstaking and time-consuming ethnographic methods to research nonprofessional, noncommercial gospel musicians. The same is true of white gospel musicians; see, for example Jeff Todd Titon's *Powerhouse for God* on Appalachian sacred music and William Lynwood Montell's *Singing the Glory Down,* about amateur gospel musicians in south central Kentucky.[14]

This denial of commercial motives (and material, bodily desires) to black musicians has a long tradition among white writers, as John Lincoln Collier argues. White jazz critics, who often were on the political left and certainly didn't want to see their idols as selling out to Mammon, have written similarly about black jazz players, describing them as having come up in poverty and as having pretty much remained in that condition because they insisted on pursuing their art rather than worldly gain. Compared to the peril of selling out, their well-known drug addictions are untroubling to white chroniclers. In similar fashion, the most dedicated gospel musicians remain poor and serene for the sake of their art and, even more important, their Lord. Heilbut described Delois Barrett Campbell, despite her fame, as earning a living very modestly, singing the round of funeral parlors on Chicago's South Side.

Accordingly, white writers echo approvingly the negative judgments in the black churches upon those gospel singers who have gone over to pop. The propensity of church members and gospel singers to shun those who have thus "sold out" is legendary. So is the repeated refusal of Mahalia Jackson to sing in any other venue than a church or concert hall. Her white biographer, Laurraine Goreau, makes much of this, including Jackson's refusal to enter a public drinking place even when not performing. Jackson is said to have even regretted her appearance at the Newport Jazz Festival and to have drawn some criticism from clergy for it.

13. Heilbut, *Gospel Sound,* 305.

14. Burt Feintuch, "A Noncommercial Black Gospel Group in Context: We Live the Life We Sing About," *Black Music Research Journal* 1 (1980): 37-50.

Yet this celebration of the "faithful" singers and the condemnation of those who crossed over ignores the truth that in fact some singers did divide their time successfully between "religious" and "commercial" venues. The renowned Rosetta Tharpe, for instance, spent her career in both kinds of place, and Aretha Franklin switched back and forth. And in the documentary, "Say Amen, Somebody," an elderly Thomas Dorsey makes light of others' propensity to think of the blues as dangerous ("The blues is just a good woman feeling down").

Along with commercialism, white writers protect their subjects from the usual ills of celebrity status. They maintain, sometimes against the evidence, that gospel musicians — even the most successful — are underappreciated, except in the black churches, which are their real, loyal audiences. Thus, a corollary is that black musicians belong to their people, to the truly faithful. For instance, Heilbut opens his book by describing the funeral of one of the early gospel singers and organizers, Roberta Martin:

> In January 1969, 50,000 black Chicagoans trooped through Mount Pisgah Baptist Church on the newly named Dr. Martin Luther King Drive. They were viewing the body of Roberta Martin, a gospel singer whose obituary did not appear in The *New York Times* and whose funeral not even *Jet* reported. Roberta had grown rich from her gospel group and publishing studio. But she began her career in store-front churches, singing for nickels and dimes, and the poor who supported her then gathered now to pay their final respects. Roberta Martin belonged to them, to all the impoverished singers who tell you, "We're not here for form or fashion. We're here to be ourselves." She's helped give them a way to be themselves through a musical style that could lure the most depressed. While she reigned they rejoiced, now they honored her as someone who'd "stuck with her own." Miss Martin's origins and struggles meant a lot more that week than all her worldly success.[15]

Likewise, white critics have preferred to characterize black jazz musicians as underrated and misunderstood, except by the "real" people — and the white cognoscenti. For this reason, they gladly embraced the bebop innovators, who in fact were deliberately thumbing their noses at popular taste

15. Heilbut, *Gospel Sound,* ix.

— successfully for a time. Bebop, incidentally, discouraged dancing, thus putting the body at greater distance.

Ironically, when gospel singers have made it big in the white world — when they have received the recognition their talent is said to deserve — this is a danger sign that they have turned their backs on black audiences, have succumbed to the seductions of the market, and have "whitened" and weakened their art. John Hammond was apparently caught in this contradiction when he courted Mahalia Jackson for the Columbia label but simultaneously urged her to think carefully about signing the contract, because he feared she'd lose her black audiences.

When I argue that white writers on gospel speak out of both sides of their mouths — for the healing of the binaries on the one hand and the reassertion of those very binaries in new purer form on the other hand — I am not of course accusing them of falsity or deviousness, merely of a contradiction that many of us — black and white and especially middle class — share and have yet to resolve. We do not know whether we can trust any good at all to come from commercialism, and many of us don't feel so very comfortable in our bodies at times. Especially us academics. Most importantly, our culture is ambivalent about whether it wants its divinity immanent or transcendent, judgmental or friendly, or, indeed, there at all.

To return to the beginning and the encounter between Studs Terkel and Mahalia Jackson: Terkel and others like to believe that *somebody* is sure about all these things that puzzle them — Mahalia Jackson, Marion Williams, Delois Barrett Campbell, and their black listeners. It's quite probable that in doing so we're indulging in a bit of mythmaking and romanticizing. It would not be the first time whites have done this to blacks, nor probably the last. The mythmaking is not all bad, but we whites might help ourselves if we are conscious that our responses tell us also about our own longings as well as about the gospel singers we love.

HYMNS AS GOOD (OR BAD?) THEOLOGY

CHAPTER NINE

Singing about Death in American Protestant Hymnody

Jeffrey VanderWilt

And am I born to die?
To lay this body down!
And must my trembling spirit fly
Into a world unknown?

CHARLES WESLEY, 1763

Hundreds of hymns like this one by Charles Wesley speak to the experience and the consequences of death. These hymns seek to inform the attitudes and affections by which singers may understand the death of relatives, strangers, and the self. Such texts portray the human being crying out to God, "Is this life all the life that I shall ever know?" The consistent Christian response to the question of death has been to declare the promise of the resurrection and eternal life. But do Christians ever adequately describe their conceptions of the resurrection and the life beyond death? When painting a portrait of heavenly life, the hymn writer uses a palette of images that appeal to the emotions. This palette typically consists of theological conceptions along with the sights and the sounds of earthly life. Descriptions of death and resurrection are necessarily located within particular cultural circumstances. The language and images of death in American hymnody have therefore developed within the context of the history of changing attitudes toward death, the deceased, and their fate beyond this life.

The Rhetoric for Death in American Protestant Hymnody

In this chapter I explore the language and images found in American Protestant hymns on death. How have American Protestants sung about death? What language and images are found in the main body of such hymns? How do they function theologically? And can they continue to serve us? To answer these questions, I suggest, first, that the imagery for death in Protestant hymns suggests a strong hunger for transcendence rooted in our nature as mortal, finite creatures. Second, I ask whether hymns on death nourish us in our hunger for the transcendent or merely provide a palliative escape. Finally, these two concerns prepare the way for reflecting on the future of hymnody on death.

Images in our hymnody correspond closely to shifts in American cultural attitudes toward death that scholars such as Phillippe Ariès, John Stannard, Gary Laderman, and others have identified.[1] My focus is on the typological meanings found within one selection of American hymns. Given the themes found in this sample of American Protestant hymnody on death, where does the language come from? Toward what overall theological consequences may it lead?

The selection is the three hundred "most published" hymns as identified in the database prepared by Stephen Marini [See Appendix I]. Of this three hundred, there are eighty-one hymns that contain significant references to death, heaven, hell, or the tomb. As useful as the list of hymns may be, however, they hardly represent the fullness of Protestant hymnody on death. Most of the hymns are from the eighteenth and nineteenth centuries. Hymns by Isaac Watts and Charles Wesley predominate over all others. Spirituals and early twentieth-century gospel hymns are not represented.[2] Hymns written by women are under-

1. See as examples of a huge literature, Philippe Ariès, *Western Attitudes toward Death: From the Middle Ages to the Present,* trans. Patricia M. Ranum (Baltimore: Johns Hopkins University Press, 1974); C. Charles Bachmann, "More on The American Way of Death : [by J. Mitford; readers' forum]," *Pastoral Psychology* 15 (1964): 54-55; Gary Laderman, *The Sacred Remains: American Attitudes Toward Death, 1799-1883* (New Haven: Yale University Press, 1996); Jessica Mitford, *The American Way of Death Revisited* (New York: Alfred A. Knopf, 1998); and David E. Stannard, *The Puritan Way of Death: A Study in Religion, Culture, and Social Change* (New York: Oxford University Press, 1977).

2. On spirituals, see David R. Roediger, "'And Die in Dixie': Funeral Customs of the

represented.[3] Since it is a subset of the most commonly published hymns over a very broad period, the sample can only indicate the broad, general stream of American Protestant hymnody on death.

With limitations duly noted, what does this selection of hymns say about death and the possible theological convictions of the men and women who presumably sang them? Within the texts of these eighty-one hymns, I have identified thirty typologies for death in seven major categories arranged in three groups (see the table on p. 182). Of these thirty, the seven major categories are natural, paschal, physical, affectional, social, political, and anti-types. I list the natural and paschal categories under the heading "transcendent" typologies since these images refer to events and forces that are outside the power of human control. I group the physical, affectional, social, and political categories under the heading "human" typologies since these images speak to the nature of human life. Within the "human" typologies, physical, psychological, cultural, and social phenomena stand in as metaphors for heaven and the afterlife. Finally, the heading of "anti-types" stands alone. For every given image for heaven or paradise, there is a corresponding, negative image for hell and the eternal death. Thus, images for hell may correspond to transcendent or human typologies, though scenes of "slippery rocks" and "fiery depths" predominate. This life, too, may be described by way of anti-types. If life is called a "mourning vale," then heaven may be a "sweet field of living green." The binary opposition of imagery for life and death, eternal life and the eternal death, is a standard rhetorical technique in hymnody on death.

Rhetoric in the Hymns

The rhetoric on death in the sample hymns comes in two main varieties: monitory or consolatory. The monitory hymns are "cautionary tales in verse." They demand that people consider their inevitable mortality. The

---

American Slave Community 1700-1865," *Massachusetts Review* 22 (1981): 163-183. On gospel hymns, see Sandra S. Sizer, *Gospel Hymns and Social Religion: The Rhetoric of Nineteenth-Century Revivalism* (Philadelphia: Temple University Press, 1978), and James Crissman, *Death and Dying in Central Appalachia* (Urbana: University of Illinois Press, 1994).

3. See June Hadden Hobbs, *"I Sing for I Cannot be Silent": The Feminization of American Hymnody, 1870-1920*, Pittsburgh Series in Composition, Literacy, and Culture (Pittsburgh, PA: University of Pittsburgh Press, 1997).

Transcendent Typologies

- Natural images
  - Cosmic images
  - Nautical images
  - Pastoral images
  - Temporal images
- Paschal images
  - Resurrection images
  - Images of Second Coming and Resurrection
  - Apocalyptic images
  - Images of paradoxical death

Human Typologies

- Physical images
  - Images of bodiliness and corporeality
- Affectional images
  - Tomb affectional images
  - Intimacy images
  - Fear images
  - Images of joy and praise
- Social images
  - Domestic images
  - Images of labor and rest
  - Reunion images
  - Musical images
  - Images of pilgrimage and transportation
- Political images
  - Legal images
  - Military and battle images
  - Images of the nation state
  - Images of promised land and Zionism
  - Royal images

Anti-Types

- Images for hell and the "eternal death"
- Images for "this life" opposed to the "heavenly life"

consolatory hymns describe death as the initiation of the fulfillment of God's promises to believers. Sickness, tribulation, and death are mere "gateways to paradise." A hymn from the *New England Sunday School Hymn Book* (1830) illustrates the monitory type: "Your sparkling eyes and blooming cheeks / must wither like the blasted rose." Then there was the hymn about a certain "wicked Polly" that is cited in Edward S. Ninde's early study, *The Story of the American Hymn*. "She [that is, wicked Polly] would go to balls and dance and play, / In spite of all her friends could say; / 'I'll turn,' said she, 'when I am old, / And God will then receive my soul.'" Unfortunately it is all too clear where Polly is heading. She dies and it is too late to repent. To her father, she sighs, "Your counsels I have slighted all, / My carnal appetite to fill. / When I am dead, remember well / Your wicked Polly groans in hell."[4] To modern ears, the vivid images of death in such hymns sound dark and intense, even harsh. It is startlingly difficult to imagine leading a rousing chorus of these hymns with American youth today. We are much more familiar with consolatory rhetoric.

For an example of the consolatory type, consider Isaac Watts's 1707 hymn: "Why do we mourn departing friends, / Or shake at death's alarms? / 'Tis but the voice that Jesus sends, / To call them to His arms."[5] Such texts seek to ameliorate the grief of survivors by calling to mind the joys of paradise. Here, death is neither dark nor harsh. It marks one's passage into the Promised Land, safely into the arms of Jesus. With its emphasis on the heavenly rewards of the "sweet by and by," the consolatory hymn may appear merely to palliate the sufferings and injustices of the present life, but this is an impression that will demand more attention.

The Hunger for Transcendence Expressed in Hymnody

The imagery for death in American culture has a rich history. James J. Farrell, for example, suggests that between 1850 and 1920 the country witnessed the "dying of death." This time period saw huge cultural shifts in the cemetery, in the preparation of the body, in the development of a funeral industry, and in the demise of "morbid" language in Protestant theologies and funeral services. The overall trend has resulted in a contemporary funerary culture that emphasizes consolatory gestures, the hegemony of funeral and ritual professionals, and the cosmetic preparation of the body for burial.[6] By contrast, eighteenth-century funerals were monitory, performed by family and community members for one another; they did not feature embalming or any other procedure to lengthen the natural process of mortal decay. During the past 250 years, the *ars moriendi* of Americans, our art of dying, has turned an about-face.

4. Edward S. Ninde, *The Story of the American Hymn* (New York: Abingdon Press, 1921), 68-69.

5. Isaac Watts, "Why do we mourn departing friends" (1707), in *The New Laudes Domini* (New York: The Century Co., 1892), 1142.

6. James J. Farrell, *Inventing the American Way of Death, 1830-1920* (Philadelphia: Temple University Press, 1980).

Should we expect our *carmina moriendi*, our songs of dying, to have changed any less? In fact, the American *carmina moriendi* have changed in a manner directly parallel to the changes in our *ars moriendi*. While the "morbid" language of Watts and Wesley has fallen into disuse, the songs of more contemporary hymnals focus on comfort and consolation at the time of bereavement.

In his study of the English hymn, Lionel Adey summarizes these sweeping changes: "The just who earlier slept in hope of joyful resurrection, then trembled in fear of the Judgment, have in latter centuries gathered at the River to meet their loved ones gone before, and finally joined the unjust in the hospital's most remote and silent corridor. . . . Heaven has appeared before longing eyes as the golden city where rust corrupts not, nor thieves break through and steal; as an unfading garden watered by the springs of grace; as a palace where the hungry dine forever at the Lord's table, and the naked and unloved put on wedding garments for the Bridegroom; as home for exiles led there through the wilderness; and finally as a gathering of long-lost friends and relatives."[7] Overall, the history of images for death stresses the continuity between the life of this world and the life of the next. Heaven is a "city," a "garden," a "picnic" near a lovely "river." These metaphors strengthen believers in their conviction that heaven is known and knowable; that the life of the world to come is continuous with the life of the world we know.

Ironically, the hymns on death in our study link this stress on continuity to an equally strong stress on discontinuity. The effect is one of paradox. To express our yearning for transcendence demands both that familiar and known forms from this life will continue and that they shall be discontinued because they have been perfected and become divine. Heaven may be a reunion, but it is not merely a reunion. Heaven may be the Promised Land, but it does not resemble the earthly Zion. Heaven may be a "golden city," but it is not Rome, New York, or Tokyo.

Images of discontinuity give a strong picture of our desire for transcendence and the revelation of God's promised gift of transcendence in the Paschal mystery of the death and resurrection of Jesus. Images of continuity, on the other hand, give a strong indication of our inability to grasp the radical "strangeness" of God's heavenly love. In the hymnody on death, the synthesis of images of continuity with images of discontinuity

7. Lionel Adey, *Class and Idol in the English Hymn* (Vancouver: University of British Columbia Press, 1988), 1-2.

is a theologically valuable strategy for coping with the need to fathom the mystery of God's heaven.

Continuity between this Life and the Next

In the eighty-one sampled hymns, "human" typologies were found to stress continuity between the world of the life to come and the world of this life. Domestic imagery, musical imagery, and songs that stress the human affections featured continuity. The home, the songs, and the feelings we know in this life were made to substitute for the "home," the "songs," and the "feelings" we may know in the life to come.

Heaven Is My Home

The image of a "domestic heaven" is one of the strongest images to stress continuity between this life and the next. The typology includes reference to "heavenly mansions" and the softness of the "death bed." This type of imagery is present in all periods of American hymnody, from Watts to Thompson. The list of hymns that speak of "heavenly mansions" (KJV: John 14:2) is long: The fourteen examples of this type range from Isaac Watts's "When I can read my title clear" from 1707 (which speaks of "heavenly mansions"); through James Montgomery's 1814 "People of the living God" ("Where you dwell shall be my home"); to Will Thompson's "Softly and tenderly Jesus is calling" from 1880 ("O Sinner, come home").[8] The domestic heaven is a "mansion" with its connotation of wealth and spaciousness. The "heavenly mansion" is prepared by the Risen Savior. It is a "blest abode" and a place of "glory." It is the place where God "dwells" with human beings. It is a place of rest where one retires at the end of one's labors. The domestic heaven is, above all, a place of peace and safety.

8. The other hymns with this image are Seagrave, "Rise, my soul, and stretch thy wings" (1742); Philip Doddridge, "And will the judge descend?" (1755); Robert Robinson, "Come thou fount of ev'ry blessing" (1758); Samuel Medley, "I know that my Redeemer lives" (1775); William Cowper, "Jesus, where'er thy people meet" (1779); George Heath, "My soul be on guard" (1781); David Denham, "Midst scenes of confusion and creature complaints" (1826); James Montgomery, "For ever with the Lord" (1835); John Mason Neale, tr. of Bernard of Cluny (1145), "Jerusalem the golden" (1853); Marcus Wells, "Holy Spirit, faithful guide" (1858); William Tappan, "There is an hour of peaceful rest" (1860); and Featherstone, "My Jesus I love thee" (1864).

Imagery of a "domestic heaven" was especially common in hymns about the death of children and in songs for children to sing about death. For example, in her book *Mother's Child,* Lydia Maria Child wrote in 1831 that child rearing is aimed at preparing beings "for another world as well as for this."[9] Children, she wrote, should regard death "like going to a happy home." For nineteenth-century authors like Child, the next life is an "extension of this one." Death recapitulates "a common repetitive activity of childhood: going home when the day is done."[10]

If hymns for children spoke of death as "going home when the day is done," this "return home" must be viewed in the context of one's daily activities: domestic chores, playtime, or other, more masculine pursuits. June Hadden Hobbs observes that the "domestic heaven" hymns tend to differ according to the gender of the author. The "coming home" hymns by male hymn writers, Hobbs writes, "could well be scenes of men returning home after battle to a reward or escape." By contrast, the "coming home" hymns by female authors "sacralize a place where service . . . is the order of the day." Hymns by men "require a linear concept of time and place their primary emphasis on the future." The hymns by women more typically emphasized continuity between heaven and earth, the present with eternity.[11]

The imagery of the domestic heaven recontextualizes one's present experience of "home." As Lionel Adey writes: "The Methodist or Evangelical sought to bring home to the homeless by creating a heaven in their hearts as [an] earnest of that to come. 'I'm but a stranger here,' sang one such in 1836, 'Earth is a desert drear. . . . Whate'er my earthly lot, / Heaven is my home.'"[12] If one's earthly home is something less than "mansionly," the image of a sumptuous, heavenly home is likely to be quite appealing.

The Heavenly Choirs

Musical imagery for heaven also stresses continuity between this life and the next. Five hymns represent the imagery of a musical heaven in this study, including Isaac Watts's 1719 "I'll praise my Maker with my breath" ("And, when my voice is lost in death") and Robert Lowry, "Shall we gather

9. Lydia Maria Child, *Mother's Child* (Cambridge: Applewood, 1831), 74. Cited in Hobbs, *"I Sing for I Cannot be Silent,"* 43.

10. Child, *Mother's Child,* 81. Cited in Hobbs, *"I Sing for I Cannot be Silent,"* 43.

11. Hobbs, *"I Sing for I Cannot be Silent,"* 101.

12. Adey, *Class and Idol,* 68.

at the river," from 1864 ("Saints whom death will never sever,/Lift Their songs of saving grace").[13] These hymns describe heaven as a place for eternal choirs, for ceaseless hymns of praise. Continuity is stressed when singers pledge to begin the ceaseless and eternal songs today. In the hymns about a musical heaven, death is compared either to a loss of voice or to admission into the angelic choirs. The "loss of voice" is temporary, since the "poor lisping, stammering tongue" of one's mortal body will be raised to sing an immortal song. The singing assembly is thus given over to the feeling that they are caught up now in an activity they will perform in a superlative fashion forever.

The feeling is familiar to many Christians. The "humble songs" performed by "poor lisping, stammering tongues" are a foretaste of the "nobler sounds" we expect to make with the saints in glory. From this perspective the singing of hymns exhibits a nearly "sacramental" quality. The finite hymns of this life symbolize and effect the sense of one's participation in the transcendent "hymns" of heaven both now and for ages to come.

Why Must We Fear to Die?

Among the hymns on responses to death that stress the emotional response to death, heaven, or judgment, two emotions predominate: the desire for intimacy with God and others, and the fear of death. Hymns that mention the desire for intimacy with God and others tend to stress continuity between the desires of this life and their fulfillment in the next life. Hymns that mention the fear of death tend to stress the paradoxical quality of Christian death. Given the Resurrection of Jesus, death is not to be feared but greeted warmly.

Intimacy

Hymns stressing our desire for intimacy with God and others include eleven examples, from Joseph Addison, "How are thy servants blest, O Lord," from 1712 (with the lines "And death, when death shall be our lot, I shall join our souls to thee); through John Newton's 1775 "Though troubles assail, and dangers affright" ("Not tearing or doubting/with Christ on

13. The other three are Watts, "And must this body die" (1707); Watts, "Come, we that love the Lord" (1707); and William Cowper, "There is a fountain filled with blood" (1772).

our side"); to Henry Lyte, "Abide with me," in 1881 ("I triumph still, if Thou abide with me").[14]

These hymns suggest that, while intimacy with God or Jesus is available in this life, such intimacy will be infinitely greater in the next life. For example, in the gospel hymns studied by Sandra Sizer, Jesus is the focus. He is not a distant redeemer but an intimate friend. He is not the hero who "rushes out to do battle with . . . chaotic forces." Rather, he reaches inward to save us. He is a "shelter" and a "refuge." This, Sizer notes, is not a "sphere of passivity but of passion."[15] Thus, when she examines Wesley's "Jesus, lover of my soul," Sizer concludes: "Within one brief compass, we find the metaphors of Jesus as an intimate, the Savior (and heaven) as a haven, and life as a tempest. . . . The significant language context is the ideology of evangelical domesticity and the forms of the community of feeling, especially prayer and testimony."[16]

Feeling lies at the core of authentic relationship as conceived by the late-nineteenth-century hymn writers. As Hobbs observes, Fanny Crosby's hymn, "Safe in the arms of Jesus," describes "an entire theological system centered on a Savior whose power lies in bonds of relationship that not only continue, but are refined and strengthened after death."[17] The language of the heart predominates, and lyrics describing how one will rest in the "bosom" of the Redeemer are sung unself-consciously. To sing such hymns is to express in public one's desire for closeness with God. It situates one's self as already in some form of intimacy with God, while yearning for more closeness. The hymns of intimacy both express and limit the desire for transcendent relationship with God. God will draw us nearer, though never so near as will be experienced after death.

14. The other eight are Charles Wesley, "And let this feeble body fail" (1759); Philip Doddridge, "Thine earthly Sabbaths, Lord we love" (1737); Samuel Stennett, "On Jordan's stormy banks I stand" (1787); John Leland, "The day is past and gone" (1792); John Leland, "O when shall I see Jesus, and reign with him above" (1793); Sarah F. Adams, "Nearer my God, to thee, nearer to thee!" (1841); and Fanny J. Crosby, "I am thine, O Lord, I have heard thy voice" (1875).

15. Sizer, *Gospel Hymns and Social Religion,* 33.

16. Ibid., 127.

17. Hobbs, *"I Sing for I Cannot be Silent,"* 182.

Fear

Hymns stressing the fear of death or seeking to inspire an absence of fear of death include Thomas Ken, "Glory to thee, my God, this night" from 1709 (that one may learn to "dread death" no more than one's "bed") and John Fawcett's 1782 "Blest be the tie that binds" ("When we asunder part, / It gives us inward pain").[18] Watts's "Why should we start, and fear to die?" from 1707 is perhaps the most direct of the texts to address the emotion of fear. Fear is a sign of our timidity. Whereas the death of Christ has made death the "gate of endless joy," we treat it as a place of "dread." With this theological view, as Gary Laderman concludes, "death was transformed into a time of hope and promise rather than gloom and despair."[19] By the end of the nineteenth century, hymns that cultivated the fear of death as a tool for evangelism were replaced with texts that emphasized consolation in the midst of emotional discomfort. Fawcett's "Blest be the tie that binds" is a good example with its indirect and ambiguous reference to "inward pain" at the time of parting.

Note how, in this small sample, there are at least three different characterizations of the fear of death. If Fawcett has softened the "fear of death" into an "inward pain," then the emotional response to death has been submerged into the realm of private feelings. Watts's imagery, by contrast, remains in the public sphere. One of his texts alludes to the public ritual of burying the dead: "Why should we tremble to convey / Their bodies to the tomb?" Muhlenberg's text understands the emotions facing the Christian in death in a thoroughly "Paschal" fashion. The rationale for "welcoming the tomb" is not that it ends the miseries and sufferings of this life. Rather, believers should welcome the tomb because Christ has first lain there. Its "gloom" is resolved in resurrection glory. Clearly, these hymns confront us with our own fears of death and proclaim our need for a new emotional response to death because of the resurrection of Jesus. The proclamation that death ought "no longer appall us" begins to stress the distance between typical responses to death and the Christian faith.

18. Others are Watts, "Why do we mourn departing friends" (1707); Watts, "Why should we start, and fear to die?" (1707); William Williams, "Guide me, O thou great Jehovah" (1745); and Joseph Fawcett, "Lord, dismiss us with thy blessing" (1773).

19. Laderman, "Locating the Dead: A Cultural History of Death in the Antebellum, Anglo-Protestant Communities of the Northeast," *Journal of the American Academy of Religion* 63 (1995): 40.

Discontinuity between This Life and the Next

The hymnody on death stresses the distance between this life and the next in a variety of ways. Binary opposition between "earthly" and "heavenly" categories is a standard technique. Thus, many hymn writers contrast "earthly labor" to "heavenly rest." They may oppose the mortality of one's "earthly body" to the immortality of one's "heavenly soul." "Paschal" and "paradoxical" typologies also function to maintain distance between the world of the life to come and the world of this life. These images stress the distance between this life and the next and the paradoxical character of finding "life" in death at the heart of the Christian message. The stress on distance highlights the unknown and unknowable character of death itself.

The Land of Rest

The labor versus rest typology is an interesting example of contrast and distance. So, in 1818, William Tappan, a Congregationalist, wrote "Heaven, a place of rest." Ann Douglas notes that this "title might well have served for hundreds of the popular hymns that succeeded it."[20] Watts's "Hear what the voice from heaven proclaims" is perhaps the earliest example of labor versus rest imagery. In this hymn death is portrayed as a "soft sleeping bed," while life is marked by suffering, sin, toils, and strife. Labors performed in life will bring a great reward in heaven.[21]

Other examples include verse four of Phoebe Brown's "I love to steal away from every cumbering care," where death marks the end of the "toilsome day";[22] Joseph Gilmore's "He leadeth me, O blessed thought" speaks of the end of earth's labors;[23] Knowles Shaw's "Sowing in the morning, sowing seeds of kindness," is a loose paraphrase of Psalm 126. The binary opposition in the text of the psalm, "sowing in tears" versus

20. Ann Douglas, *The Feminization of American Culture* (New York: Alfred A. Knopf, 1978), 219.

21. Watts, "Hear what the voice from heaven proclaims" (1707).

22. Phoebe H. Brown, "I love to steal away, from every cumbering care" (1828): "Thus, when life's toilsome day is o'er, / May its departing ray / Be calm at this impressive hour, / And lead to endless day."

23. Joseph H. Gilmore, "He leadeth me: O blessed thought!" (1861), with the words, "And when my task on earth is done."

"reaping with joy," is adapted by Shaw to refer to the "Lord's harvest" at the end of time.[24]

Adey notes that images for labor will need to shift if the hymns are to survive into the future. Pastoral imagery, such as "carrying in sheaves" has a certain charm, but very few Americans harvest their wheat by hand. With the Industrial Revolution having passed into the age of information technologies, other images for labor will soon be equally outdated. Adey concludes, "Now that poets come from industrial areas, images drawn from the factory or mine are already being outdated by the new technology, which will in the foreseeable future make nonsense not only of the imagery of toil but, for most people, of any single vocation or career."[25]

There is a risk whenever earthly images of labor are opposed to a conception of heaven. Earthly technologies and cultural norms shift, often dramatically. Thus, one wonders how many members of the American leisure class need a "restful place" in order to think about heaven. If my earthly mansion is situated a few yards from the tennis courts, how much may I be expected to yearn for a "heavenly mansion" or for my heart to be "taken [and] sealed to . . . courts above?"[26] If the labor versus rest typology once indicated a yearning for transcendence, does it still?

I'll Lay This Body Down

One of the chief means of signaling the human yearning for transcendence is found in a "love-hate" relationship with our own bodies. The desire to escape finitude and bodiliness is closely related to desires for experiencing limitless freedom in loving relationships. The nearly limitless desire to love and to be loved can scarcely ever be expressed within the confines of one's body as presently constituted. This reality goes to the heart of the Christian conception of incarnation. If Jesus Christ was, in fact, an adequate expression of God's limitless love expressed within the confines of a human body, are Christians ever enabled to express God's love adequately? How one views the body and consequently its mortality controls one's answer to this question.

24. Knowles Shaw, "Sowing in the morning, sowing seeds of kindness" (1874); with its chorus, "We shall come rejoicing, / Bringing in the sheaves."

25. Adey, *Class and Idol*, 252.

26. Robert Robinson, "Come thou fount of ev'ry blessing" (1758).

Calvinist theologies, for instance, use statements about human bodiliness and finitude to characterize the absolute distance that exists between God and creatures.[27] For Puritans, the "corruptible, decomposing body" was mere "food for worms." The body chiefly signifies human sin. Puritan rhetoric, with its emphasis on "predestination and the tortures of hell," had fallen by the wayside by the middle of the nineteenth century. This type of rhetoric is chiefly observed in the hymns of Isaac Watts, who emphasized the corruptibility and transience of the body with words like "clay," "prison," "vanity," and "dust."

A corruptible, decaying body is one of the most inescapable outcomes of human death. One of the main strategies for coping with the decay of the body was to stress the immediate and invisible life of the deceased after death. Laderman notes that, after the Civil War, Protestants, especially in the North, preferred to emphasize the state of the soul in death. The souls of the deceased had "flown away" to "worlds unknown" and are no longer "here."[28] Nonetheless, pre-Civil War Protestants still needed to find a theological meaning for the body of the deceased.[29] Few hymns give a stronger impression of the "meaninglessness" of the body than Montgomery's "Servant of God, well done!" which describes the corpse as an "empty tent," and a "darkened ruin."[30] Ironically, at this time the "beautification" of the corpse became common in Victorian America. Even as the meaning of the body was becoming void of Christian signification, it was given over to cosmetic and sentimental adornment.

Hymns that stress human bodiliness and physicality tend to speak of the decay of the body, of the body as a metaphor for one's limitations, or of life as an athletic event. They use "tomb" imagery or medical language. Nine out of nineteen hymns using images for the body in this study were written by Isaac Watts, including from 1707, "Hark from the tombs a doleful sound" ("Then when we drop this dying flesh, / We'll rise above the

27. Laderman, *Sacred Remains,* 52.

28. At the same time, the public dissection of corpses became more common as medical research advanced. Concerns for public health and sanitation also impacted the mortuary practices of the mid-nineteenth century. Overall, the care for the deceased was transferred from the religious sphere to the public sector. The nearly complete transfer of mortuary practice to the private corporation would not occur until the twentieth century. See Laderman, "Locating the Dead," 44.

29. Ibid., 38.

30. James Montgomery, "Servant of God, well done!" (1819).

sky.") Similar images are found in hymns by, among others, Philip Doddridge, "Awake my soul, stretch every nerve" from 1755 ("When Victor's wreaths and monarchs' / Shall blend in common dust") and Samuel Medley's 1782 "Awake my soul to joyful lays" ("Oh may my last expiring breath / His loving kindness sing in death").[31]

Marching onward into Zion

Earthly pilgrimage is one of the great themes of human bodiliness within a social context. In hymnody it is "marching onward into Zion." The movement of the body from lower to higher ground, from the wilderness into the Promised Land certainly represents the movement of an individual person. It may also represent the movement of the social body with its rich allusions to the pilgrimage of Israel from Egypt into Canaan. The six pilgrimage hymns in this study include Watts, "Why do we mourn departing friends?" from 1707 ("Awake! ye nations under ground; / Ye saints! Ascend the skies.") and William Cowper, "Jesus, wher'er thy people meet" from 1779 ("And going, take thee to their home").[32] Louis F. Benson is only one of several historians to note that the "pilgrimage" song became quite popular in American camp meetings: "The companionships of the rough journey to the camp reappear in songs of a common pilgrimage to Canaan, the meetings and partings on the ground typify the reunions of believers in Heaven, and the military suggestions of the encampment furnish many themes for songs of the militant host, brothers in arms in the battle of the Lord."[33]

31. The others are Watts, "And must this body die" (1707); Watts, "Thee we adore, eternal name" (1707); Watts, "Thus far the Lord has led me on" (1709); Watts, "Why do we mourn departing friends" (1707); Watts, "Why should we start, and fear to die?" (1707); Watts, "Life is the time to serve the Lord" (1709); Watts, "I'll praise my Maker with my breath" (1719); Watts, "Teach me the measure of my days" (1719); John Newton, "Day of judgment! Day of wonders!" (1774); Samuel Medley, "I know that my Redeemer lives" (1775); George Heath, "My soul be on guard" (1781); David Denham, "Midst scenes of confusion and creature complaints" (1826); James Montgomery, "People of the living God" (1814); James Montgomery, "Servant of God, well done!" (1819); Margaret Mackay, "Asleep in Jesus! Blessed sleep" (1832); and William B. Tappan, "There is an hour of peaceful rest" (1860).

32. The other four are Philip Doddridge, "Thine earthly Sabbaths, Lord we love" (1773); Watts, "Broad is the road that leads to death" (1707); James Montgomery, "People of the living God" (1814); and Watts, "Thee we adore, eternal name" (1707).

33. Louis F. Benson, *The English Hymn: Its Development and Use in Worship* (New York: George H. Doran Co., 1915), 293.

If they make the camp meeting an exciting metaphor for heaven, these hymns make everyday life seem bleak by comparison. The journey is lonely and it inevitably ends in death. Nonetheless, these hymn writers suggest we should rather not leave the road on which we are traveling. Our journeys may even continue after death, as in Montgomery's hymn where the lost soul wanders about after death while it seeks the heavenly home.

A natural extension of the theme of earthly pilgrimage appears in hymns and songs describing modes of transportation. Chariots, boats, ships, trains, clouds of bright angels, and human flight transport people to the realm of heaven.[34] Common to such images is the idea that heaven is very much a "place" distinct and removed from "here." The idea of movement predominates, with a strong note of verticality and transience.

Transportation motifs are not universal, but they are complemented by a number of hymns that speak of a more "immediate" change in location. The late-nineteenth and early-twentieth-century gospel hymns, Sandra Sizer observes, sometimes speak of salvation as something "accomplished by simple translation ('I will be there') or, at most, by the action of Jesus ('He'll carry me over Jordan')."[35] Sizer notes that many of the pilgrimage hymns "emphasize the transient nature of this-worldly life." They use verbs in their progressive form, "thus making grammar conform to the content they express."[36] If heaven is not "here," then death involves a sudden movement "there." If heaven is our "destination," then earthly life is nothing but a "conduit." To suggest that earthly life is only a means to a higher end has been an essential, though potentially troublesome, part of the Christian message.

Paschal Imagery

To proclaim the resurrected life of heaven at the end of every journey means that, for Christians, the central meaning of death must depend upon the doctrine of the Paschal mystery of Jesus' death and resurrection. Paschal imagery in the hymns of this sample underscores the "paradoxi-

34. See for example, Sarah F. Adams, "Nearer my God, to thee, nearer to thee!" (1841), with the words, "Or if on joyful wing, / Cleaving the sky, / Sun, moon, and stars forgot, / Upward I fly."

35. Sizer, *Gospel Hymns and Social Religion*, 32.

36. Ibid., 31.

cal" character of death and the doctrine of hope for the general resurrection. The "paradox of death" comes closest to the classical Christian understandings. The classic, "paradoxical" imagery emphasizes the "defeat of death by death." Hymns that speak of one's hope for the general resurrection also rely on the language and images of Easter. They focus on the promise that those who "die a death like his" shall also "rise like him" on the last day.

The General Resurrection

Hymns from my sample that speak of the resurrection on the last day include Watts, "And must this body die" from 1707 ("God, my Redeemer, lives, / And often from the skies / Looks down and watches all my dust, / Till he shall bid it rise") and Charles Wesley, "And am I born to die" from 1763 ("Waked by the trumpet sound, / I from my grave shall rise").[37] These hymns uniformly describe the resuscitation of corpses and "rising" or "awakening" from the tomb. One's bodily integrity will be restored from the "dust." As Laderman notes, "In spite of natural laws that ordained bodily disintegration, God had the power to restore life to the dead and 'awaken' the body from its lifeless state. The death and resurrection of Jesus provided the faithful with primary evidence for the validity of such a belief."[38] For the authors of these hymns new life would return at the appropriate moment and the corpse retained a religious significance.

This sample included no hymns on death written after the Civil War to stress the image of the general resurrection. This would seem to corroborate Laderman's observation when he concludes that, after the Civil War,

> in virtually every facet of Protestant theology the physical remains of the dead were *persona non grata,* so to speak. While much of the dominant theology in the Gilded Age focused on the improvement of social conditions in cities, the saving of souls in this life, and the status of the spirit in the next, the corpse itself had become useless to religious instruction.[39]

37. Others include Watts, "Thus far the Lord has led me on" (1709); Thomas Ken, "Glory to thee, my God, this night" (1709); and John Newton, "Day of judgment! Day of wonders!" (1774).

38. Laderman, *The Sacred Remains,* 53.

39. Ibid., 169.

After Watts and Wesley, hymn writers would find the corpse and the resuscitated body less primary. Instead, the later hymns focus on the disembodied spirit's immediate departure to heavenly comforts or infernal punishments.

Paradoxical Death

A. Gregory Schneider suggests that evangelical responses to death are centered on images of the paradoxical character of death. He writes that "evangelical religion [is characterized by] an effort to steal a march on death, a strategy for conquering death by living a dying life."[40] However, only six hymns from my sample illustrate such paradoxical imagery for death, including Charles Wesley's "Christ the Lord is ris'n today" ("Where, O death, is now thy sting? / Once He died our souls to save: / Where's thy victory, O grave?") and James Montgomery's "For ever with the Lord!" from 1849 ("By death I shall escape from death, / And life eternal gain").[41]

"Paradoxical" language for death is far more common in Eastern Orthodox hymnody. Montgomery's line, "By death I shall escape from death," comes closest to the classic conception inherited from Hebrews 2:14 and the hymns of the Byzantine Easter liturgy: "Christ has trampled down death by death." The other hymns in our sample offer paraphrases of 1 Corinthians 15:55. The hymns of Watts, therefore, speak of "stingless death" and "victoryless tomb." These hymns locate death within the context of the resurrection without minimizing its horror. On the one hand, the imagery of "paradoxical death" insures that we do not turn death and the corpse into a fetish; on the other hand, this type of imagery insures we do not evacuate their proper, Christian meaning.

Anti-Types of Heaven and the Collapse of Hell

Ariès points out that "one of the most fundamental changes in the vision of the afterlife since the Enlightenment has been the virtual erasure of im-

40. A. Gregory Schneider, "The Ritual of Happy Dying Among Early American Methodists," *Church History* 56 (1987): 353.

41. Others are Watts, "Hear what the voice from heav'n declares" (1707); Watts, "He dies; the heavenly Savior [friend of sinners] dies" (1709); and Henry F. Lyte, "Abide with me" (1881).

ages of hell from the Christian imagination."[42] The hymns in our sample that feature the anti-types of heaven and speak to the image of hell include Charles Wesley's, "Sinners, turn, why will ye die?" from 1741, ("Sinners, turn: why will you die? / Why, you thankless creatures, why / Will you cross his love and die?") and Thomas Hastings, "Delay not, delay not; O sinner, draw near," from 1831 ("Delay not, delay not, the Spirit of grace, / Long grieved and resisted, may take his sad flight, / And leave thee in darkness to finish thy race, / To sink in the gloom of eternity's night").[43] The text by Hastings is the most recent example of the hymn to mention hell in this sample. His image of an eternal "night" is one of the more common images for eternal death and hell. The eternal "night" also appears in the texts of Leland, Thompson, and Hastings. In texts that suggest a more naturalist conception of death, Wesley and Montgomery hearken back to an ancient conception when they speak of God's negative judgment resulting in an "eternal death."[44] In Hunter's "My heav'nly home is bright and fair," one also finds the anti-type of the "domestic heaven" hymn: the rather surprising image of a "domestic hell." One expects that most people singing this hymn would prefer the bright, fair heavenly home to the fiery, flooded infernal home of Hunter's hymn.

Life, too, can be an "anti-type" for heaven. As blissful and green as heaven may be portrayed, so many hymn writers will stress a corresponding misery and drought in the present. As Sandra Sizer notes with respect to some gospel hymns, "The hymns are sharply dualistic in this respect, describing the world and its woes in opposition to the bliss of heaven and the beauty of Jesus."[45] Stannard concludes much the same of the Puritans when he states, ". . . for a people to logically have contempt for the world they must also hold with conviction a picture of a superior alternative to

42. Ariès, *The Hour of Our Death*, 474.

43. Others are Watts, "That awful day will surely come" (1707); Watts, "Teach me the measure of my days" (1719); Charles Wesley, "A charge to keep I have" (1762); Timothy Dwight, "While life prolongs its precious light" (1800); John Leland, "The day is past and gone" (1792); William Hunter, "My heav'nly home is bright and fair" (uncertain date); and Will L. Thompson, "Softly and tenderly Jesus is calling" (1880).

44. Ariès, *Western Attitudes*, 31: Speaking of the conception apparent in early Medieval texts and art, Ariès writes, "The wicked, that is to say those who were not members of the Church, would doubtlessly not live after their death; they would not awaken and would be abandoned to a state of nonexistence."

45. Sizer, *Gospel Hymns and Social Religion*, 24.

earthly existence."[46] In a word, the anti-types of heaven in the hymnody on death function primarily to create discontinuity between the life that we know and the kind of life we hope to embrace (or avoid) in the life to come.

Death, a Great Unknown

Expressions of continuity and discontinuity in hymnody on death may result from the desire to understand a radically "unknown" and "unknowable" mode of existence in terms that are both familiar and consoling, yet foreign and superlative. Earlier in American history, the Puritans believed that, although the bodily resurrection would occur some time in the future, one should avoid contemplating the details. The details, they thought, are beyond the power of human beings to imagine or understand.[47] In a fascinating twist of theology for the sake of emotional consolation, the hymnody in this sample, to the contrary, helps believers eagerly to imagine and contemplate the details of their heavenly existence. We have seen how the hymn writers' imagination includes, among many others, "soaring spirits in flight," "gates ajar," "sleeping in the arms of Jesus," "decaying flesh," and "winding sheets." There are the Jordan and the Promised Land, the fields of "living green," and "broad highways" full of pilgrims treading toward death.

The streets of the holy city are paved in gold, and trumpets will call us to walk there. Golden streets and a world devoid of pain and suffering are vital, rich descriptors of the resurrected life revealed to Christian faith. Such images are appealing since they imply that death is the great economic equalizer. As James Crissman writes, "Heaven in song is a concrete, tangible place where people look just like they do on earth. . . . The dead will encounter streets of gold and no pain, sorrow, suffering, poverty, struggling, or inequality."[48] One's overall impression is that the hymnody on death both disparages this life and makes the life after death sound very appealing. But, does its appeal lie in its normalcy (a life so comfortably familiar) or in its superlative and unknowable qualities (a life uncomfortably strange)? Who could bear to imagine — let alone survive — the infinite love of God?

David Stannard perceptively directs attention to a key passage from

46. Stannard, *The Puritan Way of Death*, 185.

47. Laderman, *The Sacred Remains*, 52.

48. Crissman, *Death and Dying in Central Appalachia*, 170.

the late eighteenth century. "It was becoming the norm, the accepted norm, for the godly to die 'in Raptures of holy Joy': They wish, and even long for Death, for the sake of that happy state it will carry them into."[49] Likewise, nineteenth-century Americans were equally fascinated with death. Their writings indicate a near desire for death. They spoke of death as a step toward the "reunions of eternity." For example the 1864 hymn, "Shall we gather at the river," describes the other side of death as a "gathering of saints . . . whom death will never sever."[50] Ariès is therefore justified when he concludes: "In heaven people found everything that made them happy on earth — that is, love, affection, family — without what made them sad — that is, separation."[51] One must therefore ask, if our hymnody depicts death so appealingly and life so unattractively, is our singing about death nourishment for faith or an invitation to escape from the struggles we face in life?

Hymnody on Death: Nourishment or Escapist Palliative?

Lionel Adey restates the uneasy question: "Do hymn lyrics voice only the thankfulness of the comfortable or the longings of the homeless? Does man make God in the likeness of the time, to quell the rebellious, stir the zealous into teaching natives their conqueror's religion, reinforce father's authority, sanctify mother's tenderness, bless their child's obedience, cozen the masses into submission and prompt the children of wealth and privilege to expiate their guilt in social service?"[52] In other words, do the images for death in hymns nourish the desire for transcendence? Or are the hymns about death mainly palliative, another "opiate" in a culture eager to overlook present-day, earthly injustices?

Hymns on death nourish a desire for transcendence precisely when they maintain a tension between this world and the world revealed in Christ. Similarly, hymns on death are palliative when they focus exclusively on the next world as the place where all desires will be fulfilled and all injustices redressed.

49. For example, William Thompson, *The Duty of a People Respecting Their Deceased Ministers* (Boston, 1743), 22. Cited in Stannard, *The Puritan Way of Death*, 150.

50. Robert Lowry, "Shall we gather at the river" (1864).

51. Ariès, *The Hour of Our Death*, 452.

52. Adey, *Class and Idol*, 243.

Escapism: Collapsing the Tension

The hymnody on death would seem to palliate our desire for transcendence when it collapses the tension between the world as we now experience it and the world as Christ reveals it will become. The experience of death is then primarily an escape from the ambiguities of this world into a world of untold bliss. The collapse of tension is seen especially in the images of the "domestic heaven" and in the language of hymns on death for children.

Whose Home Is in Heaven?

The imagery of the "domestic heaven" easily collapses the tension between this world and the next. Songs of "heavenly home" may project an eternal compensation for injustices suffered in this life.[53] For example, Jesus' parable of Dives and Lazarus (Luke 16:19-31) is eminently appealing with its stress on the equity of divine justice for all. Those who cause suffering in this life will receive it in the next; those who suffer in this life will escape it in the next. The moral equation is absolute and offers solace to victims of real injustice.

On the other side, hymns like Thompson's "Softly and tenderly" that call sinners to a "home" without consequences may risk collapsing the biblical imagery of God's justice. If modern Christians are given to imagine the "heavenly mansion" of Medley's "I know that my Redeemer lives" as privately owned "real estate" in a "gated community," are they not more likely to overlook the propagation of injustice by those who hold and who protect the right to unbridled wealth?

If heaven is our life "at home with God," it is also our life "at home with all whom God has chosen to love." The gospel calls believers to maintain a tension in the image of the "domestic heaven." It is a home, yes; but it is not home only for ourselves. It is God's home prepared for many. The problem with songs of "heavenly Zion" does not originate in their "Zionism"; it originates in the false idea that God has arbitrarily limited the group of those who love and long for the heavenly Jerusalem. The sin of Dives was his belief that there was not enough room for people like Lazarus in the bosom of Abraham. The notion of a universal salvation is quite appealing. But the notion cannot be bought at the expense of biblical im-

53. Ibid., 68.

ages for God's absolute justice. It must be founded, rather, upon the accentuation of imagery for God's omnipotent love.

Should Children Sing about Death?

Nowhere is the collapse of tension in the hymnody on death more apparent than in the number of hymns on death written for or about children. For evidence, one need only compare the 1854 *Hymns for Sunday Schools, Youth & Children* with thirty-five entries on the subject of death to the 1911 *Methodist Sunday School Hymnal* with its three entries under "death" and eight entries under "heaven."

The Puritan child was, in Stannard's words, "immersed in death at the earliest age possible." His or her salvation was at stake and the "terrifying prospects of separation and damnation" were not hidden from them.[54] By contrast, nineteenth-century children were also taught about death, but they were taught, not to fear death, "but to desire it, to see death as a glorious removal to a better world and as reunion with departed and soon-to-depart loved ones."[55] The modern experience, however, represents a third way. We tend to reject the fundamental *agreement* between the Puritan and the nineteenth-century children. Where those children were encouraged to be present for the death of relatives and loved ones, to confront death and not to deny it, today Americans strive mightily to conceal mortality from their children. Ariès puts the matter starkly, "Formerly children were told that they were brought by the stork, but they were admitted to the great farewell scene about the bed of the dying person. Today they are initiated in their early years to the physiology of love; but when they no longer see their grandfather and express astonishment, they are told that he is resting in a beautiful garden among the flowers."[56]

Prior to the Civil War, American parents could realistically expect to lose at least one child in infancy.[57] By 1860 the experience of infant death

54. Stannard, *The Puritan Way of Death*, 188.

55. Ibid., 188-189.

56. Ariès, *Western Attitudes*, 92-93.

57. Laderman estimates that the death rate before the Civil War was around 15 per thousand live births in rural towns and went as high as 20 to 40 per thousand in cities. Eighty percent of all Americans died before the age of 70. In Massachusetts circa 1849, life expectancy for women was between 36.3 and 38.3 years; for men it was slightly lower. Laderman, *The Sacred Remains*, 24-25.

had reoriented Protestant theologies of "infant depravity" at least as expressed in popular media, like hymns.[58] Even those who were ideologically committed to the doctrine, such as Cotton Mather, had difficulty applying it in the context of their own families. Mather was thus "unwilling to accept the possibility that his own child, who had died soon after birth in 1693 without benefit of baptism, would go any place but Heaven."[59] In the past three hundred years it is not surprising, in light of shifting attitudes toward the death of children, that the doctrine of double predestination has all but vanished.

Changes in attitudes with respect to the death of children may be attributed to a great number of social and cultural factors. Chief among them is the dramatic decrease in infant mortality in the industrialized West. Consumer cultures valorize youth and routinely associate the acquisition of material goods with youthful vigor. Is it not possible that Christians who live in such a culture might also come to valorize youth and associate the acquisition of spiritual goods with youthful vigor? While Christian parents want only the best for their children, is it possible that the comfortable words we sing at the time of death may in fact insulate them from grief? It may be possible that more honest songs about death and dying — simple, direct, hopeful, and without euphemism — have yet to be written.

Nourishment: Maintaining Tension

The earlier hymnody on death nourished transcendence when it maintained a tension between the world as we experience it and the future world as revealed by Christ. In the hymns by Watts and Wesley, for example, the experience of death is regularly described as an inherent fact of one's life, for which one must adequately prepare, which one may never avoid. For them, however, Christian faith finds in death the basis of hope for an unlimited and eternal life of loving and being loved. Death need not be feared.

If we seek to nourish contemporary believers in their desire for tran-

58. Stannard, *The Puritan Way of Death,* 59: "To the Puritan the child was more than a loved one extremely vulnerable to the ravages of the environment; he was also a loved one polluted with sin and natural depravity."

59. Sylvia D. Hoffert, "'A Very Peculiar Sorrow': Attitudes Toward Infant Death in the Urban Northeast, 1800-1860," *American Quarterly* 39 (1987): 606.

scendent love, perhaps we ought to seek out those hymns that reflect the paradox and tension inherent in the biblical revelation of the Paschal mystery of Jesus' death and resurrection. The relative popularity of hymns that speak to the "stinglessness" of death and the "victorylessness" of the grave suggest that Christian faith resonates strongly with these images. The hymns about Christ, who "tramples down death by death," easily situate our experience of death within the transcendent love of God, but do not give us the "cheap grace" and "consolation" of a world where we can avoid the costly struggle for justice.

But the single most crucial test for the future must certainly be whether American Christians will continue singing hymns about death at all. The "death" of hymnody on death in the American context parallels the concealment of death in a culture that has made the "proper funeral" into just another saleable commodity.

The Future of Hymnody on Death

Is there a future for hymnody on death? There are signs of stirring in the present, of which three deserve brief mention. First is the ecumenical influence in English language hymnody. Second is the renewed focus in theology and liturgy upon the Paschal mystery of Jesus' death and resurrection. Third is a renewed emphasis on psalmody and psalm paraphrases.

The new *United Methodist Hymnal* provides an excellent example of the ecumenical influence on hymnody. The book suggests four hymns for funerals. These include a setting of Wisdom 3:1-6 (commonly used in Roman Catholic funeral rites); a translation of the Russian hymn, "Christ, the Victorious"; a new hymn by Fred Pratt Green, "How blest are they who trust in Christ"; and an African-American spiritual, "Fix me, Jesus (for my long white robe)."[60]

When considering the emphasis on the Paschal Mystery two contemporary hymns spring to mind. Natalie Sleeth's "Hymn of Promise" highlights the paradoxical character of death when considered from a Christian perspective. She writes, "In our end is our beginning / In our death a resurrection; the last a victory." Suzanne Toolan's setting of John

60. *The United Methodist Hymnal* (Nashville, TN: The United Methodist Publishing House, 1989).

6: "I am the bread of life" has a strong Paschal emphasis in verse 4 where the congregation sings Christ's words to Martha, "I am the Resurrection, / I am the life. / If you believe in me, / even though you die, you shall live for ever." This hymn is slowly working its way into the Protestant repertoire (witness its inclusion in the Episcopalian *Hymnal 1982*).

Finally, there is a renewed emphasis on psalmody and psalm paraphrases in contemporary American worship. Are we now reclaiming the heritage of Isaac Watts, with his project to consider the psalms in light of the Christian gospel? Modern psalm settings tend to provide more literal and accurate translations than Watts. Many modern settings are faithful to the genre of lamentation. They speak bluntly and honestly about human affairs before God. Songs such as Michael Joncas's "On Eagle's Wings," a loose paraphrase of Psalm 91, bring death before us in a fashion that is gentle and complex, yet honest. Its broad popular appeal was boosted by association with memorial services held after the bombing of the Oklahoma City Federal Building. "On Eagle's Wings" represents only the tip of the iceberg of newly composed settings of the psalms for Christian worship.

Peter L. Berger once noted that "The power of religion depends, in the last resort, upon the credibility of the banners it puts in the hands of men *[sic]* as they stand before death, or more accurately, as they walk, inevitably, toward it."[61] We must continue to be concerned to place before the Christian people faithful, honest, and direct references to the Christian message with respect to death and the life of the world to come. These references must be timely and understandable, contemporary yet faithful to our traditions, comforting yet full of integrity. They must be grounded in Scripture even while they form our desire to participate more deeply in the transcendent love of God. They must not insulate us from the vicissitudes of our present life, nor should they merely "numb the pain" we feel in the present age. With respect to these needs, we must look to our past for both negative and positive instruction. More importantly, I believe we must look to future hymn writers if these needs are going to be addressed adequately in the context of twenty-first-century American Christianity.

61. Peter L. Berger, *The Sacred Canopy: Elements of a Sociological Theory of Religion* (1967; New York: Anchor Books, 1990), 51. Cited in Stannard, "Death and Dying," 1328.

CHAPTER TEN

Stories and Syllogisms: Protestant Hymns, Narrative Theology, and Heresy

Susan Wise Bauer

American Protestantism is, in the words of Nancey Murphy, a two-party system; the "division between 'liberals' and 'conservatives' (including both fundamentalists and evangelicals) is a deep one, and often marked by acrimony and stereotypes."[1] My first Easter at conservative Westminster Theological Seminar in Philadelphia introduced me to this acrimonious division; I suggested to the campus music director that we sing a hymn which was regularly used at my more liberal Presbyterian church in college days. "I serve a risen Saviour, he's in the world today," the hymn affirmed, ". . . You ask me how I know he lives; he lives within my heart."

He was deeply shocked. "I certainly hope that's not the basis of your faith!" he warned me. "That's not how you know Christ is risen! We have the testimony of the eyewitnesses! We have the account in Scripture! We have the changed behavior of the disciples! To say that you just know he lives within your heart is to appeal to experience. That can lead you straight to liberal heresy!"

We did not sing "He lives," and other hymns celebrating personal experience were equally suspect; many such hymns were not even in the seminary's *Trinity Hymnal,* and those that were ("Moment by moment I'm kept in his love," or "I am thine, O Lord, I have heard thy voice, and it told thy love to me") were hidden away in the back of the book, in a section en-

1. Nancey Murphy, *Beyond Liberalism & Fundamentalism: How Modern and Postmodern Philosophy Set the Theological Agenda* (New York: Trinity Press International, 1996), 1.

titled, "Hymns for Informal Occasions." Clearly these were inappropriate for the church's ordinary worship. Soon I learned that the reaction of the music director was hardly unique. Michael Horton is typical of the conservative suspicion of these hymns:

> Hymns chart progression from classic hymns of the 17th and 18th centuries (especially those of Charles Wesley, Augustus Toplady, John Newton and William Cowper) to the Romantic "songs and choruses" of the nineteenth [century]. . . . They reflect the shift from Reformation categories (God, sin and grace, Christ's saving work, the Word, church, sacraments, etc.) to Romantic individualism. . . . The number of nineteenth-century hymns that talk about the objective truth of Scripture, and that which God has done outside of my personal experience, is overwhelmed by the number of hymns that focus on my personal experience. It is my heart, not God and his saving work, that receives top billing. . . . [These hymns] are not only burdened with this self-centered and Gnostic tendency, but often contain outright heresy probably not intentionally, but as a result of sloppy theology.[2]

This divide between objective truth and personal experience, central to the split between Protestant liberals and conservatives, is based partly upon opposing views of human nature: is it essentially sinful and untrustworthy, and so needing to be rescued by an external Divine, or essentially divine, though perhaps distorted by external pressures of sin?

The conservative Protestantism that objects to the use of personal experience in hymns usually subscribes to a Calvinistic theology of original sin, affirming that although man was created in the image of God, the fall of Adam introduced sin into the human race. Sin comes from the human heart, and humans require the intervention of the personal Other in order to restore spiritual sight; no unredeemed man has the capacity to see and respond to truth on his own. And even the redeemed are in danger if they rely on their own perceptions of the world to establish truth. Michael Horton explains this danger:

> Pietism, a reaction against Reformation orthodoxy, represented a turn inward, from God to self. Instead of focusing on God and his saving

2. Michael Horton, "Are Your Hymns Too Spiritual?" *Modern Reformation* 4, no. 4 (July/August 1995).

> work in Christ, it shifted the focus to me and my personal relationship with Jesus. While no cardinal evangelical truth was rejected, the objective focus on Christ's justification of the sinner was subverted by the subjective focus on the experience of the believer. . . . [T]he purpose of worship now was not to provide the context in which God addressed his people and saved them by preaching and sacrament, but to provide an opportunity for the unconverted to express their commitment and determination to live a holy life. God was pushed into the background.[3]

Horton's fear that experience is dangerous — "subversive" to the "objective" truth of Christ's justification — stems from the conservative conviction that experience (even for the redeemed) is a part of the sinful, fallen world and will prove deceptive.

Liberal Protestantism, on the other hand, both celebrates and trusts experience (unless, of course, such experience might affirm a moral code that rates others' experiences as unhealthy or untrustworthy). Liberal worship becomes a time when experience is plumbed for meaning. Consider the worship directions used by the liberal Mountain View United Methodist Church in Boulder, Colorado: "Take these few minutes of quiet time to get in touch with the calm places, the still deep places in you; the spirit. Relax your body. Quiet the inner dialogue of your mind. Focus on feeling, on being. Be receptive to your center — your reservoir of inner peace, strength, love. Be aware of being with others. Feel the spirit of the community."[4] This trust of experience stems from a theological understanding of the human person as essentially divine, as carrying within itself a seed of God. Sin is external to the divine self, pushing against it from society outside. The way of redemption is not to trust in the objective work of an external divine God, but rather to nourish and attend to the divine within. In the words of liberal theologian Virginia Mollenkott, the human person is "a sinless self traveling through eternity . . . we are empowered toward co-creatorship."[5]

3. Michael Horton, "Leading the Church Into the 20th Century." A paper published by the Alliance of Confessing Evangelicals (Philadelphia, PA), 1997.

4. From the 1999 bulletins of the Mountain View United Methodist Church (355 Ponca Place, Boulder, CO).

5. Virginia Mollenkott, transcript of a speech given at the Re-Imagining Conference, sponsored by the Women's Ministry Unit, PCUSA (Minneapolis, MN, January 1993). Transcript prepared from tapes and published by the organization "Good News: A Forum for Scriptural Christianity Within the United Methodist Church" (January 1994), p. 13.

The "sinless self" of liberal Protestantism is able to understand and interpret the events of life; experiences of this sinless self are loci of divine truth.

This opposition between conservative and liberal theologies of the person helps to explain the conservative suspicion of hymns that celebrate personal experience. Yet Horton's simple breakdown between seventeenth- and eighteenth-century hymns as trustworthy and doctrinal, and nineteenth-century hymns as experiential and even heretical — a categorization repeated in the writings of other conservative theologians[6] — does not square with the evidence offered by American Protestant hymnals. There we find hymns of doctrine and hymns of experience side by side, written by the same authors, occurring within the same period, and often celebrating the same truths.

Analysis of the 150 most frequently reprinted hymns in Stephen Marini's American Protestant Hymns Project database, reveals that experiential and doctrinal — narrative and systematic — ways of thinking have always existed side by side in American Protestantism. Of these most frequently reprinted hymns, 77 qualify as "narrative hymns," while 56 follow the pattern "systematic."[7] (See Appendix I.)

Narrative Hymns

I am defining narrative hymns as those centered on the believer's experience: A character has a problem or dilemma; this leads either to an encounter or a journey; this encounter or journey brings a change in heart and/or circumstances, producing a new state of existence. Repeating refrains are common, although not inevitable, and usually deal with the encounter/journey stage of the narrative's central character, who is also the

6. See, for example, Peter Jones, *The Gnostic Empire Strikes Back: An Old Heresy for a New Age* (Phillipsburg, NJ: Presbyterian & Reformed, 1992); John MacArthur, *Charismatic Chaos* (Grand Rapids, MI: Zondervan, 1993); Horton, "Are Your Hymns Too Spiritual?"; and R. Kent Hughes, et al., eds., *The Coming Evangelical Crisis: Current Challenges to the Authority of Scripture and the Gospel* (Chicago: Moody Press, 1997).

7. The twenty-one remaining hymns do not fit either pattern. Twelve are occasional hymns; four are hymns of exhortation to a single act; three are hymns explaining or celebrating a single state of mind, without any progression throughout the hymn; two retell biblical stories. See Appendix I.

narrative voice. Samuel Stennett's 1797 hymn "On Jordan's stormy banks" illustrates this narrative structure:

> On Jordan's stormy banks I stand,
> and cast a wishful eye
> to Canaan's fair and happy land,
> where my possessions lie.
> *Refrain:* I am bound for the promised land,
> I am bound for the promised land,
> Oh, who will come and go with me?
> I am bound for the promised land.
>
> O'er all those wide extended plains
> shines one eternal day;
> there God the Son forever reigns,
> and scatters night away. [*Ref.*]
>
> No chilling winds or poisonous breath
> can reach that healthful shore;
> sickness and sorrow, pain and death,
> are felt and feared no more. [*Ref.*]
>
> When I shall reach that happy place,
> I'll be forever blest,
> For I shall see my Father's face,
> and in his bosom rest. [*Ref.*]

The central character of this narrative is "I," the inevitable persona in story hymns, and the refrain is focused on his (the default persona of narrative hymns appears to be male) journey towards Canaan.[8] In this story hymn,

8. Although a discussion of gender, story, and syllogistic hymns is beyond the scope of this introductory analysis, an argument could be made gendering story hymns as feminine and syllogistic hymns as masculine. Such an argument would draw on the work of Nancy Hardesty, *Women Called to Witness: Evangelical Feminism in the Nineteenth Century* (Nashville: Abingdon Press, 1984); Virginia Lieson Brereton, *From Sin to Salvation: Stories of Women's Conversions, 1800 to the Present* (Bloomington: Indiana University Press, 1991); Susan Juster, "The Spirit and the Flesh: Gender, Language, and Sexuality in American Protestantism," in *New Directions in American Religious History*, ed. Harry S. Stout and D. G. Hart (New York: Oxford University Press, 1997); and June Hadden Hobbs, *"I Sing for I Cannot Be Silent": The Feminization of American Hymnody, 1870-1920* (Pittsburgh: University of Pittsburgh Press, 1997).

the journey and enlightenment stages are cast in the future tense: (1) The individual's problem: He's in a world full of sin, looking forward to the sinless perfection of Heaven ("Jordan" is here indicative of death). (2) The encounter: The "I" meets God the Son (note the physical metaphors of landscape and light). (3) The journey: Death must be passed through in order to reach the "healthful shore." (4) The enlightenment and transformation: the "I" achieves a new state of (future) happiness, blessing, and rest.

For another example, Sarah Flower Adams' "Nearer, my God, to thee," first published in 1841, is a narrative hymn patterned after the story of Jacob's dream in Genesis 28:

> Nearer, my God, to thee, nearer to thee!
> E'en though it be a cross that raiseth me.
> Still all my song shall be,
> Nearer, my God! To thee, nearer to thee.
>
> Though, like the wanderer, the sun gone down,
> Darkness be over me, my rest a stone;
> Yet in my dreams I'd be
> Nearer, my God, to thee, nearer to thee.
>
> There let the way appear, steps unto heaven;
> All that thou sendest me in mercy given;
> Angels to beckon me
> Nearer, my God, to thee, nearer to thee.
>
> Then with my waking thoughts, bright with thy praise,
> Out of my stony griefs Bethel I'll raise;
> So by my woes to be
> Nearer, my God, to thee, nearer to thee.
>
> Or if on joyful wing, cleaving the sky,
> Sun, moon and stars forgot, upward I fly;
> Still all my song shall be,
> Nearer, my God, to thee, nearer to thee.

The repeated refrain here expresses the wished-for encounter of the central character, who progresses in a dreamlike state from a place of distance from God, into a new state of closeness and praise. (1) Individual problem:

the distance of God from the narrator. (2) The beginning of the journey towards encounter. (3) The encounter, brought about by angels. (4) A new state of existence: enlightenment and a willingness to praise God; "Bethel" is an altar acknowledging God's faithfulness. Notice the light metaphor (the narrator is now "bright with thy praise"). (5) Looking forward to an even more enlightened, future state of existence.

This pattern of development is consistent throughout the seventy-seven hymns identified as narrative hymns by the use of story (individual problem or dilemma), encounter, or journey that results in an encounter, enlightenment, and new state of existence.[9]

An examination of the seventy-seven narrative hymns (see Appendix I) reveals a number of commonalities. In each, the singer/narrator, not God, is the central character. The individual problem/dilemma may be internal (sin, despair), external (circumstances, Satan's attack), or a matter of lacking capability (I want to sing — but need divine help). In 17 of the 77, the initial situation leads to a journey or pilgrimage. In the remaining 60 hymns, the initial situation leads to a divine encounter. These encounters are of four kinds:

1. An encounter with a member of the Trinity. These may be intensely personal ("Jesus speaks," "Jesus whispers, I am his," "He flew to my relief"), or may take place through the mediation of a sacred object ("Low before His cross [I] lie," "Here [in the Word of God] springs of consolation rise," "There is a place where Jesus sheds / The oil of gladness on our heads. . . . It is the blood bought mercy seat").
2. A rhetorical request made with obvious assurance of an answer. These include such requests as "Jesus, Savior, pilot me!" "Increase my courage, Lord," "Hide me, O my savior, hide," and "Return, O holy dove, return!" The rhetorical nature of these requests is made clear by the shift in the hymn towards a new state of existence following the request; thus, they stand in for the more explicit encounters of (1).

9. This attempt to define a single pattern uniting seventy-seven hymns owes a great deal to the semiotics of narrative, as pioneered by Vladimir Propp in his application of Russian formalism to the analysis of folk tales. For applications to Christian hermeneutics and theology, see especially Paul Ricoeur, *Figuring the Sacred: Religion, Narrative, and Imagination,* trans. David Pellauer, ed. Mark Wallace (Minneapolis: Augsburg, 1995).

3. An act of God directed towards the narrator personally ("... [T]hou send'st to me ... Angels to beckon me").
4. An experience of grace ("Thy love unknown / Has broken every barrier down"; "Sudden expired the legal strife, / 'Twas then I ceased to grieve").

Following these encounters, the narrator progresses to a new state of mind or being. It is this progression or resolution that distinguishes the narrative hymn from other hymn forms. The seventy-seven narrative hymns under study show four types of resolution:

1. Thirty-six of the hymns end in heaven or in the believer's glorified state ("There I shall bathe my weary soul, / In seas of heavenly rest," "Land me safe on Canaan's side," "Heaven's morning breaks, and earth's vain shadows flee").
2. Twenty-one end with an improvement in the believer's state of mind, happiness, or standing before God ("[I] weep, believe, and sin no more"; "I hear and will follow Thy call").
3. Sixteen end with an expression of greater devotion to God, a greater feeling of love for God, or a greater sense of the nearness of God ("Now to be thine, yea, thine alone"; "Had I a thousand hearts to give, / Lord, they should all be thine").
4. Two end with the narrator pointing other sinners towards God ("I'll point to thy redeeming blood, / And say, 'Behold the way to God'").

One narrative hymn in which the elements are very clear is William Cowper's "O for a closer walk with God," which appeared in *Olney Hymns* (1779):

O for a closer walk with God, — *[Introduction to the narrator's problem: a desire for greater nearness to God]*
a calm and heavenly frame,
a light to shine upon the road
that leads me to the Lamb!

Where is the blessedness I knew — *[Elaboration on the problem: once, he was nearer than he now is.]*
when first I saw the Lord?
Where is the soul-refreshing view
of Jesus and his word?

What peaceful hours I once enjoy'ed!
how sweet their mem'ry still!
But they have left an aching void
the world can never fill.

Return, O holy Dove, return,
sweet messenger of rest; [Gen. 8:11]
I hate the sins that made thee mourn [Eph. 4:30]
and drove thee from my breast.

[The encounter with a person of the Trinity, phrased as a rhetorical request.]

The dearest idol I have known,
whate'er that idol be,
help me to tear it from thy throne
and worship only thee.

[The narrator's willingness to make the holy Dove welcome; the beginning of the transition to a new state of mind/being.]

So shall my walk be close with God,
calm and serene my frame;
so purer light shall mark the road
that leads me to the Lamb.

[The final state: an improvement in the believer's state of mind and standing with God.]

Like the Gospel narratives themselves, hymns can be explicated using semiotics of narrative — but certain cautions apply. Ricoeur, identifying the narratemes of the passion narratives, points out that semiotics of narrative is not entirely successful in accounting for the Gospels' occasional subversion of narrative patterns. He writes, for example, that Peter figures as the hero's helper, while Judas acts as opponent. Yet these codified rules are "subverted by the figurization in the passion narratives."[10] Peter also acts as opposition to Christ, while Judas becomes the instrument of the hero's triumph. To explain this subversion, Ricouer turns to the notion of narrative voice; a Gospel narrative is not only an arrangement of narratemes, but also the product of a speaking voice. This "someone speaking" has the ability to make a theological point through use and subversion of the narratemes; Peter acts as both helper and opposition because the narrative voice is constructing a truth about the "refractory nature of man."

In the same way, narrative hymns occasionally "subvert" the narratemes described above. Consider the 1787 hymn by Edmund Jones:

10. Ricoeur, *Figuring the Sacred*, 189-190.

Come, humble sinner, in whose breast
A thousand thoughts revolve;
Come with your guilt and fear oppressed,
And make this last resolve.

I'll go to Jesus, though my sin
Hath like a mountain rose;
I know His courts, I'll enter in,
Whatever may oppose.

Perhaps He may admit my plea,
Perhaps will hear my prayer;
But if I perish I will pray,
And perish only there.

I can but perish if I go;
I am resolved to try,
For if I stay away, I know
I must forever die.

The initial problem is clear; the narrator's guilt and sin produces an oppression that impels the narrator on a journey towards Christ ("His courts"). Yet the hymn ends with a negative resolution: rather than receiving a positive affirmation of life, the narrator recognizes that the failure to journey towards Christ will inevitably bring death. All other destinations will result in his death, leaving him with no other choice. This subversion of the expected resolution makes a point about the believer's experience. A journey towards God in faith may be undertaken without any emotional assurance of forgiveness; yet it is begun anyway, because of the conviction that God's forgiveness is central to life. Significantly, this narrative hymn also contradicts Michael Horton's assertion that stories about experience focus on self, rather than God; the character of God and His promise of life are at the center of the narrator's resolution.

Systematic Hymns

Systematic hymns cannot be analyzed using the semiotics of narrative, since there is no "narrative" or story present. Rather, systematic hymns explore a point of Christian doctrine in a logical manner. Consider, for example, this syllogistic hymn, written by Isaac Watts in 1707:

Alas! and did my Saviour bleed,
and did my Sovereign die!
Would he devote that sacred head
for such a worm as I!

Was it for crimes that I had done
He groaned upon the tree?
Amazing pity! Grace unknown!
And love beyond degree!

Well might the sun in darkness hide,
and shut his glories in,
When Christ, the mighty Maker died
for man the creature's sin.

Thus might I hide my blushing face,
while his dear cross appears;
Dissolve my heart in thankfulness,
and melt mine eyes in tears.

But drops of grief can ne'er repay
the debt of love I owe;
Here, Lord, I give myself away.
'Tis all that I can do.

Although this hymn does not ignore the experience of the believer, its structure is governed by a progression through the systematic theology of a Christian life. The orthodox Protestant systematic theology is a series of statements related both logically and in sequence: God existed first, as sinless Creator and King; man was created, but fell; man is, first and foremost, a sinner; God, the sinless Creator and King, was bound to condemn him to death; Christ came to earth to "stand in" as the victim of God's wrath; this sacrifice satisfied divine justice; the believer accepts this sacrifice through faith and thus attains the legal status of sinlessness ("justification"); justification is followed by a slow progression towards an actual state of sinlessness ("sanctification"); this state of sinlessness will become final only at the resurrection of the believer in the last days. This hymn of Watts typifies systematic thought: it progresses from the initial state of sin (v. 1), through Christ's sacrifice (vv. 2-3), to the believer's justifying acceptance of Christ in faith (v. 4) and the state of sanctification that follows (v. 5; the phrase "give myself away" is typical of the rhetoric of sanctification).

Such hymns can also be called syllogistic because each stanza builds logically on a premise established by the preceding lines in order to reach a conclusion which can then be applied to the Christian's life. In the case of Watts, the hymn takes the form: (1) My sin was so great that it required the sacrifice of One much greater than I. (2-3) This sacrifice was made out of love. (4) I respond in thankfulness and acceptance (justifying faith). (5) I continue to respond for the rest of my life by binding myself to God's service (sanctification).

Ironically, the later printings of this hymn were transformed into a narrative, thanks to the addition of a repeated refrain provided by Ralph E. Hudson around 1885:

> At the cross, at the cross, where I first saw the light
> And the burden of my heart rolled away;
> It was there by faith I received my sight
> And now I am happy all the day.

This refrain recasts the sin of the first two stanzas as the narrator's initial problem, posits an encounter at the cross (modeled on the experience of Bunyan's Christian in *Pilgrim's Progress*), and winds up with a resolution that comes from that encounter: improved sight and happiness. The radically different nature of the resulting hybrid hymn is reflected in its new title, "At the Cross."

Watts, who carried on a secondary career as a logician, undoubtedly influenced generations of hymn writers. His 1724 textbook on logic, *Logic: The Right Use of Reason in the Inquiry After Truth,* demonstrated a high respect for human intellect: "Reason is the glory of human nature, and one of the chief eminencies whereby we are raised above our fellow-creatures, the brutes, in this lower world. . . . Now the design of Logic is to teach us the right use of our reason, or intellectual powers, and the improvement of them in ourselves and others. . . . It is the cultivation of our reason by which we are better enabled to distinguish good from evil, as well as truth from falsehood. . . . The art of logic, even as it assists us to gain the knowledge of the sciences, leads us on towards virtue and happiness, for all our speculative acquaintance with things should be made subservient to our better conduct in the civil and the religious life."[11] Watts's textbook proceeds through a rigorous course of logic, treating the subjects of perception, judgment, argumentation, and disposition, and recommending that the proper logic be applied to the sciences, ethics, and theology equally. "The connexion of truths should arise and appear in their successive ranks and order," he advises in his conclusion, "as the several parts of a fine prospect ascend just behind each other in their natural and regular elevations and distances, and invite the eye to climb onward with constant pleasure till it reach the sky."[12] The systematic method of hymn writing was intended to do exactly that.

The pattern of systematic explication appears throughout the fifty-six systematic hymns of Stephen Marini's list. Consider, for example, "Come, thou Fount of every blessing" (Robert Robinson, 1758):

> Come, thou Fount of every blessing,
> Tune my heart to sing thy grace;
> Streams of mercy, never ceasing,
> Call for songs of loudest praise.
> Teach me some melodious sonnet,
> Sung by flaming tongues above;
> Praise the mount! I'm fixed upon it,
> Mount of God's unchanging love.
>
> Here I raise my Ebenezer;
> Hither by thy help I'm come.
> And I hope, by thy good pleasure,
> Safely to arrive at home.
> Jesus sought me when a stranger,
> Wandering from the fold of God:
> He, to rescue me from danger,
> Interposed his precious blood.

11. Isaac Watts, *Logic: The Right Use of Reason in the Inquiry After Truth* (Morgan, PA: Soli Deo Gloria, 1996 [from 1847 American ed.]), 2-4.

12. Ibid., 351.

O to grace how great a debtor,
Daily I'm constrained to be;
Let that grace now, like a fetter,
Bind my wandering heart to thee.
Prone to wander, Lord, I feel it,
Prone to leave the God I love;
Here's my heart, O take and seal it,
Seal it for thy courts above.

Once more, the syllogistic form appears, with each of Robinson's statements about the Christian life depending on the statement before: (1) The love and mercy of the Creator God precedes all human action. (2) Man is a sinner (far from "home," a wandering "stranger"). Christ's sacrifice ("precious blood") stood in for the sinner in the face of God's wrath ("danger"). (3) The sinner accepts God's grace (justification). This grace continues to work towards a daily absence of sin. The redeemed sinner looks forward to final sinlessness at the resurrection ("courts above").

Although many systematic hymns do explore soteriology, not all proceed through the stages of salvation in this manner. Others are christological, following the order of Christ's earthly work (incarnation, ministry, death, resurrection, glorification, second coming) or focusing in on two to three segments of this progression. Still others explore a Christian doctrine, systematically building up a theory of the incarnation, the Resurrection, the Trinity, or some other doctrine.

Of the 56 systematic hymns in the 150 most frequently reprinted, seven move through the entire progress of soteriology (from original sin to justification, sanctification, and glorification), while 19 deal only with redemption and the resulting sanctification. Sixteen follow the pattern of Christ's work on earth; 41 develop specific Christian doctrines, as specified below. There is some overlap, since longer systematic hymns often pause in the exploration of soteriology or Christ's work in order to develop some point of Christian doctrine.

Christ's exaltation	9
God's faithfulness	5
God's sovereign power	4
The Church's foundation and existence	3
The Great Commission	2

The Resurrection	2
The Trinity	2
Zion/Jerusalem and its meaning	2
General revelation	1
God's love for his people	1
Perseverance	1
Prayer	1
The Incarnation	1

While narrative hymns begin with a vignette illustrating the narrator's place, systematic hymns begin with a statement of fact, an assertion of faith (six hymns) or a command (seven hymns). Five end with a call to conversion; 12 end with a call to praise. Twenty-five are addressed to God; 31 are addressed to men; three alternate between the two.

"Hail, thou once despised Jesus" is an example of a hymn that explores the doctrine of Christ's exaltation, while also following a soteriological order from sin through glorification. It was written by John Bakewell in 1757 and altered by Martin Madan in 1760, giving it its present form:

Hail, thou once despised Jesus!
Hail, thou Galilean King! *[Addressed to God]*
Thou didst suffer to release us;
Thou didst free salvation bring.
Hail, thou universal Savior,
Who hast borne our sin and shame! *[Soteriology: Sin]*
By thy merits we find favor;
Life is given through thy Name.

Paschal Lamb, by God appointed,
All our sins on thee were laid; *[Soteriology: Justification]*
By almighty love anointed,
Thou hast full atonement made.
Every sin may be forgiven
Through the virtue of thy blood;
Opened is the gate of heaven,
Reconciled are we with God.

Jesus, hail! enthroned in glory,
There forever to abide; *[Christ exalted]*

All the heavenly hosts adore thee,
Seated at thy Father's side. *[Christ exalted, seated at God's right hand]*
There for sinners thou art pleading; *[Soteriology: sanctification]*
There thou dost our place prepare; *[Christ exalted and interceding]*
Thou for saints art interceding
Till in glory they appear. *[Soteriology: glorification]*

Worship, honor, power and blessing
Christ is worthy to receive; *[Christ exalted and praised by all]*
Loudest praises, without ceasing,
Right it is for us to give.
Help, ye bright angelic spirits,
Bring your sweetest, noblest lays;
Help to sing of Jesus' merits,
Help to chant Emmanuel's praise!

This hymn not only develops the order of salvation (from sin to justification by Christ's blood, to sanctification as Christ continues to plead for those saints who are still working their salvation out on earth, to glorification), but also lays out the parts of Christ's exaltation: He suffered, but is now in glory, seated at the Father's side, interceding for sinners, and eventually all created beings will acknowledge his lordship.

A systematic hymn addressed to man is William Cowper's 1774 "God moves in a mysterious way," originally titled, "Light Shining Out of Darkness":

God moves in a mysterious way,
His wonders to perform;
He plants his footsteps in the sea, *[Doctrine: God's sovereign power*
And rides upon the storm. *involves power of nature]*

Deep in unfathomable mines
of never-failing skill
he treasures up his bright designs
and works his sovereign will. *[The carrying out of God's will]*

Ye fearful saints, fresh courage take; *[The address to redeemed man]*
The clouds ye so much dread

Are big with mercy, and shall break
With blessings on your head. *[The preservation of God's people]*

Judge not the Lord by feeble sense,
But trust him for his grace;
Behind a frowning providence
He hides a smiling face.

His purposes will ripen fast,
Unfolding every hour;
The bud may have a bitter taste,
But sweet will be the flower.

Blind unbelief is sure to err,
And scan his work in vain;
God is his own interpreter, *[The interpretation of God's own work]*
And he will make it plain.

The hymn builds a definition of God's sovereign power, while stanzas 3-5 teach the believer how to respond to this doctrine with an appropriate attitude of trust.

Comparing the Styles

The narrative and systematic ways of expressing truth are markedly different. Narratives are, by their nature, more flexible and contain more ambiguity than statements of doctrine; compare the uncertainty of "Come, humble sinner, in whose breast" with the triumphant assertions of "Arise, my soul, arise!" Systematic hymns, on the other hand, prioritize doctrine, the products of logical thought, as a vehicle for truth. This narrative-systematic divide reflects not only varying views of man as essentially trustworthy or essentially deceived, but also divergent views of God and authority.

Conservatives view God as a personal Being, outside the cosmos and independent from it; in the words of D. Marty Lasley, the "material universe is made up of minerals, chemicals, atoms, electrons, quarks, and energy," while the "spiritual realm consists of a personal God, miracles, prophecy, visions, dreams, healing, prayer and soul." The two aren't completely separate, but they are ontologically distinct; Lasley writes that "Christian reality consists of us goldfish, in water, with clear boundaries between the water and the transcendent spiritual realm beyond the glass. There is some Other out there that feeds us every day and changes the water."[13] Liberals, in contrast, view God as primarily internal, not external; as transcendent, not ineffable; as participating in the same reality as humans. Liberal Episcopalian John Shelby Spong draws on Paul Tillich's categorization of God, not as a personal Being, but as the Ground of All Being, when he writes that God is "not a person, but . . . the mystical presence in which all personhood could flourish. . . . This God was not a being but rather the power that called being forth in all creatures. This God was not an external, personal force that could be invoked but rather an internal reality that, when confronted, opened us to the meaning of life itself."[14]

A God who is a personal Other can be understood through reason; God as "personal" is conceived in theistic terms, including the capacity to reason. The capacity for reason is what conservative Christians usually define as the image of God; it is the only human capacity which can be pictured as "other," in some way independent of the "goldfish bowl" Marty Lasley describes. Systematic thinking becomes a "bridge" to this Other God. But a God who is an internal reality, transcendent and yet participating in our earthly lives, can be met and known in the experiences of life. This God can be encountered in many different ways and in many different experiences; in fact, relating a story of a personal, individualistic encounter with the divine is the best way to experience God.

The equally important issue of authority ("Who can say what is true?") derives from the identity of God. For conservatives, authority is located in a place understood as outside human experience and having some independence from it. The Bible is the central location of this outside authority, as the conservative wing of the Southern Baptist Convention makes clear: "What the Bible says, God says; what the Bible says happened, really happened; every miracle, every event, in every book of the

13. D. Marty Lasley, "Rescuing Christianity from Bishop Kevorkian," *The Anglican Voice: The Online Magazine of Episcopalians United* (2 June 1999), http://www.anglicanvoice.org/voice/spong0699.asp.

14. Bishop John Shelby Spong, *Why Christianity Must Change or Die* (San Francisco: HarperSanFrancisco, 1998), 42. In the book's opening chapter, Spong argues that any conservative/evangelical definition of God as "external, supernatural, and invasive" is intellectually bankrupt.

Old and New Testament is altogether true and trustworthy."[15] Conservatives attribute to the written words of Scripture an independence from material existence. Since these written words are grasped and understood by the mind, the mind and theological understanding become a more trustworthy locus of authority than experience. Syllogism, derived from the written Scripture, becomes the highest form of truth; theological statements possess an objective reality, as summarized by David F. Wells:

> [The prophets of the Bible] were interpreting the external acts of God in a history that was objective, by a Word that was divinely given and was not a result of their own sagacity or personal insight. And we need that same objectivity if we are to find again a fully active Christian mind today. . . . It is simply incontrovertible that the disappearance of a belief in truth of this order destroys both the soil in which any theology must grow and the criterion by which it must be judged. Without this criterion, theology becomes autobiography, and, no matter how revealing it is of the person who shares it, it can have no public significance. . . . Unless truth is objective, it cannot be declared to others, cannot be taught to others, cannot be required of others.[16]

Implicit in this judgment, but apparently unrecognized, is a Platonic understanding of the intellect as possessing a degree of freedom over against the deceptive appearance of material things.

This conservative trust in the Bible's authority is accompanied by a suspicion of any moral pronouncements based on the individual or even collective experience of Christians.[17] Experience is seen by conservatives as both attractive and deceptive, and as a potentially dangerous challenge to the Bible's inerrancy.[18]

15. Report of the Presidential Theological Study Committee, Part II, Article I (SBC, 1994). Adopted by the Southern Baptist Convention, meeting in committee, June 1994; recently republished in *Baptist Confessions, Covenants, and Catechisms*, ed. Timothy George and Denise George (Nashville, TN: Broadman & Holman, 1996).

16. David F. Wells, *No Place For Truth: Or Whatever Happened to Evangelical Theology* (Grand Rapids: Eerdmans, 1993), 281-282.

17. See, for example, Harold Lindsell, *The Battle for the Bible* (Grand Rapids, MI: Zondervan, 1976); and Kern Robert Trembath, *Evangelical Theories of Biblical Inspiration: A Review and Proposal* (New York: Oxford University Press, 1987).

18. An examination of evangelical attitudes towards the Bible is obviously beyond the scope of this chapter. In *The Evangelical Renaissance* (Grand Rapids, MI: Eerdmans, 1973),

Liberal Protestants, on the other hand, see ethical authority as evolving within the experiences of everyday life. The ongoing history and experience of God's people thus becomes as important as God's actual words. Paul Beeman of the United Methodist Church quotes approvingly from liberal theologians Victor Paul Furnish and Gerhard Ebeling to make this point:

> New Testament scholar Victor Paul Furnish puts it this way: "Specific moral teaching of the Bible is less important than the Bible's total witness to God in history." . . . [A]n evolving understanding of what beliefs and behaviors should be normative for Christian discipleship. . . . Experience is theologian Gerhard Ebeling's definition of the Word of God. He wrote that God's Word is not the Bible itself; not the printer's ink on a printed page. The Word is the event, when words spring off the page, grasp us by the collar, and claim us. Word is event; experience.[19]

Liberal theology conflates Scripture and experience, suggesting that the two are co-dependent; the written words of Scripture arose from the experiences and stories of God's people; thus, the ongoing stories of God's people are also "Scripture," and in a sense are authoritative.

For liberalism, stories of experience are trustworthy because they reveal the divine within; dogmatic theology is suspect because it takes cat-

---

evangelical theologian Donald G. Bloesch was able to point out, quite accurately, that modern evangelicals "acknowledge that the Bible is the word of man as well as the Word of God, and that the divine Word is made known through a human word that bears the marks of cultural conditioning" (33). This view has gained strength in the decades since Bloesch's survey. However, Bloesch qualifies his conclusion, noting that evangelicals remain "adamant in their contention . . . that the revealed Word of God, Jesus Christ, must not be set against the written Word, that the latter is the original and definitive witness to Jesus Christ" (34). In other words, Scripture (even qualified as culturally shaped) remains interpretive of ALL experience — not only the experience of the individual believer, but the experience of Christ Himself. That Bloesch's qualification was still accurate for 1990s evangelicalism is made clear in Wells' *No Place for Truth,* a book that won the 1994 Gold Medal from the Evangelical Press Association.

19. Transcript of a speech given by Paul Beeman, retired clergy of the United Methodist Church (Pacific Northwest Annual Conference) and president of PFLAG (Parents, Families, and Friends of Lesbians and Gays), at the Reconciling Congregation Program Annual Dinner, Pacific Northwest Annual Conference of the United Methodist Church, Moscow, Idaho, June 18, 1999.

egories that might work for one person's experience and imposes them on another person's experience. For conservatives, doctrine is trustworthy because it is derived from Scripture, and the mind which apprehends Scripture (in contrast to the whole person/emotion/soul that is involved in experience) can grasp truth. Even after redemption, however, experience is suspect; apparently, the mind which reads and understands Scripture is more trustworthy than the entire person who experiences God.

This summary should clearly reveal one similarity between liberal and conservative points of view: Both "parties" of Protestantism are united in seeing human existence on earth as not completely flawed. Conservatives trust the mind, while liberals (ironically enough) do not. But both posit a reliable way of knowing the divine, and their preferences influence their chosen methods of communication and of worship. They also bear on how they judge the value of different kinds of hymns.

There are obvious differences between the narrative and systematic groups of hymns: nine of the narrative hymns were written by women, while none of the systematic hymns are female-authored; 28 of the narrative hymns were written after 1800, and of those, 15 were written after 1850. Only nine of the systematic hymns were written after 1800; of those, only two were written after 1850. These divisions correspond with the conservative claim that storytelling and reliance on experience represents a nineteenth-century corruption of right doctrine, coinciding with a sentimental "feminization" and weakening of biblical Christianity.[20]

But on closer examination, this division becomes problematic. Sentimental language and images also characterize systematic hymns (consider, for example, Philip Doddridge's "Grace, 'tis a charming sound"). More importantly, the basic pattern of the narrative hymn is thoroughly biblical: the progression of difficulty/encounter/enlightenment/new state of being characterizes dozens of scriptural stories, including those of Jacob and Israel, that have been used as conscious models for narrative hymns. As a matter of fact, the systematic progression of redemption (sin/redemption/sanctification/glorification) is itself an example of this progression.

Furthermore, Watts, the logician, wrote ten of the narrative hymns

20. See, for example, Ann Douglas's *The Feminization of American Culture* (1977; New York: Farrer, Straus, Giroux, 1998), a feminist history from the 1970s which, despite its questionable historical judgments, has suddenly become a frequently-cited source for conservatives lamenting the decline of American evangelicalism.

— along with eighteen of the systematic hymns. And the revivalist Wesleys, while writing eleven of the narrative hymns, also produced four systematic hymns.

An examination of nineteenth-century evangelical reflection on emotion and reason does not make it any easier to separate the two. Watts's concern for right reason is shared, not only by his fellow hymn writers, but by later evangelical Protestant preachers — even those who are more commonly portrayed as focused on revivalistic emotion, rather than the right use of the mind. Charles Finney's introduction to his 1851 work on systematic theology, *Lectures on Systematic Theology*, for example, relies heavily on the practice of syllogism. Finney's own introduction to his work begins:

> In this work I have endeavoured to define the terms used by Christian divines, and the doctrines of Christianity, as I understand them, and to push to their logical consequences the cardinal admissions of the more recent and standard theological writers. . . . I regard the assertion, that the doctrines of theology cannot preserve a logical consistency throughout, as both dangerous and ridiculous.[21]

Finney is characterized as a revivalist in studies of American Protestantism[22] — a label which does not always carry positive connotations. Paul K. Conkin, in *The Uneasy Center: Reformed Christianity in Antebellum America,* remarks primly that the revival meetings of Charles Finney and his Methodist compatriots involved "excitement and innovative physical exercises."[23] In fact, he defines evangelicalism as a movement that puts "warm and spontaneous worship [and] frequent revivals" at the center of religious expression. Yet this warmth and innovative physical demonstration clearly does not involve skepticism about the importance of the intellect, as Finney's words make clear:

> My brother, sister, friend — read, study, think, and read again. You were made to think. It will do you good to think; to develop your pow-

21. Charles Grandison Finney, Jr. *Lectures on Systematic Theology: Embracing Moral Government, the Atonement, Moral and Physical Depravity, Natural, Moral, and Gracious Ability, Repentance, Faith, Justification, Sanctification, &c.* (London: William Tegg and Co., 1851), no page numbers.

22. Mark A. Noll, *A History of Christianity in the United States and Canada* (Grand Rapids, MI: Eerdmans, 1992), 174, characterizes Finney as "the best-known revivalist in the United States."

23. Paul K. Conkin, *The Uneasy Center: Reformed Christianity in Antebellum America* (Chapel Hill: University of North Carolina Press, 1995), 126.

ers by study. God designed that religion should require thought, intense thought, and should thoroughly develop our powers of thought. The Bible itself is written in a style so condensed as to require much intense study. Many know nothing of the Bible or of religion, because they will not think and study.[24]

John Wesley, another Methodist revivalist and the author of several narrative hymns, is sometimes criticized for his stress on emotionalism. Yet Wesley's seventieth sermon in his *Standard Sermons,* entitled, "The Case of Reason Impartially Considered," had this to say: "Among them that despise and vilify reason, you may always expect to find those enthusiasts who suppose the dreams of their own imagination to be revelations from God. We cannot expect that men of this turn will pay much regard to reason. Having an infallible guide, they are very little moved by the reasonings of fallible men." Wesley also criticized those who "run into the contrary" error: "While they are strongly impressed with the absurdity of undervaluing reason, how apt are they to overvalue it! Accordingly, we are surrounded with those (we find them on every side) who lay it down as an undoubted principle, that reason is the highest gift of God. They paint it in the fairest colours; they extol it to the skies. They are fond of expatiating in its praise; they make it little less than divine. They are wont to describe it as very near, if not quite, infallible. They look upon it as the all-sufficient director of all the children of men; able, by its native light, to guide them into all truth, and lead them into all virtue."[25]

This balance is also present in the narrative hymns of the Wesleys, which appeal to experience and emotion, yet do not hesitate to draw from the reasoned doctrines of orthodoxy to describe highly personal encounters with God. A classic case is the narrative hymn "O, for a heart to praise my God," written by Charles Wesley (c. 1742):

O for a heart to praise my God, *[Opening dilemma: wish to be set free*
A heart from sin set free, *from sin to praise God without hindrance]*
A heart that always feels thy blood
So freely shed for me. *[Soteriology: justification]*

24. Finney, *Lectures.*

25. John Wesley, Sermon 70, "The Case of Reason Impartially Considered." Posted on the Christian Classics Ethereal Server (1999), no page numbers.

A heart resigned, submissive, meek,
My great Redeemer's throne,
Where only Christ is heard to speak,
Where Jesus reigns alone. *[Doctrine: Christ's exaltation]*

A humble, lowly, contrite, heart,
Believing, true and clean, *[Soteriology: sanctification]*
Which neither life nor death can part
From Christ who dwells within.

A heart in every thought renewed
And full of love divine, *[Soteriology: sanctification]*
Perfect and right and pure and good,
A copy, Lord, of thine.

My heart, thou know'st, can never rest *[Repetition of the dilemma,*
Till thou create my peace; *with the addition of restlessness]*
Till of mine Eden repossest,
From self, and sin, I cease.

Thy nature, gracious Lord, impart;
Come quickly from above; *[The encounter: phrased as a request]*
Write thy new name upon my heart,
Thy new, best name of Love. *[The resolution: after the encounter, the heart is in better standing and experiences greater devotion to God]*

It is undeniable that proportionately, a greater number of narrative hymns were written after 1800 than before. Although little work has been done on the rhetorical patterns of hymns, David Reynolds has documented a shift between 1774 and 1912 in pulpit rhetoric — from an emphasis on the logical development of an intellectual idea found in Scripture, to an emphasis on stories about people's lives, including their moral problems and the proper resolutions of these problems.[26]

Reynolds sees the primary shift from "logical" to "narrative" rhetoric

26. David Reynolds, "From Doctrine to Narrative: The Rise of Pulpit Storytelling in America," *American Quarterly* 32 (Winter 1980): 479-498. The argument is amplified in Reynolds's book, *Faith in Fiction: The Emergence of Religious Literature in America* (Cambridge, MA: Harvard University Press, 1981).

as taking place between 1776 and the late 1850s. He suggests that the ecclesiastical "disestablishment" provided by the Constitution put all churches into a buyer's market where they had to attract as many congregants as possible while competing with other churches — and so religious speech in preaching, as well as in worship, began to shift towards the popular and attractive, and away from the "elite," educated model of rational discourse. In Reynolds's view, this transition happened both within the nascent conservative wing of Protestantism (the populist evangelicals/revivalists) and within the newly forming liberal wing — the elite, New England, Unitarian churches. Revivalists and evangelicals made "emotional appeals to the masses, thereby simplifying and often sentimentalizing doctrine," while Unitarians "preferred stylistic and rhetorical beauty to theological investigation."[27] In other words, evangelicals wanted converts, and Unitarians wanted beauty; both turned to stories to fulfill their needs.

Reynolds' analysis, however, takes no account of studies suggesting that the American religious scene was a little more complicated than the two-party system he describes (conservative populists on the one hand, and liberal elites on the other); both Nathan Hatch's *The Democratization of American Christianity* and Robert Abzug's *Cosmos Crumbling* offer a more complex portrait of American religion. Furthermore, the shift from doctrine to storytelling is not as complete or as chronologically simple as Reynolds implies. Reynolds writes that theology was "overthrown" by the time of the Civil War; he describes the nineteenth-century "dissolution" of theology, and concludes that nineteenth-century religion prospered in America, while theology went slowly bankrupt.[28]

But examination of the 150 most frequently reprinted hymns shows no clear chronological division. Narrative hymns were more frequently composed in the nineteenth century, but their use was pioneered by Watts; systematic hymns continued to be written and used. This collection of hymns implies that both ways of understanding faith — the narrative and the doctrinal — have existed side by side in American religious thought from 1700 on. A more satisfying explanation seems to be that both of these two ways of thinking have been related to common intellectual currents.

Conservative thought has been greatly influenced by "Scottish com-

27. Reynolds, "From Doctrine to Narrative," 491.

28. Ibid., 498.

mon sense," a philosophy traced back to Thomas Reid, who reacted to the skepticism of David Hume by objecting that "everyone in his senses believes such truths as the existence of the real world, cause and effect, and the continuity of the self. The ability to know such things is as natural as the ability to breathe air."[29] As developed in America, common sense philosophy has three elements: epistemological common sense, which asserts that truth in propositional form can be grasped by all, not simply by the learned elite; ethical common sense, which asserts that humans know "by the nature of their own being certain foundational principles of morality"; and methodological common sense, which suggests that any truth about the world, religion, or consciousness can be built by a "strict induction" from the "first principles" of knowledge.[30] Charles Hodge's 1872 statement is typical of a conservative reliance on methodological common sense: "The Bible is to the theologian what nature is to the man of science. It is his storehouse of facts; and his method of ascertaining what the Bible teaches is the same as that which the natural philosopher adopts to ascertain what nature teaches."[31] This equation of the Bible with objective fact is further explored by Nancey Murphy in *Beyond Liberalism and Fundamentalism*. Murphy's brief survey of Western philosophical thought begins with Descartes' innovation: replacing the idea of authority resting in a "self" or author with the modern notion of "indubitable beliefs *available to each individual*."[32] This is foundationalism — a system of knowledge built on an objective, universally available foundation. Locke, following conceptually after Descartes, distinguished three kinds of knowledge: empirical science (based on sensory experience), indubitable knowledge (based on ideas and deduction), and revelation. Revelation depends on the existence of God, which Locke classifies as indubitable knowledge. Murphy writes that modern conservatives are Cartesian foundationalists, seeking to use Scripture as an inerrant, "indubitable foundation for theological construction."[33] Conservative exaltation of doctrine, based on Scripture, relies on methodological common sense and a foundationalist view of Scripture.

29. Mark A. Noll, "Common Sense Traditions and American Evangelical Thought," *American Quarterly* 37 (1989): 220.

30. Ibid., 221.

31. Quoted in Noll, "Common Sense Traditions," 223.

32. Murphy, *Beyond Liberalism and Fundamentalism*, 12.

33. Ibid., 17.

Yet Nancey Murphy claims that liberals too are committed to foundationalist thought. She cites Stephen Toulmin's *Cosmopolis: The Hidden Agenda of Modernity* on the origin of Cartesian foundationalism: "The bloodshed and chaos that followed upon seventeenth-century differences of belief lent urgency to the quest for universal agreement; the epistemologist could render a service to humanity by finding a way to produce such agreement. . . . So, from Descartes's time, the ideal of human knowledge focused on the general, the universal, the timeless, the theoretical — in contrast to the local, the particular, the timely, the practical. In short, it is the quest for universal knowledge that drives the modern quest for indubitable foundations."[34]

Locke's "indubitable knowledge" relied on the universal sway of reason; but a new kind of foundationalism, first articulated by Friedrich Schleiermacher, proposed that the essence of all religion is "a certain sort of feeling or awareness." This God-consciousness is universal and unmediated, available (in principle) to all human beings; it is "the true source or origin of religion, not a product of anything prior." Scripture is no longer foundational; rather, it is "undergirded by a theory of universal religious experience."[35] In contemporary liberalism, the descriptions of "experience" become highly nuanced and complex, but the central point remains: any scriptural claim must be "tested against the criterion of adequacy to common human experience."

The liberal exaltation of experience and the conservative reliance on doctrine ultimately rest on the same foundationalist assumptions. The interconnections between these ways of thinking is clearly seen as they overlap in the hymns most commonly used by American Protestants, who wrote — and sang — hymns of experience and hymns of doctrine with equal vigor.

Reclaiming a Confidence in Narrative

As a child of evangelicalism, and as a worship leader, and a novelist, I find myself returning to the question: Why is Michael Horton frightened of experience? Why do conservatives treat stories with such suspicion?

34. Ibid., 13.
35. Ibid., 22-24.

Conservative wariness of narratives may have to do with a desire to police identities. The flexibility and ambiguity of narrative allow for experiences of faith different than our own. Narrative theologian Johann Baptist Metz writes that marginal groups always employ "not argument and reasoning, but narrative"; they tell stories about their experience because this "refusal to speak the language of ritual and theology" is the only way to express a different grasp of reality than those who rule a culture or a situation.[36] Those who view themselves at the "center" are much more likely to employ doctrinal, logical language. If this is so, conservatives are trying to position themselves at the center of American Protestantism, and are reluctant to admit any method of discovering truth that might edge them from this contested spot.

Yet narrative can accomplish important purposes that doctrine cannot. Paul Ricoeur writes:

> The most important lesson to be gained from [Robert] Alter's work [in *The Art of Biblical Narrative*], a lesson that had already been formulated with much power by Eric Auerbach in his *Mimesis*, is that it is precisely the narrative composition, the organizing of the events in the narrative, that is the vehicle for, or, better, that foments, the theological interpretation. . . . What struck Alter in the more dramatic of these narratives is the fact that the text aims at communicating the conviction that the divine plan, although ineluctable, gets realized only by means of what he calls "the refractory nature of man." . . . Taking this problem up from the other end, we might say that a theology that confronts the inevitability of the divine plan with the refractory nature of human actions and passions is a theology that engenders narrative; better, it is a theology that calls for the narrative mode as its major hermeneutical mode. . . . Thus the closing words of Alter's book are relevant to our investigation: "It is in the stubbornness of human individuality that each man and woman encounters God or ignores Him, responds to or resists Him 'in' the perilously momentous realm of history."[37]

Narrative structure, where the inevitable divine plan collides with the re-

36. Johann Baptist Metz, "A Short Apology of Narrative," trans. David Smith, in *Why Narrative? Readings in Narrative Theology,* ed. Stanley Hauerwas and L. Gregory Jones (Grand Rapids: Eerdmans, 1989), 255.

37. Ricoeur, *Figuring the Sacred,* 182-183.

fractoriness of human nature, makes a theological statement too complex and painful to be put into systematic form, yet too important to be ignored. Conservatives who recaptured narrative and sanctioned the use of the narrative hymns, could regain in worship this element of struggle and mystery; narrative theology, as Terrence Tilley writes, "recognizes the irreducible and provocative multiplicity in Christianity. . . . The God who bargains with Abraham and Moses will not budge with Jonah. . . . The loving Father of Jesus does not visit the death of his Son. The stories of God cannot be captured in a system."[38] What is true for Christian reality in general, should be regarded as also true in our hymns.

38. Terrence Tilley, *Story Theology* (Wilmington, DE: Michael Glazier, 1985), 17.

CHAPTER ELEVEN

"Some Poor Sailor, Tempest Tossed": Nautical Rescue Themes in Evangelical Hymnody

Richard J. Mouw

Two motives sparked the writing of this chapter. The first was simply the wish to take a closer look at hymns that I have loved since I first sang them in my childhood and teenage years. In those days I regularly visited local rescue missions with church groups, and it was in those visits that I learned to sing about rescuing the perishing and throwing out lifelines. Although I had almost no direct experience with the dangers of sea travel, the imagery of those hymns nevertheless seemed to convey important truths about our human condition and the good news of the Christian story.

Secondly, I wanted to interact with some of the interpretations that Sandra Sizer set forth in her important book, *Gospel Hymns and Social Religion* (1978). I find her "rhetorical" analysis of nineteenth-century hymnody to be both creative and illuminating. Her project of exploring gospel hymns in order to explicate their portrayal of social reality is an important one. But I do have some serious questions about what she sees as the social implications of the rescue imagery employed by nineteenth-century hymn writers, and I will explore my disagreements with her on these matters in what follows.

My personal acquaintance with at least one kind of twentieth-century setting in which hymns employing nautical imagery were featured makes me skeptical about any claim that these musical expressions have some sort of intrinsic connection to unworthy social goals. I learned many of my earliest lessons about God's deep concern for poverty and oppression during my regular visits to evangelical skid-row rescue missions during childhood and teenage years. There, long before I knew anything about Saint Francis and Mother Teresa, I saw dedicated Christians offering a loving embrace to the addicted, the hungry, and the homeless. And because it was precisely in those contexts that I also learned to sing nautical-image hymns, it seems obvious to me that the "rescue" motif was intended to highlight a sense of mission that went beyond an exclusively "spiritual" scope. The connection between the imagery and the sense of mission is what I will explore here.

Elements of Nautical Imagery

My special focus here are gospel hymns that feature seafaring themes. In their use of nautical imagery, evangelical hymn writers have typically focused on one or more of four elements.

First, *life as a stormy sea:* This is a basic theme that is presupposed in the use of other elements. The troubles and challenges that human beings face in life are likened to the perils encountered at sea, as in Edward Hopper's oft-sung verse:

Jesus, Savior, pilot me
Over life's tempestuous sea;
Unknown waves before me roll,
Hiding rock and treacherous shoal;
Chart and compass came from Thee:
Jesus, Savior, pilot me.[1]

Second, *the plea for a reliable pilot/navigator:* Hopper's verse also illustrates the way in which God (often Jesus) is depicted as helping people make their way across the stormy sea of life.

Third, *the quest for safety:* The benefits of the Christian life are portrayed in terms of finding refuge from the dangers of the sea. Preaching and evangelism are likened to lighthouse functions. A positive relationship with God is seen as residing in a calm harbor or a haven. Sometimes anchorage motifs are also employed, as in:

1. Edward Hopper, "Jesus, Savior, pilot me" (1871), *Tabernacle Hymns, Number Three: For the Church and Sunday School* (Chicago: Tabernacle, 1949), no. 308.

Will your anchor hold
in the storms of life,
When the clouds unfold
their wings of strife?
When the strong tides lift
and the cables strain,
Will your anchor drift,
or firm remain?
We have an anchor
that keeps the soul
Steadfast and sure
while the billows roll,
Fastened to the Rock
which cannot move,
Grounded firm and deep
in the Savior's love.[2]

Fourth, *the call to rescue those in peril:* The Christian community is seen as having been given an urgent rescue mandate, as in the final verse of Edward Ufford's "Throw out the Life-Line":

Soon will the season of rescue be o'er,
Soon they will drift to eternity's shore,
Haste then, my brother, no time for delay,
But throw out the Lifeline and save them today.[3]

Features

I turn now to a brief look at some key features — mostly obvious ones — of the hymns that emphasize nautical rescue.

2. Priscilla Jane Owens, "We have an anchor" (1882), *The Cyber Hymnal* (http://www.cyberhymnal.org/htm/w/e/h/wehavean.htm).

3. Edward Ufford, "Throw out the Lifeline" (1888), *Tabernacle Hymns,* no. 16.

The Focus on the Individual

In his 1974 encyclical "Redemptor Hominis," Pope John Paul II referred to his immediate predecessor, Paul VI, as the "helmsman of the Church, the bark of Peter."[4] In doing so, he was making use of an ecclesial image that has a long history. Indeed, as Gertrude Grace Sill points out, the continuing designation of the central portion of a church building as the "nave" derives from the ancient practice of depicting the church as a sailing vessel that, as St. Hippolytus put it, "is beaten by the waves, but not submerged."[5]

This same image is employed in a well-known African-American hymn: "The winds may blow and the billows may foam, / Oh, glory hallelujah, / But she is able to land us all home. / Oh, glory hallelujah. / 'Tis the old ship of Zion, hallelujah."[6] This use of the sailing vessel image to refer to the church as a corporate body does not seem to come as naturally to nineteenth-century white evangelicals. Take, for example, Dwight L. Moody's well-known "lifeboat" comment: "I look upon this world as a wrecked vessel. God has given me a lifeboat and said to me, 'Moody, save all that you can.'"[7] Here Moody sees the sailing vessel as being given to him individually — " God has given *me* a lifeboat" — as an instrument for his own evangelistic ministry. Similarly, the sung request is that "Jesus, Savior, [will] pilot *me*"; and individual believers know that their only means of safety in the storms of life is to have their *personal* anchors firmly secured to the Rock: "Blow your wildest, then, O gale, / On my bark so small and frail: / By His grace I shall not fail, / For my anchor holds."[8]

This is obviously the kind of spiritual expression that typically gets labeled "individualism" by evangelicalism's critics. Is such judgment fair? I think not. For example, in a recent volume in which three mainline Protestant pastors tell the stories of their pilgrimage "beyond liberalism,"

4. Pope John Paul II, "*Redemptor Hominis:* An Encyclical Letter of the Redeemer of Man," March 4, 1979, Part I, Section 3 (http://www.newadvent.org/docs/jp02rh.htm).

5. Gertude Grace Sill, *A Handbook of Symbols in Christian Art* (New York: Macmillan, 1975), 134.

6. Thomas W. Carter "The old ship Zion" (1844), *The Sacred Harp Composer Index* (http://fasola.org/index/L/079.html).

7. Quoted in William G. McLoughlin, *Revivals, Awakenings, and Reform: An Essay on Religion and Social Change in America, 1607-1977* (Chicago: University of Chicago Press, 1978), 144.

8. W. C. Martin, "My Anchor Holds" (1902), *The Cyber Hymnal* (http://www.cyberhymnal.org/htm/m/myanchor.htm).

Anthony B. Robinson testifies to a new emphasis in his ministry on the importance of "conversion." But he quickly adds: "I am not much interested in fundamentalist versions of conversion, which seem to me too privatistic, too scripted, and too inclined to [view conversion] as the end of suffering or problems, when it may be the beginning of them."[9] This characterization does not seem to portray the view of reality we are exploring here, where human life — even the Christian life — is viewed as a journey on a stormy sea, and where the available "chart and compass" hardly seem to provide a well-scripted path of clear sailing. Nor is the "other-directedness" of the believer's journey — constantly hearing the urgent call to throw out the lifelines and to aid struggling persons into the lifeboat — easily thought of as a "privatistic" understanding of how God wants believers to make their way through the world.

"Mode of Address"

I borrow this category from Sandra Sizer, who has distinguished three basic patterns in nineteenth-century gospel hymns.[10] One is where no particular "audience" is specified. The hymn may simply make an affirmation ("O, how I love Jesus") or tell a story ("There were ninety and nine").

A second mode is that of exhorting human audiences. The hymn may issue a plea to sinners to turn from their wicked ways ("Come to the Savior now"), or it may urge Christians to get on with an important task ("Sound the battle cry").

Sizer's third mode is the direct address to the deity, either with supplications and requests ("Guide me, O Thou great Jehovah") or expressions of praise or thanks ("Holy, holy, holy, Lord God almighty").

This last mode of address is perhaps the most common in classical hymnody; indeed, a case can be made for it being the proper form of the hymn as such. But it is not the dominant mode of address in nineteenth-century evangelical hymns. Here the first and second modes dominate. And in those hymns employing nautical rescue themes, exhortation is the

9. Martin B. Copenhaver, Anthony B. Robinson, and William H. Willimon, *Good News in Exile: Three Pastors Offer a Hopeful Vision for the Church* (Grand Rapids: Eerdmans, 1999), 24.

10. Sandra Sizer, *Gospel Hymns and Social Religion: The Rhetoric of 19th Century Revivalism* (Philadelphia: Temple University Press, 1978), 169.

typical pattern: they address the Christian community, and they feature an urgent call-to-action: "Throw out the lifeline," "Rescue the perishing," "Let the lower lights be burning." That this is the typical mode should not be surprising: when the subject matter is seeking the lost who are somewhere "out there," it makes more sense to encourage the seekers than to address directly those who have not yet been "found."

Recommended "Posture"

I use this term to point to a set of issues that Sizer discusses in terms of "passivity and passion," two closely related qualities that she sees as characterizing, with varying degrees of intensity, nineteenth-century gospel hymns. Her examples illustrate the ways in which — as she sees it — Christians are called in these hymns to a passive, albeit passionate, surrender to the divine will.[11]

The songs that would seem on the face of it to resist being grouped under the "passivity-passion" rubric are those calling Christians to engage in battle — there is obviously much passion in these hymns, but the passivity is not obvious. But Sizer points out that calls to action — as exemplified clearly in "Onward, Christian Soldiers, marching as to war" — are not typical of the genre. "Most battle hymns," Sizer observes, "are not those of the conquistador"; rather, they put more of an emphasis on "the kingly role of Jesus than on the battle itself; and most of the rest portray not a conquering army, but rather bands of fighters exhorted to 'stand,' 'display' the banner, be 'firm' and 'steady,' 'not turn away.'" In "Hold the Fort," for example, believers are "on the defensive, waiting to be saved by the action of Jesus, but not going out to conquer territory."[12]

While all of this makes good sense, Sizer's case is less convincing when she turns to an analysis of "missionary hymns." Here too she finds examples of bold activism. In "From Greenland's Icy Mountains," for example, various nations are portrayed as pleading with Christians "to deliver their land from error's chain." This Sizer sees as displaying the "imperial mission" spirit. But the "rescue mission" hymns are, on her analysis, better understood in terms of the "passivity-passion" pattern. She sees

11. Sizer, *Gospel Hymns,* 38-40.

12. Ibid., 41.

signs of this "shift from a more active to a more passive conception of the religious life" in a hymn like Fanny Crosby's "Rescue the perishing." But the shift reaches "its logical conclusion in hymns in which Christians say and do nothing, but are simply lights shining in the darkness."[13] She offers Philip Bliss's "Let the lower lights be burning" as a case in point:

> Brightly beams our Father's mercy
> From His lighthouse evermore,
> But to us He gives the keeping
> Of the lights along the shore.
> Let the lower lights be burning!
> Send a gleam across the wave!
> Some poor fainting, struggling seaman
> You may rescue, you may save.[14]

This hymn, says Sizer, totally dispels the notion that saving people from a shipwreck might be a strenuous task. Again, people passively tossed about by the forces of chaos are rescued, brought into the circle of salvation by another passive force, the "lights along the shore."[15]

According to Sizer, this imagery reinforces a pattern wherein "Christian workers do not move far from their territory," inviting sinners to come to them, rather than venturing into dangerous regions themselves.[16]

Again, I do not think Sizer's analysis holds up. Take her primary example, Philip Bliss's "Let the lower lights be burning." Bliss had borrowed the imagery for this hymn from a story he heard from D. L. Moody, about a ship that had attempted to dock at Cleveland on a stormy night. The single light from the main lighthouse was visible, but no one had lit the smaller lights that lined the shore. Thus, the ship missed the channel and crashed onto the rocks, and many lives were lost. Moody used this story to issue a call to Christian faithfulness: "Brethren, the Master will take care of the great light-house: let us keep the lower lights burning."[17]

13. Ibid., 43-44.

14. Quoted by Sizer, *Gospel Hymns,* 44.

15. Ibid., 44.

16. Ibid., 43.

17. Victor C. Detty, *P. P. Bliss: A Centennial Sketch of His Life and Work, 1838-1938* (Wyssox, PA: by the Author, 1938), 34.

There is an obvious call to action in Moody's story. The ship in question had not made it safely to shore because people had failed to *do* something: they had neglected to light the lamps that marked the coastline. Bliss, echoing Moody's use of this illustration, was urging Christians to be diligent in maintaining these "lower lights" in actively pursuing the evangelistic mission. To be sure, an even more aggressive action is thinkable — launching an active rescue operation into the churning waters. But the whole point of the Moody-Bliss example seems to be that Christians should actively send signals out to persons at sea, even when actually taking lifeboats into a stormy night is not feasible.

Sizer is mistaken, then, when she construes the imagery employed by Moody and Bliss as simply encouraging a passive posture in the Christian life. The real shift that *is* worth noting in this kind of hymn, however, is one toward a more dramatic depiction of the conditions in which sinners find themselves. The "imperial mission" imagery that Sizer reads as encouraging passionate Christian action presupposes a context in which captive lands are hoping for a military invasion. The image, then, is that of active Christians moving into a context that is passively waiting for something to happen. The nautical imagery, on the other hand, presupposes a dangerously active sea — a condition that is not susceptible to alteration by Christian efforts. The only plausible rescue operation in such a situation is an active program of guiding seafarers to safety.

Actually, Sizer can make a case for passivity with reference to Bliss's hymn only by describing the situation in a way that leaves human effort out of the picture altogether. In the comment quoted above, she denies "that saving people from a shipwreck might be a strenuous task" by setting up a contrast between "people passively tossed about by the forces of chaos" and the salvation afforded by "another passive force, the 'lights along the shore.'" The important factor that she fails to mention — and the one that Moody and Bliss intended to emphasize — is the *active human maintenance* of "the lower lights."

"These Poor Sinners"

Samuel Hopkins Hadley, an important leader in the urban rescue mission movement of the nineteenth century, was himself one of the "rescued." An alcoholic who was contemplating suicide, he attended a service in New

York's Cremorne Mission one evening in 1882. When he heard the mission's founder, Jerry McAuley, tell how he, as a "thief, an outcast," and "one of the worst drunkards in the Fourth Ward," had experienced a dramatic conversion, Hadley knelt at the altar rail. He later testified that he was especially moved by the words — ones he would "never forget" — that McAuley prayed on behalf of the penitents that night: "Dear Savior, won't You look down in pity upon these poor souls? They need Your help, Lord; they cannot get along without it. Blessed Jesus! These poor sinners have got themselves into a bad hole. Won't You help them out? Speak to them, Lord; do, for Jesus' sake. Amen."[18]

This brief prayer captures much of the mood of the theological perspective that employed rescue themes. Sandra Sizer may have been wrong in insisting that Christians were relatively passive participants in the divine rescue operation, but she is certainly right when she sees the corresponding portrayal of the sinful "human condition as that of a passive victim."[19] In McAuley's prayer the "poor sinners" are helpless, having fallen "into a bad hole" with no means of deliverance apart from divine mercy.

Sizer imagines a debate between hymn writers of two very different theological periods: Ira Sankey, who represents the kind of theology associated with rescue themes, and Isaac Watts, whose convictions comported well with the more traditional patterns of Calvinist thought. Sizer summarizes their differences in this proposed debate topic: "Human Beings: Worms or Wanderers?" The worm image comes, of course, from the well-known Watts line: "Would he devote that sacred head for such a worm as I?" Sizer notes (with substantiating evidence from other hymns by Watts) that the "worm" is all the more despicable because he tries to exert his will against God, the ruler of all; that is, he is a *rebel* worm, a blasphemer, a criminal, a backslider, an upstart challenging God's rightful government; and such a worm deserves only to be damned.[20]

Sizer's observation that the rescue hymns signal a shift in the understanding of the sinful condition is well taken. These nineteenth-century hymns focus, not so much on arrogant rebels as on "these poor sinners."

18. S. H. Hadley, *Down in Water Street: A Story of Sixteen Years Life and Work in a Water Street Mission* (New York, 1902); quoted in Norris Magnuson, *Salvation in the Slums: Evangelical Social Work, 1865-1920* (Metuchen, NJ: Scarecrow Press and the American Theological Library Association, 1977), 11.

19. Sizer, *Gospel Hymns*, 30.

20. Ibid., 27.

This shift had much to do with the increasing numbers of evangelicals who were personally encountering the harsh realities of poverty. During this period in the nineteenth century, the Salvation Army's magazine, *War Cry,* regularly described the plight of the urban poor: the magazine's cover illustrations and articles graphically portrayed their distress, picturing barren and dirty rooms, shabbily clothed children playing in treeless streets beside the tenements, and evicted families standing helpless on the sidewalk.[21]

The sense of personal compassion for the urban sinner extended even to categories of persons who might otherwise be thought of by Christians in terms of arrogant rebellion. When Charles Crittendom, for example, urged New York prostitutes to turn from their wicked ways, he was soon overwhelmed by the futility of his pleas: the women, he realized, were trapped in a way of life with no plausible alternatives. Thereafter he emphasized the establishment of living quarters for "fallen women," including programs that would enable them to find a different way of life.[22]

Sizer acknowledges that the older elements of guilt, rebellion, and the need for pardon are not completely absent from the rescue hymns; "yet the former scenario of a court of judgment is softer and more diffuse."[23] There seems to be an obvious reason for this softening. The evangelicals who were attempting to minister to the urban destitute, including those desperate persons whose patterns of life were in open conflict with biblical values, were able to see — in ways that previous generations of evangelicals had not found it possible — that there were indeed structural-systemic factors that needed to be considered when assessing the sinful patterns of urban life. Prostitution and alcoholism were still viewed as behavioral sins displeasing to God. But the urban evangelists were unable to ignore the ways in which social conditions made it virtually impossible for many individuals *not* to fall into these sinful patterns. Our collective rebellion against God may have created the context in which systemic injustices were inevitable. But it was still necessary to see some classes of individuals as victimized *by* those unjust patterns. Thus the drunkard and the prostitute were viewed as both legal offenders *and* pitiable victims.

21. Magnuson, *Salvation in the Slums,* 31.

22. Ibid., 80.

23. Sizer, *Gospel Hymns,* 29.

On this point, Sizer seriously misinterprets an important line from P. P. Bliss's "Once for all": "Curs'd by the law and bruised by the fall." She insists that the use of "by" in both cases is meant to signal a denial of the sinner's active agency.[24] But here she fails to grasp the theological meaning of Bliss's use of the law image. The picture is one of a person, having actively broken the law, standing condemned ("curs'd") in a courtroom.[25] In pairing this image with that of the "bruised" character of our fallenness, Bliss is giving equal treatment to both our active rebellion and our passive "victim" status.

Political Implications

Sizer is especially interested, as she analyzes the "rhetoric" of these hymns, in their political implications. The emphasis that we have been noting on a personal compassion for victims of impersonal social forces was not, she insists, consciously intended to set forth a political program. Instead that compassion embodied a strategy — by focusing especially on conversion efforts that would produce changed hearts knit together in Christian fellowship — "for transcending [the political] by defining a sacred community."[26]

This conclusion seems to capture accurately the social aims that were served by the hymns in question. And as stated, these aims seem commendable. Unfortunately, however, Sizer seems to see something more insidious being promoted by the rescue hymns. The "community of feeling" that is reinforced by these hymns, she says, is detachable from the specific "structures of mass meetings" in which they were created, and are thus capable of being transplanted into "a home, a church, or an amorphous group which chose to sing together."

So far so good. But now Sizer quickly extends the argument. "Once the tradition was established" of relocating the "community of feeling" in the manner just described, "the hymns could float indefinitely," so that "evangelicals could appropriate them as symbols of unity in the face of

24. Ibid., 28-29.

25. This interpretation comports best with the sense of Galatians 3:10 (which is the likely source for Bliss's language): "For it is written, 'Cursed is everyone who does not observe and obey all things written in the book of the law.'"

26. Sizer, *Gospel Hymns*, 156.

potential threats from groups perceived as alien, whether aristocratic Southerners or despotic Catholics, or later, Jews or communists or homosexuals." Having posited these links, Sizer goes even further: "The popular evangelical tradition has a propensity to see conspiracies lurking around every corner; it is probably no accident that Billy Graham rose to fame in the late 1940s during the Communist scare which culminated in the atrocities of the McCarthy era."[27]

Needless to say, Sizer's clause — "it is probably no accident" — is itself the stuff of which conspiracy theories are woven. In a few short steps Sizer has gone from a helpful characterization of the social ethic implied by rescue hymns and other gospel songs of the nineteenth century to the insistence that the rhetorical trajectory of these hymns points to recent manifestations of anti-Semitism and homophobia. Having suggested that the nineteenth-century hymns created a community of feeling that not only included some people, but also excluded others, she goes on to blame the "rhetoric" of these hymns for all of the ways that later evangelicals defined themselves over against an alien "other."

Suppose, however, that we go back to the earlier stage of the argument, where she has established — correctly, in my view — that the rescue hymns reinforce a "sacred community" whose social strategy features a reaching out to the dispossessed in the hopes of incorporating them, by means of conversion, into fellowship that transcends political ideology. As stated, this account has a remarkably contemporary ring. The position described is not very different from, say, the influential view of the contemporary Christian ethicist Stanley Hauerwas, who is known for his contention that the church doesn't *have* a social ethic — it *is* one: "Put starkly, the first social ethical task of the church is to be the church — servant community." The church, says Hauerwas, is called primarily to be a countercultural model of the ways in which God wants human community to be organized. As such, he argues, the Christian community "must set its own agenda, caring in very personal ways for the widow, the poor, and the orphan. Such care, from the world's perspective, may seem to contribute little to the cause of justice, yet it is our conviction that unless we take the time for such care neither we nor the world can know what justice looks like."[28]

27. Ibid., 157.

28. Stanley Hauerwas, *The Peaceable Kingdom* (Notre Dame, IN: University of Notre Dame Press, 1983), 99-100.

Of course, one could insist that Hauerwas's model community also excludes even as it includes, since it too sees the Christian community as embodying a social ethic contradicting that of the larger culture — and that therefore it too can lead to conspiracy-inspired atrocities against the "other." But such a conclusion would require a rather lengthy argument, one that goes beyond simply speculating about the implications of Hauerwas's "rhetoric." Much the same would be needed, I suggest, to establish links between the content of nineteenth-century rescue hymns and the more recent evangelical behaviors of which Sizer so strongly disapproves. The argument in this latter case would have to take into account the important fact that the people who sang the rescue hymns in their nineteenth-century setting demonstrated strong impulses toward extending the boundaries of their "community of feeling" in remarkably inclusive ways, given their cultural setting — reaching out, for example, to black Americans and Asian immigrants in clear opposition to prevailing patterns of racist thought and practice.[29]

"Rescue" as an Organizing Image

Rescue, it should be clear by now, was a dominant motif for many nineteenth-century evangelicals as they attempted to spell out their conception of the Christian mission in the world. Does the rescue imagery still speak to our lives in the twenty-first century?

To suggest that it does would seem to be a rather bold move. For one thing, rescue has had a negative connotation in the contemporary therapeutic culture, where the role of "Rescuer" is typically treated as a form of pathology.[30] And even if we insist on taking our cues from the Bible rather than from contemporary culture, it still is not intuitively obvious that rescue deserves the prominent *theological* status that the nineteenth-century evangelicals gave it.

Not that the Bible ignores rescue imagery. The Psalms certainly contain many rescue themes: for example, "How long, O Lord, will you look on? Rescue . . . my life from the lions" (Ps. 35: 18), and the Psalmist's hymn

29. Magnuson, *Salvation in the Slums,* 118-131.

30. See, for example, the analysis of the Rescuer role in the alcoholic "game," in Eric Berne's bestseller, *Games People Play* (New York: Grove Press, 1964), 73-81.

of praise to the One "who redeems your life from the pit" (Ps. 103:4) — a motif that is echoed in Jerry McAuley's rescue mission prayer on behalf of "these poor sinners" who "have got themselves into a bad hole." In the New Testament, there is not much by way of explicit rescue imagery in the epistles, but the Gospels do display the theme on occasion — with perhaps the most notable example being the Good Shepherd's rescue mission on behalf of the one lost sheep.

We must still wonder, though, whether these biblical data justify the utilization of rescue imagery as anything more than one among many scriptural motifs. It is interesting to note that at least one scholar has recently given an affirmative answer to this question. In 1995 Peter Selby, a British theologian and former Anglican bishop, published a small monograph entitled *Rescue: Jesus and Salvation Today.* Even though Selby gives no indication that he cares about — or is even familiar with — the attention to rescue imagery in nineteenth-century evangelicalism, he does treat rescue as a central theme in biblical thought. "At the centre of the Christian enterprise lies a promise of rescue," says Selby; and the point of his book is "[t]o understand more adequately what Jesus offers in the way of rescue and how we are to appropriate that offer."[31]

In making his case for rescue as an image that can be plausibly used to explicate what the Bible has to say about God's overall redemptive purposes for humankind, Selby gives considerable attention to issues of structural sin. Indeed, many of his concerns echo those of liberation theologians — one could even plausibly substitute "liberation" for "rescue" at many points in his discussion.

But Selby's choice of rescue as an organizing theme gives his theology a broader scope than typically allowed by liberation theologies. He can incorporate the liberationist's concern for the ways in which individuals and societies are often oppressed by structural factors, while at the same time maintaining a central focus on the ways in which sin — both structural and individual — affects persons. It is most natural, after all, to think about *people* being rescued, and not economic or political systems.

Selby's approach, however, also produces a broader notion of rescue than was typical of the nineteenth-century evangelicals. Moody and others tended to depict a certain subgroup of human beings as needing rescue, with their own calling being that of rescuers. In contrast, Selby con-

31. Peter Selby, *Rescue: Jesus and Salvation Today* (London: SPCK, 1995), 1.

sistently portrays all human beings as proper objects of the divine rescue operation, not only the most obvious social "victims" — the poor, the political oppressed, persons who suffer from racist and genocidal schemes — but also those who are the perpetrators of programs of injustice. "Of course, the 'rescue' needed by the marginalized is not the same as that needed by those who are accomplices in causing them to be marginalized," Selby explains; "but the question, 'Who needs rescue?' is nevertheless the one that turns back on those who assume too quickly that they know it is others rather than themselves."[32]

While I will not pursue further Selby's development of the rescue theme as a theological organizing principle, I do want to underscore the way in which he uses this motif to cover both the passive and active dimensions of social presence. By insisting that both oppressor and oppressed are caught up in predicaments for which the only effective mode of deliverance is divine rescue, Selby means to emphasize the fact that our proper human response to the divine rescue operation is one of *both* passive reception of rescue as a gift *and* an active recognition that God will judge us for our failure to act in ways that are appropriate to the "rescued" life.[33]

Selby has demonstrated in an impressive manner that the rescue motif can be employed so as to give full theological attention to issues of structural injustice even while promising release from the things that enslave us in very personal ways. His nuanced account provides an attractive alternative to Sizer's depiction of our human role in God's overall rescue operation as a relatively passive one.

Continuing Storms at Sea

Any sensible theological evaluation of nautical rescue hymns must acknowledge, of course, that the Bible does not really make much use of the kind of seafaring imagery employed by the nineteenth-century hymn writers. To be sure, we have in the Scriptures stories about Noah and the ark, Jonah and the big fish, and allusions in the Psalms to angry waves. And there are a few obvious examples of nautical events in the Gospels —

32. Ibid., 110.

33. Ibid., 111.

even some cases where Jesus and his disciples faced life-threatening situations while traveling by boat. The epistles, on the other hand, contain nothing that has any real relevance to this subject.

But hymnic images do not have to be borrowed directly from the Scriptures in order to have theological legitimacy. What is important is that they comport well with underlying biblical themes, and that they "contextualize" these themes for believers in their present life situations.

This seems to be exactly what was happening in the nineteenth-century. For example, in his study of Victorian hymnody, Ian Bradley reports that when these American nautical hymns were "imported" to the British isles, they were embraced enthusiastically by Christians there. The British responded in a manner similar to their American counterparts to the depiction of "the human condition as one of being object rather than subject, tossed in the billows, shipwrecked, and then rescued and saved entirely by the actions of Jesus."[34]

Of course, all of this occurred — both in North America and Great Britain — in times and places where people were quite conscious of the dangers of the sea, so that images of angry waters and vulnerable barks and the real threat of shipwreck were appropriate vehicles for some deep spiritual impulses. Have these images become less compelling in our own day, when reports of tragedies on highways and air travel routes are more likely to occupy our attention than stories of accidents at sea? I think not. The continuing fascination with the story of the *Titanic* is one piece of evidence for a hypothesis that can only be suggested here, namely, that images associated with "the angry deep" have an enduring power in the human imagination that has little to do with our geography or our level of technological sophistication.

Indeed, it was not all that long ago when some of the most "advanced" discussions of the distribution of resources in our global community were being debated in terms of "lifeboat ethics." And I cannot refrain from pointing out that in those discussions the emphasis was primarily on exclusion — who needs to be kept out of the lifeboat in a global crisis — in sharp contrast to Dwight L. Moody's more inclusive insistence that the Lord had commissioned him to get as many people as possible into his rescue craft.

34. Ian Bradley, *Abide With Me: The World of Victorian Hymns* (London: SCM Press, 1997), 174.

Perhaps the best place to begin assessing the continuing theological relevance of nautical rescue imagery is where the Bible itself begins. "In the beginning," writes the author of Genesis, the earth "was a formless void and darkness covered the face of the deep" — and then "a wind from God swept over the face of the waters" and the divine "let there be" brought light out of darkness and order out of chaos (Gen. 1:1-11).

But because of the entry of sin into the world, darkness and chaos continued to threaten the divinely created order. In the Old Testament the encounters between God's power and the forces of destruction are regularly depicted in terms of mighty waves challenging the Creator's good purposes: "O Lord God of hosts, who is as mighty as you, O Lord? Your faithfulness surrounds you. You rule the raging of the sea; When its waves rise, you still them." (Ps. 89:8-9). It is against the background of this ancient depiction of God's power that we must understand the response of Jesus' disciples when they witnessed his calming of the sea: "And they were filled with great awe and said to one another, 'Who then is this, that even the wind and the sea obey him?'" (Mark 4:41).

Darkness and chaos are only too familiar characteristics of our own "postmodern" era — a state of affairs made even more frightening by the fact that so many these days actually find reason to celebrate the absence of light and the presence of disorder. For some of us the terrors symbolized by images of individuals being tossed about by threatening waves on dark nights are not beyond our ken. Nor is it alien to our spiritual imaginations to understand our own mandate — as persons who have ourselves been rescued from those terrors — as a call to throw out lifelines and to keep lit the lights along the shore. Such an understanding of the human condition, and of God's instructions to Christians as to how to respond to that condition, will continue to have poignancy until such a time when the darkness is fully banished and the sea becomes as smooth as glass.

APPENDIX I

American Protestant Hymns Project: A Ranked List of Most Frequently Printed Hymns, 1737-1960

Prepared by Stephen A. Marini

This ranked list of 300 hymns represents the most often reprinted hymns found in 175 American Protestant hymnals and hymnbooks that were published from 1737 to 1960. It was prepared by Professor Stephen A. Marini of Wellesley College for a project, "Hymnody in American Protestantism," coordinated by the Institute for the Study of American Evangelicals (ISAE) at Wheaton College and funded by generous support from Wheaton College and the Lilly Endowment. This list was made available to participants in the ISAE project, and it was used extensively by Robert Schneider, Felicia Piscitelli, Jeffrey VanderWilt, and Susan Wise Bauer for the chapters they prepared for this book.

In this appendix, the hymns are ranked by the frequency of their apperance and then keyed to the use made of them by these four authors. The "first line" sometimes amalgamates hymn variations under the most-often used variant (e.g., "Come ye that love the Lord" and "Come we that love the Lord" are counted together under "Come we that love the Lord"). Author and date of initial publication follow (in parentheses), and then the number of hymnbooks out of the 175 in which the particular hymn was found is provided after the parenthesis.

The next column, designated by "M," is keyed to Schneider's chapter, "Jesus Shall Reign: Hymns and Foreign Missions, 1800-1870." It employs a listing of missionary hymns from nineteenth-century American Protestant hymnals compiled by Richard Steadman Mauney for his doctoral thesis, "The Development of Missionary Hymnody in the United States of America in the Nineteenth Century" (D.M.A. diss., Southwestern Baptist Theological Seminary, 1993), pp. 148-151. The numbers after the letter "M" designate the rank order of the hymn in the Mauney list followed (in parentheses) by the number of hymnals in which Mauney found it. Thus, "From Greenland's icy mountains" was the most frequently published missionary hymn, which Mauney found in 53 of the nineteenth-century hymnbooks that made up his sample.

The next column, designated by "RC," is keyed to Piscitelli's chapter, "Protestant Hymnody in Contemporary Roman Catholic Worship." It provides information that Piscitelli gathered about the use made of the Marini Protestant hymns in 67 modern Roman Catholic hymnbooks. (Those 67 books are listed with Appendix II.) The number after the letters "RC" designate the rank order of the hymn by frequency as found in the Catholic hymnbooks followed (in parenthesis) by the number of Catholic hymnals in which Piscitelli found it. Thus, the first-ranked hymn in the Marini list, "All hail the power," was the third most often reprinted of all the Marini hymns in the 67 Catholic hymnbooks, and it was found 36 times. In these 67 hymnbooks the most often reprinted hymn from the Marini list was "Faith of our fathers" (which had been ranked in a tie for 65th in the Marini list), and it was reprinted in 43 out of the 67 Catholic hymnals. It is an interesting sidelight to note that, although many Protestants do not know about the origin of this hymn, it was actually written by a nineteenth-century convert to Roman Catholicism, Frederick Faber, for whom the "fathers" who braved "dungeon, fire and sword" were Jesuits and other Catholic priests suffering persecution in the reign of Elizabeth I (1558-1603).

The third column, designated by "D," is keyed to VanderWilt's chapter, "Singing about Death in American Protestant Hymnody." It designates the hymns used by VanderWilt for his analyses.

The fourth and last column, designated by "B," is keyed to Bauer's chapter, "Stories and Syllogisms: Protestant Hymns, Narrative Theology, and Heresy." It designates the hymns that Bauer examined, divided by those that feature a narrative structure (N), a systematic structure (S), or both (both).

Rank	First Line (Author, Date) — Publications				
1	All hail the power (Perronet, 1779) — 160		RC — 3(36)		B(S)
2	Jesus, lover of my soul (C. Wesley, 1740) — 153		RC — 37(4)	D	B(N)
3	Alas and did my Savior bleed (Watts, 1707) — 143		RC — 37 (4)		B(both)
4	How firm a foundation (Rippon, 1787) — 145				B(S)
5	Am I a soldier of the cross (Watts, 1721-1724) — 133		RC — 23 (13)	D	B(N)
6	Come, thou fount (Robinson, 1758) — 126			D	B(S)
7	Guide me O thou great Jehovah (Williams, 1745) — 120		RC — 48 (2)	D	B(N)
8	On Jordan's stormy banks (Stennett, 1787) — 119		RC — 69 (1)	D	B(N)
9	Rock of ages (Toplady, 1776) — 114		RC — 33(5)	D	B(S)
10	When I can read my title clear (Watts, 1707) — 113			D	B(N)
11	Joy to the world (Watts, 1719) — 111		RC — 8 (30)		B(S)
12	When I survey the wondrous cross (Watts, 1707) — 110		RC — 48 (2)		B(S)
13	Blest be the tie (Fawcett, 1782) — 108		RC — 69 (1)	D	B(N)
14	There is a fountain (Cowper, 1771) — 107		RC — 69 (1)	D	B(S)
15	From Greenland's icy mountains (Heber, 1823) — 105	M — 1(53)	RC — 69 (1)		B(S)
16	Amazing grace, how sweet the sound (Newton, 1779) — 104		RC — 5 (34)	D	B(S)
17	Jesus, my all to heaven is gone (Cennick, 1743) — 102				B(N)
	Just as I am (Elliot, 1834) — 102		RC — 69 (1)		B(N)
18	Come, we that love the Lord (Watts, 1707) — 100		RC — 41(3)	D	B(N)
	My faith looks up to thee (Palmer, 1830) — 100		RC — 48(2)		B(N)
	O for a closer walk with God (Cowper, 1772) — 100		RC — 48(2)		B(N)
19	Blow ye the trumpet, blow (C. Wesley, 1750) — 99				B(S)

	Come thou almighty king (Anonymous, 1757) — 99		RC — 3(36)		B(S)
20	O for a thousand tongues (C. Wesley, 1738) — 96		RC — 33(5)		B(both)
21	Jesus shall reign (Watts, 1719) — 95	M — 2(50)	RC — 19(15)	D	B(S)
22	Come, Holy Spirit, heavenly dove (Watts, 1707) — 94				B(N)
	Glorious things of thee are spoken (Newton, 1779) — 94	M — 2(50)	RC — 27 (7)		B(S)
	Nearer my God to thee (Adams, 1841) — 94		RC — 41(3)	D	B(N)
23	I love thy kingdom, Lord (Dwight, 1801) — 93	M — 105(5)	RC — 48(2)		B(S)
	There is a land of pure delight (Watts, 1707) — 93		RC — 69 (1)	D	B(N)
24	Lord, dismiss us with thy blessing (Fawcett, 1773) — 92		RC — 27(7)	D	B(N)
25	Children of the heavenly king (Cennick, 1742) — 91			D	B(N)
	Christ the Lord is ris'n today (C. Wesley, 1739) — 91		RC — 21(14)	D	B(S)
26	Hark the herald angels sing (C. Wesley, 1739) — 90		RC — 6(33)		B(S)
	How sweet the name of Jesus sounds (Newton, 1779) — 90		RC — 41(3)		B(S)
27	I know that my redeemer lives (Medley, 1775) — 89		RC — 15(18)	D	B(S)
28	Holy, holy, holy (Heber, 1826) — 88		RC — 11(26)		B(S)
29	O happy day that fixed my choice (Doddridge, 1775) — 87		RC — 69 (1)		B(N)
30	Come ye disconsolate (Moore, 1816) — 86		RC — 69 (1)		B(N)
	Father of mercies, in thy word (Steele, 1760)				B(N)
	Grace, 'tis a charming sound (Doddridge, 1755) — 86				B(S)
31	Abide with me (Lyte, 1847) — 85		RC — 27(7)	D	B(N)
32	Before Jehovah's awful throne (Watts, 1719) — 84				B(S)
	He dies, the friend of sinners dies (Watts, 1709) — 84			D	B(S)
	Jesus, and shall it ever be (Grigg, 1765) — 84				

33	God moves in a mysterious way (Cowper, 1774) — 83		RC — 41(3)		B(S)
34	A charge to keep I have (C. Wesley, 1762) — 81			D	B(N)
	From all that dwell (Watts, 1719) — 81	M — 7(38)	RC — 14(20)		B(S)
	Jesus, I my cross have taken (Lyte, 1824) — 81			D	B(N)
35	Come, humble sinner, in whose breast (E. Jones, 1787) — 80			D	B(N)
36	From every stormy wind that blows (Stowell, 1828) — 79				B(N)
	I love to steal a while away (Brown, 1824) — 79			D	B(N)
37	Jerusalem, my happy home (Anonymous, c. 1600) — 78		RC — 21(14)		B(N)
	My soul, be on thy guard (Heath, 1781) — 78			D	B(N)
	Salvation, O the joyful sound (Watts, 1707) — 78				B(S)
	When all thy mercies (Addison, 1712) — 78				B(N)
38	Father, whate'er of earthly bliss (Steele, 1776) — 77				B(N)
	How tedious and tasteless the hours (Newton, 1779) — 77				B(N)
	Rise my soul and stretch thy wings (Seagraves, 1742) — 77			D	B(N)
39	I would not live alway (Muhlenburg, 1826) — 74			D	B(N)
40	How beauteous are their feet (Watts, 1707) — 73	M — 5(45)			B(S)
	Prayer is the soul's sincere desire (Montgomery, 1818) — 73			D	B(S)
41	Majestic sweetness sits enthroned (Stennett, 1787) — 71				B(N)
	Stand up (stand up) for Jesus (Duffield, 1858) — 71		RC — 69 (1)		
42	Hark, ten thousand harps (Kelly, 1804) — 70	M — 50(12)			B(S)
	My country 'tis of thee (Smith, 1843) — 70		RC — 10 (27)		
43	Love divine, all loves excelling (C. Wesley, 1747) — 69		RC — 15(18)	D	B(S)
44	Lord in the morning (Watts, 1719) — 68				B(S)

	Must Jesus bear the cross alone (Shepherd, 1694) — 68			D	B(N)
	Sweet hour of prayer (Walford, 1845) — 68		RC — 69(1)		B(N)
45	Awake and sing the song (Hammond, 1745) — 67				B(S)
	Did Christ o'er sinners weep (Beddome, 1787) — 67				B(both)
	Hark, the glad sound! the Savior comes (Doddridge, 1755) — 67		RC — 37(4)		
	Plunged in a gulf of dark despair (Watts, 1707) — 67				B(N)
	I'm not ashamed to own my Lord (Watts, 1720) — 67				B(S)
46	Why do we mourn departing friends (Watts, 1707) — 66			D	
47	In the cross of Christ (Bowring, 1825) — 65		RC — 37(4)		B(N)
	Welcome, sweet day of rest (Watts, 1719) — 65				
48	Depth of mercy can there be (C. Wesley, 1740) — 63				B(N)
	O beautiful for spacious skies (Bates, 1904) — 63		RC — 12(25)		
	Onward Christian soldiers (Baring-Gould, 1864) — 63		RC — 41(3)		B(S)
	Safely through another week (Newton, 1779) — 63				B(N)
	While shepherds watched their flocks (Tate, 1700) — 63		RC — 23(13)		
49	Arise, my soul, arise (C. Wesley, 1739/1742) — 62				B(S)
	Awake, my soul, and with the sun (Ken, 1695/1709) — 62		RC — 69(1)		
	He leadeth me: O blessed thought (Gilmore, 1862) — 62		RC — 69(1)	D	B(N)
	Lord, we come before thee now (Hammond, 1745) — 62				B(N)
	Watchman, tell us of the night (Bowring, 1825) — 62	M — 4(47)	RC — 48(2)		
50	Asleep in Jesus, blessed sleep (Mackay, 1854) — 61			D	
	Hark from the tombs a doleful sound (Watts, 1707) — 61			D	B(N)
	Show pity, Lord (Watts, 1719) — 61				B(N)

	Sun of my soul (Keble, 1827) — 61		RC — 41(3)		B(N)
51	Awake my soul in joyful lays (Medley, 1782) — 60			D	B(N)
	Glory to thee my God this night (Ken, 1695/1709) — 60		RC — 48(2)	D	
	I love to tell the story (Hankey, c. 1868) — 60		RC — 69(1)		B(N)
	The morning light is breaking (Smith, 1843) — 60	M — 16(29)			B(S)
	The spacious firmament on high (Addison, 1712) — 60		RC — 69(1)		B(S)
52	Broad is the road that leads to death (Watts, 1707) — 59			D	
	Come, let us join our cheerful songs (Watts, 1707) — 59		RC — 31(6)		B(S)
	How precious is the book divine (Fawcett, 1782) — 59				B(N)
	Jesus, Savior, pilot me (Hopper, 1871) — 59		RC — 48(2)		B(N)
	Praise God from whom all blessings flow (Ken, 1674) — 59		RC — 13(22)		
	What a friend we have in Jesus (Scriven, c. 1855) — 59		RC — 48(2)		B(N)
53	Sweet is the work, my God and king (Watts, 1719) — 58				B(S)
	'Tis midnight and on olive's brow (Tappan, 1822) — 58				
	Work, for the night is coming (Coghill, 1868) — 58				B(both)
54	Come, let us anew our journey pursue (C. Wesley, 1749) — 57				B(N)
55	And let this feeble body fail (C. Wesley, 1759) — 56			D	B(N)
	I need thee every hour (Hawks, 1872) — 56		RC — 69(1)		B(N)
	My Jesus, I love thee (Featherstone, 1864) — 56		RC — 48(2)	D	B(N)
56	Awake, my soul, stretch every nerve (Doddridge, 1755) — 55				B(S)
	Jesus, keep me near the cross (Crosby, 1869) — 55		RC — 69(1)		B(N)
	Lead, kindly light, amid the encircling gloom (Newman, 1833) — 55		RC — 26(10)		B(N)
	'Mid scenes of confusion (Denham, 1837) — 55			D	

	O worship the King (Grant, 1833) — 55	RC — 25(11)		B(S)
	Pass me not, O gentle Savior (Crosby, 1868) — 55	RC — 48(2)		B(N)
	Sinner turn, why will ye die (J. Wesley, 1742) — 55		D	B(S)
	Sweet the moments rich in blessing (Shirley, 1770) — 55			B(N)
57	As on the cross the Savior hung (Stennett, 1787) — 54			
	Hark, my soul, it is the Lord (Cowper, 1779) — 54			B(N)
	Not all the blood of beasts (Watts, 1707) — 54			B(S)
	O for a heart to praise my God (C. Wesley, 1742) — 54	RC — 48(2)		B(N)
58	Blessed assurance (Crosby, 1873) — 53	RC — 48(2)		
	Come, Holy Spirit, come, with energy divine (Beddome, 1800) — 53			B(N)
	Dismiss us with thy blessing, Lord (Hart, 1759) — 53			B(neither)
	God be with you till we meet again (Rankin, 1880) — 53	RC — 69 (1)		B(N)
	Lo! he comes with clouds descending (C. Wesley, 1758) — 53	RC — 41(3)		B(S)
	My God, the spring of all my joys (Watts, 1707) — 53			B(N)
	My hope is built on nothing less (Mote, 1834) — 53			B(N)
	My God, my life, my love (Watts, 1707) — 53			B(N)
	O God, our help in ages past (Watts, 1719) — 53	RC — 2(40)		B(S)
	Savior, breathe an evening blessing (Edmeston, n.d.) — 53			
	The day is past and gone (Leland, 1792) — 53		D	B(N)
	We praise thee, O God (Mackay, 1854) — 53	RC — 48(2)		B(S)
59	And must this body die (Watts, 1707) — 52		D	
	Great God attend, while Zion sings (Watts, 1719) — 52			B(S)
	O thou in whose presence (Swain, 1791) — 52			B(N)

	O where shall rest be found (Montgomery, 1819) — 52			D	B(N)
	On the mountain's top appearing (Kelly, 1802) — 52	M — 7(38)			B(N)
	Take my life and let it be (Havergal, 1873) — 52		RC — 33(5)		
60	How sweet, how heavenly is the sight (Swain, 1792) — 51				
	Savior, visit thy plantation (Newton, n.d.) — 51	M — 86(7)			B(S)
	When peace like a river (Spafford, 1873) — 51		RC — 69(1)		B(N)
61	Hail the day that sees him rise (C. Wesley, 1739) — 50		RC — 18(16)		B(S)
	Let every mortal ear attend (Anonymous, n.d.) — 50				B(S)
	O could I speak the matchless worth (Medley, 1787) — 50				B(N)
62	Almost persuaded (Bliss, 1871) — 49				
	Early my God without delay (Watts, 1719) — 49				B(N)
	Hail, thou once despised Jesus (Anonymous, n.d.) — 49				B(S)
	I can hear my Savior calling (Blandy, 1890) — 49		RC — 69(1)		B(N)
	I heard the voice of Jesus say (Bonar, 1846) — 49		RC — 19(15)		B(N)
	O that my load of sin were gone (C. Wesley, 1742) — 49				B(N)
	Once more, my soul, the rising day (Watts, 1707) — 49				
	One there is above all others (Newton, 1779) — 49		RC — 69(1)		B(S)
	Our Lord is risen from the dead (C. Wesley, 1743) — 49				B(S)
	This is the day the Lord hath made (Watts, 1719) — 49		RC — 69(1)		B(S)
63	Angels, roll the rock away (Gibbons, n.d.) — 48				
	Approach, my soul, the mercy seat (Newton, 1779) — 48				
	Behold a stranger at the door (Grigg, 1806) — 48				
	Sing them over again to me (Bliss, 1874) — 48				

	Father, I stretch my hands to thee (C. Wesley, n.d.) — 48		RC — 69(1)	
	Hail to the Lord's anointed (Montgomery, 1821) — 48	M — 10(36)	RC — 48(2)	
	Hark, the voice of love and mercy (Evans, 1782) — 48			
	Holy Ghost with light divine (Reed, 1816) — 48			
	Thus far the Lord has led me (Watts, 1707) — 48			D
	Why should we start and fear to die (Watts, 1707) — 48			D
64	By cool Siloam's shady rill (Heber, 1812) — 47			
	Come, every soul by sin oppressed (Stockton, 1874) — 47			
	Come, sound his praise abroad (Watts, 1719) — 47			
	Jesus, I love thy charming name (Doddridge, 1755) — 47			
	Jesus, the very thought of thee (Bernard of Clairvaux, 12th c.) — 47		RC — 27(7)	
	Give me the wings of faith (Watts, 1707) — 47			
	I'll praise my maker while I've breath (Watts, 1719) — 47			D
	That awful day will surely come (Watts, 1707) — 47			D
	The Lord my pasture shall prepare (Addison, 1712) — 47			
65	Another six days' work is done (Stennett, 1732) — 46			
	Faith of our fathers (Faber, 1849) — 46		RC — 1(43)	
	Glory to God on high (Allen, 1761) — 46		RC — 69(1)	
	My dear redeemer and my Lord (Watts, 1707) — 46			
	Rejoice the Lord is King (Wesley, 1746) — 46		RC — 15(18)	
	Softly now the light of day (Doane, 1824) — 46		RC — 69(1)	
66	Come, gracious Spirit, heavenly dove (Browne, 1720) — 45		RC — 48(2)	
	Holy Spirit, faithful guide (Wells, 1864) — 45			D

Rank	Hymn	M	RC	D
	How pleasant, how divinely fair (Watts, 1719) — 45			
	More love to thee, O Christ (Prentiss, 1869) — 45		RC — 69(1)	
	My soul, repeat his praise (Watts, 1719) — 45			
	O day of rest and gladness (Wordsworth, 1862) — 45		RC — 69(1)	
	O'er the gloomy hills of darkness (W. Williams, 1772) — 45	M — 5(45)		
	What various hindrances we meet (Cowper, 1779) — 45			
	Ye servants of God, your master proclaim (C. Wesley, 1744) — 45		RC — 48(2)	
67	Glory be to the Father (Doxology, 3rd-4th c.) — 44			
	God is love, his mercy brightens (Bowring, 1825) — 44			
	Hasten sinner to be wise (Scott, 1773) — 44			
	Lord Jesus, I long to be perfectly (Nicholson, 1878) — 44			
	My God, how endless is thy love (Watts, 1707) — 44			
	There's a land that is fairer (Bennett, n.d.) — 44			D
	While thee I seek protecting power (H. Williams, 1790) — 44			
68	Go preach my gospel, saith the Lord (Watts, 1707) — 43	M — 9(37)		
	God is the refuge of his saints (Watts, 1719) — 43			
	Mortals awake, with angels join (Medley, 1782) — 43			
	Take the name of Jesus with you (Baxter, 1870) — 43		RC — 69(1)	
	The heavens declare thy glory, Lord (Watts, 1719) — 43		RC — 69(1)	
	Ye wretched, hungry, starving poor (Steele, 1760) — 43			
69	I am thine, O Lord (Crosby, 1875) — 42			D
	Low in the grave he lay (Lowry, 1874) — 42			
	My life, my love I give to thee (Hudson, n.d.) — 42			

	Soldiers of Christ arise (C. Wesley, 1749) — 42	RC — 69(1)	
	'Twas on that dark that doleful night (Watts, 1707) — 42	RC — 69(1)	
	While with ceaseless course the sun (Newton, 1779) — 42		
	Your harps, ye trembling saints (Toplady, 1772) — 42		
70	Eternal source of every joy (Doddridge, 1755) — 41		
	How charming is the place (Stennett, 1787) — 41		
	Jesus, thou art the sinner's friend (Burnham, 1783) — 41		
	Lord of the worlds above (Watts, 1719) — 41		
	Softly and tenderly (Thompson, 1880) — 41	RC — 48(2)	D
	When thou my righteous judge (Rippon, 1787) — 41		
	With joy we meditate the grace (Watts, 1707) — 41		
71	Behold the Savior of mankind (S. Wesley, 1700) — 40		
	Come, thou long expected Jesus (C. Wesley, 1744) — 40	RC — 9(28)	
	Day of judgment, day of wonders (Newton, 1779) — 40		D
	How are thy servants blest, O Lord (Addison, 1712) — 40		D
	How gentle God's commands (Doddridge, 1755) — 40		
	How happy every child of grace (C. Wesley, 1759) — 40		
	Jerusalem the golden (Bernard of Cluny, 12th c.) — 40	RC — 48(2)	D
	Life is the time to serve the Lord (Watts, 1707) — 40		D
	My God, my portion and my love (Watts, 1707) — 40		
	Shall we gather at the river (Lowry, 1864) — 40	RC — 33(5)	D
	Silent night, holy night (Mohr, 1818) — 40	RC — 6(33)	
	Sowing in the morning (Shaw, n.d.) — 40	RC — 69(1)	D

72	Behold what wondrous grace (Watts, 1707) — 39		
	Down at the cross (Hoffman, n.d.) — 39		
	How did my heart rejoice to hear (Watts, 1719) — 39		
	I hear the Saviour say (Hall, n.d.) — 39		D
	Why should the children of a king (Watts, 1717) — 39		
73	And will the judge descend (Doddridge, 1755) — 38		D
	Come away to the skies (Anonymous, n.d.) — 38	RC — 48(2)	
	How sad our state by nature is (Watts, 1707) — 38		
	Jesus call us; o'er the tumult (Alexander, 1752) — 38		
	Jesus is tenderly calling (Crosby, 1869) — 38		
	Rescue the perishing (Crosby, 1869) — 38		
	Savior, thy dying love (Phelps, 1884) — 38		
	Thee we adore, eternal name (Anonymous, n.d.) — 38	RC — 69(1)	D
	When rising from the bed of death (Addison, 1712) — 38		D
74	And can I yet delay (C. Wesley, 1740) — 37		
	Bless, o my soul, the living God (Watts, 1719) — 37		
	Come my soul thy suit prepare (Anonymous, n.d.) — 37		
	How oft, alas, this wretched heart (Steele, 1757) — 37		
	Lord, I hear of showers of blessing (Anonymous, n.d.) — 37	RC — 69(1)	
	Now begin the heavenly theme (Langford, 1776) — 37		
	See Israel's gentle shepherd stand (Doddridge, 1755) — 37		
	What shall I render to my God (Watts, 1719) — 37	RC — 69(1)	
75	Hark! What mean those holy voices (Cawood, 1819) — 36		

	I send the joys of earth away (Watts, 1707) — 36		
	Let Zion's watchmen all awake (Doddridge, 1755) — 36		
	My Savior, my almighty friend (Watts, 1719) — 36		
	Now to the Lord a noble song (Watts, 1707) — 36		
	People of the living God (Montgomery, 1825) — 36		D
	Return, o wanderer, return (Collyer, 1812) — 36		
	Stay, thou insulted spirit, stay (C. Wesley, 1749) — 36		
	The Lord Jehovah reigns (Watts, 1719) — 36		
	The Lord my shepherd is (Watts, 1719) — 36		
	To our redeemer's glorious name (Steele, 1757) — 36		
76	And am I born to die (C. Wesley, 1763) — 35		D
	Let every creature join (Watts, 1719) — 35		
	On a hill far away (Bennard, 1913) — 35	RC — 48(2)	
	To God the only wise our Savior (Watts, 1707) — 35		

APPENDIX II

"*Hymns Recommended for Ecumenical Use*" *in Catholic Hymnbooks*

Simplified from a Ranking
Prepared by Felicia Piscitelli

This appendix uses another list of hymns as a way of ascertaining the use made by Roman Catholics of widely reprinted hymns. It is based on "Hymns and Tunes Recommended for Ecumenical Use," prepared by the Consultation on Ecumenical Hymnody and published first in the October 1977 issue of *The Hymn*. This appendix ranks hymns included from that recommended selection by the number of times that they were found in the 67 Catholic hymnals examined by Felicia Piscitelli. It is limited to the 50 hymns that appear most frequently. Below the ranking appears a paragraph with bibliographical information on the 67 hymn and worship books used by Piscitelli in her study (dating from the 1950s to the late 1990s, with most from the 1980s and 1990s).

1 O come, o come, Emmanuel — 49
2 Holy God, we praise thy name — 48
Praise to the Lord, the Almighty — 48
3 Faith of our fathers, living still — 44
On Jordan's banks the Baptist's cry — 44
4 Jesus Christ is risen today — 42
5 Now thank we all our God — 41
O come, all ye faithful — 41
6 O God, our help in ages past — 40
7 Alleluia, sing to Jesus — 38
8 All hail the power of Jesus' name — 36

Come, thou almighty King — 36
For all the saints who from their labors — 36
Let all mortal flesh keep silence — 36
O sacred head, now wounded — 36
The Church's one foundation — 36
9 Angels we have heard on high — 35
10 Amazing grace — 34
11 Hark! The herald angels sing — 33
Silent night — 33
12 A mighty fortress is our God — 32
The first Nowell — 32
13 Praise my soul, the King of heaven — 31
Were you there when they crucified — 31
14 Joy to the world — 30
All glory, laud and honor — 30
15 Lo, how a rose e'er blooming — 29
16 Come thou long-expected Jesus — 28
17 O little town of Bethlehem — 27
18 As with gladness men of old — 26
Holy, holy, holy, Lord God Almighty — 26
In Christ there is no east or west — 26
What child is this — 26
19 Praise the Lord! Ye heavens adore him — 24
20 All creatures of our God and King — 23
Away in a manger — 23
For the beauty of the earth — 23
Let us break bread together — 23
The strife is o'er, the battle done — 23
21 Father, we thank thee who has planted — 22
Joyful, joyful, we adore thee — 22
Praise God from whom all blessings flow — 22
Ye watchers and ye holy ones — 22
22 All people that on earth do dwell — 21
Sleepers, wake! The watch are calling — 21
23 At the name of Jesus — 20
From all that dwell below the skies — 20
Go, tell it on the mountain — 20
There's a wideness in God's mercy — 20
When I survey the wondrous cross — 20

"Hymns Recommended for Ecumenical Use" in Catholic Hymnbooks

The following Roman Catholic hymnals were surveyed for this appendix: *Adoremus Hymnal* (San Francisco: Ignatius Press, 1997); *American Catholic Hymnbook,* ed. Michael Gilligan, et al. (South Holland, IL: American Catholic Press, 1992); *Assemblybook, Cycle A* (annual publication) (Phoenix: North American Liturgy Resources, 1990); *The Book of Catholic Worship* (Washington, D.C.: The Liturgical Conference, 1966); *Brightest and Best,* by George William Rutler (San Francisco: Ignatius Press, 1998); *Catholic Community Hymnal* (Chicago: GIA Publications, 1999); *Catholic Liturgy Book,* ed. Ralph A. Keifer, et al. (Baltimore: Helicon Press, 1975); *Christian Prayer: The Liturgy of the Hours* (New York: Catholic Book Publishing Co.); *Collegeville Hymnal,* ed. Edward J. McKenna, S.J. (Collegeville, MN: Liturgical Press, 1990); *F.E.L. Hymnal,* ed. Roger Nachtwey (Los Angeles: F.E.L. Publications, 1968); *Gather,* ed. Michael J. Cymbala (Chicago: G.I.A. Publications, 1988); *Gather Comprehensive Edition* (Chicago: G.I.A. Publications, 1994); *Gather to Remember: Songs, Seasonal Psalms, Service Music,* ed. Michael J. Cymbala (Chicago: G.I.A. Publications); *Gathering to Praise* (Waco, TX: Word, Inc., 1981); *Glory & Praise, Songs for the Worshipping Assembly* (Phoenix: North American Liturgy Resources, 1977); *Glory & Praise,* vol. 2 (Phoenix: North American Liturgy Resources); *Glory & Praise,* vol. 3 (Phoenix: North American Liturgy Resources, 1982); *Glory & Praise Comprehensive Edition* (Phoenix: North American Liturgy Resources and Chicago: G.I.A. Publications, 1988); *Glory & Praise,* vol. 4 (Phoenix: North American Liturgy Resources); *Glory & Praise,* 2nd ed. (Portland: OCP Publications, 1997); *Holy Is the Lord* (Steubenville, OH: Franciscan University, 1993); *Hymnal of Christian Unity,* ed. Clifford A. Bennett, Paul Hume (Toledo, OH: Gregorian Institute of America, 1964); *Hymnal for Catholic Students,* ed. Robert J. Batastini, Gabe Huck, et al. (Chicago: G.I.A. Publications and Chicago: Liturgy Training Publications, 1988); *Hymnal for Young Christians, with Roman Catholic Mass Supplement* (Los Angeles: F.E.L. Publications, 1966); *Hymnal for Young Christians,* vol. 2 (Los Angeles: F.E.L., 1971); *Hymnal for Young Christians,* vol. 3 (Los Angeles: F.E.L., 1973); *ICEL Resource Collection of Hymns and Service Music,* International Committee for English in the Liturgy (Chicago: G.I.A); *Johannine Hymnal,* ed. Joseph Cirou and Michael Gilligan (Oak Park, IL: American Catholic Press, 1970); *JourneySongs,* ed. Bari Colombari, Paulette Vaught, Joanne Osborn, Randall DeBruyn (Portland: OCP Publications, 1994); *Lead Me, Guide Me: The African-American Catholic Hymnal* (Chicago: G.I.A. Publications); *Magnificat Missalette,* December 1998; *Maryknoll Missal* (New York: J. P. Kenedy, 1966); *Music for Catholic Worship* (Pacific, MO: Cathedral Music Press/Mel Bay Publications, 1988); *Music Issue* (annual publication, 1987 ed.) (Portland: OCP Publications); *New Catholic Hymnal,* ed. Anthony Petti and Geoffrey Laycock (New York: St. Martin's Press); *New Saint Joseph Children's Missal with*

Hymns: An Easy Way of Praying the Mass for Boys and Girls, by Rev. H. Hoever (New York: Catholic Book Publishing, 1966); *New Saint Joseph Mass Book and Hymnal* (New York: Catholic Book Publishing, 1986); *OCP Companion Missal, 1994-95* (annual publication, 1994 ed.) (Portland: OCP Publications, 1994); *Our Parish Prays and Sings* (Collegeville: Liturgical Press, 1959); *Our Parish Prays and Sings,* 2nd ed. (Collegeville, MN: Liturgical Press, 1965); *Parish Mass Book and Hymnal* (New York: Catholic Book Publishing Co., 1967); *Peoples' Hymnal,* 2nd ed. (Cincinnati: World Library of Sacred Music, 1961); *People's Mass Book,* 1st ed. (Cincinnati: World Library of Sacred Music, 1964); *People's Mass Book,* 2nd ed. (Cincinnati: World Library of Sacred Music, 1970); *People's Mass Book,* 4th ed. (Schiller Park, IL: World Library, 1984); *Pray Together,* 2nd ed., ed. William Carr and Lavern Wagner (Quincy, IL: Sunday Missal Co., 1977); *Pray Together Missalette* (Quincy, IL: Sunday Missal Co., November 1973); *Rejoice!* (Schiller Park, IL: J. S. Paluch, 1989); *Rise Up and Sing!* ed. Owen Alstott, Paulette Vaught, et al. (Portland: OCP Publications, 1992); *Songprayers,* ed. Dan F. Onley and Natalie Waugh (Phoenix: North American Liturgy Resources, 1976); *Songprayers,* revised ed., ed. Eileen E. Freeman (Phoenix: North American Liturgy Resources, 1979); *Songs for Worship,* compiled by John Michael Talbot; ed. Phil Perkins, 2nd ed. (Birdwing Music, 1985); *Songs of Praise,* vol. 1, compiled by The Word of God Music (South Bend, IN: Servant Publications, 1975); *Songs of Praise,* vol. 2, compiled by The Word of God Music (South Bend, IN: Servant Publications, 1977); *Songs of Praise,* vol. 3, compiled by The Word of God Music (South Bend, IN: Servant Publications, 1979); *Songs of Praise,* vol. 4, compiled by The Word of God Music (South Bend, IN: Servant Publications, 1981); *Spirit & Song* (Portland, OR: OCP Publications, 1999); *Sung Mass Book for Low and High Masses,* by Jan Kern (Toledo, OH: Gregorian Institute of America, 1964); *The Book of Catholic Worship* (Washington, DC: The Liturgical Conference, 1966); *The Catholic Hymnal and Service Book,* ed. Frank Campbell-Watson (New York: Benziger Editions, 1966); *The Catholic Hymnal/Cantemos al Señor* (Huntington, IN: Our Sunday Visitor, Inc., 1974); *Traditional Hymns for Guitar,* ed. Owen Alstott (Portland: Oregon Catholic Press, 1983); *Vatican II Hymnal,* ed. Terry L. Haws, revised ed. (Seattle: New Catholic Press of Seattle, 1975); *We Celebrate with Song,* ed. Charles Frischmann. J. S. Paluch, 1976); *We Celebrate,* 4th ed. (Schiller Park, IL: J. S. Paluch, 1986); *Worship II,* ed. Robert J. Batastini, Robert Oldershaw, Richard Proulx, Daniel Reuning (Chicago: G.I.A. Publications, 1975); *Worship,* 3rd ed., ed. Robert J. Batastini (Chicago: G.I.A. Publications, 1986).

APPENDIX III

Hymns in Roman Catholic Hymnals

Simplified from a Ranking
Prepared by Felicia Piscitelli

This appendix presents the most often reprinted hymns from the 67 Catholic hymn and worship books listed with Appendix II. As with the Marini list, it amalgamates variations of hymn texts with the most frequently used variant. Asterisks show hymns by non-Roman Catholic authors or translators. The number on the far right is the rank order of that particular hymn in the Marini list.

Rank	Hymn Title/First Line — Publications	Rank in Marini List
1	At that first eucharist* — 50	
2	O come, O come, Emmanuel* — 49	
3	Holy God, we praise thy name — 48	
	Praise to the Lord, the Almighty* — 48	
4	All glory, laud, and honor — 44	
	On Jordan's bank the Baptist's cry* — 44	
5	Faith of our fathers — 43	65
	O saving victim/O salutaris hostia — 43	
6	Crown Him with many crowns — 42	
	Jesus Christ is risen today* — 42	
7	O come, all ye faithful/Adeste fideles — 41	
	Immaculate Mary — 41	
	Now thank we all our God* — 41	
8	O God, our help in ages past* — 40	58
9	Creator of the stars of night — 39	

10	Alleluia! sing to Jesus* — 38	
11	All hail the power of Jesus' name* — 36	1
	Come thou almighty King* — 36	19
	For all the saints* — 36	
	Let all mortal flesh keep silence* — 36	
	O sacred head, now wounded* — 36	
	The church's one foundation* — 36	
12	Angels we have heard on high* — 35	
	O sons and daughters — 35	
	To Jesus Christ, our sovereign King — 35	
13	A mighty fortress is our God — 34	
	Amazing grace* — 34	16
14	Hark! the herald angels sing* — 33	26
	Silent night, holy night* — 33	71
15	Sing of Mary, pure (meek) and lowly* — 32	
	The first Nowell* — 32	
16	Praise, my soul, the King of heaven* — 31	
	Were you there when they crucified my Lord?* — 31	
17	Joy to the world* — 30	11
18	Lo, how a rose e'er blooming* — 29	
19	At the Lamb's high feast we sing — 28	
	Come, thou long-expected Jesus — 28	71
	Mine eyes have seen the glory* — 28	
	We gather together* — 28	
20	My country, 'tis of thee* — 27	42
	O little town of bethlehem* — 27	
	We three kings of Orient are* — 27	
21	As with gladness men of old* — 26	
	Holy, holy, holy! Lord God Almighty* — 26	28
	In Christ there is no east or west* — 26	
	On this day, the first of days* — 26	
	The coming of our God* — 26	
	What child is this* — 26	
22	At the cross her station keeping — 25	
	O beautiful, for spacious skies* — 25	48
	Songs of thankfulness and praise* — 25	
	The King of glory — 25	
23	Praise the Lord! Ye heavens adore Him* — 24	
	Tantum ergo — 24	

24 All creatures of our God and King* — 23
Away in a manger* — 23
For the beauty of the earth* — 23
Hail, Holy Queen, enthroned above* — 23
It came upon the midnight clear* — 23
Let us break bread together* — 23
The strife is o'er, the battle done* — 23
25 At the name of Jesus* — 22
Be joyful, Mary/Regina caeli, jubila — 22
Joyful, joyful, we adore thee* — 22
Praise God, from whom all blessings flow* — 22 52
Ye watchers and ye holy ones* — 22
26 All people that on earth do dwell* — 21
Father, we thank thee* — 21
Lord, who throughout these forty days* — 21
Make me a channel of your peace — 21
Praise the Lord of heaven, praise Him in the height* — 21
The God of earth and sea and sky* — 21
Wake, awake, for night is flying* — 21
When I survey the wondrous cross* — 21 12
27 From all that dwells below (beneath) the skies* — 20 34
Go, tell it on the mountain* — 20
Lord of all hopefulness* — 20
Praise to the holiest in the height — 20
Sing, my tongue, the Savior's glory — 20
There's a wideness in God's mercy — 20
28 Ave Maria — 19
Christ is made the sure foundation* — 19
God rest you merry, gentlemen* — 19
Of the Father's love begotten* — 19
Veni creator spiritus — 19
29 All hail, adored Trinity* — 18
Angels, from the realms of glory* — 18
Come, ye faithful, raise the strain* — 18
Come, ye thankful people, come* — 18
I am the bread of life — 18
I know that my Redeemer lives* — 18 27
Immortal, invisible, God only wise* — 18
Let there be peace on earth* — 18

Love divine, all loves excelling* — 18 43
How great thou art* — 18
O say can you see* — 18
Rejoice, the Lord is King* — 18 65
Take up your (thy) cross* — 18
What wondrous love is this* — 18
Whatsoever you do — 18
You satisfy the hungry heart — 18

Index of Names and Subjects

Index of Hymn (and Song) Titles